What People are Saying About
Credibility

"A refreshingly direct approach to uncovering the critical elements of leadership."
> — *Continuous Journey*

"*Credibility* is so right for the team-oriented 1990s. . . . It puts the emphasis where it should be: on how leaders can earn the support of their followers by treating them like customers. . . . This book is a winner."
> — Rosabeth Moss Kanter, professor of business administration, Harvard Business School, and author of *When Giants Learn to Dance*

"When Kouzes and Posner promise we can increase our credibility, they're not blowing smoke. Their book is the result of surveying some 15,000 people, and the upshot is that they have discovered the recipe for building credibility, step-by-step."
> — *Entrepreneur*

"Thousands of Levi Strauss & Co. employees have had the benefit of leadership training sessions based on Jim Kouzes and Barry Posner's work. At those sessions, we learned that the essence of leadership is credibility. Now, this new book provides insights that will help everyone who reads it hone their leadership skills."
> — Robert Haas, chairman and CEO, Levi Strauss & Co.

"This book is filled with ideas, models, and insights to help all leaders serve in more meaningful ways."
> — Kathryn E. Johnson, president and CEO, The Healthcare Forum

"A thoughtful and articulate discussion of credibility. Kouzes and Pozner convincingly position the concept as central to comfortable living and productive working. Most leaders and managers could benefit from their insights."
> — *Training*

"Philosophical and practical guidance for business executives at a time when computers, consultants, coproduction and ever-growing employee empowerment leave less for managers to do. . . . A penetrating survey of business methods and employee attitudes worldwide."
— PUBLISHERS WEEKLY

"Shows how all of us can be more responsive and responsible leaders."
— ANN MORRISON, author of *The New Leaders* and lead author of *Breaking the Glass Ceiling*

"Clearly, to anyone who reads the daily newspapers, there is a crisis in leadership. Kouzes and Posner, with focused research and penetrating insight, cut to the core of any strategy for building and rebuilding leadership: credibility."
— REGIS MCKENNA, author of *Relationship Marketing*

"Concepts such as seamless partnerships, collaboration, and mutual commitments, and the improvement required to achieve them, require leaders who understand how to build trust and credibility with their employees. *Credibility* speaks with clarity in an area of critical need."
— KENT STERETT, vice president of quality, Southern Pacific Lines

"Another leadership book. Unlike many, this one's right on."
— MINNEAPOLIS/ST. PAUL CITYBUSINESS

"A must-read in our fast-changing social and business environment, where our 'constituents' have growing, legitimate demands and expectations."
— CYRIL YANSOUNI, chairman and CEO, Read-Rite Corporation

"Not the quick 'how-to' manual, *Credibility* is full of concrete and credible cases that should help the thoughtful manager come to grips with this important and complex dimension of leadership."
— MIHALY CSIKSZENTMIHALYI, author of *Flow*

Credibility

JAMES M. KOUZES
BARRY Z. POSNER

Credibility

HOW LEADERS GAIN AND LOSE IT, WHY PEOPLE DEMAND IT

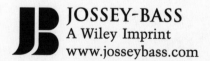

JOSSEY-BASS
A Wiley Imprint
www.josseybass.com

Published by Jossey-Bass
A Wiley Imprint
989 Market Street, San Francisco, CA 94103-1741   www.josseybass.com

The story of Frederic Hudson's illness in Chapter Eight is from Hudson, Frederic M. *The Adult Years: Mastering the Art of Self-Renewal.* Copyright © 1991 by Jossey-Bass.

Readers should be aware that Internet Web sites offered as citations and/or sources for further information may have changed or disappeared between the time this was written and when it is read.

Jossey-Bass books and products are available through most bookstores. To contact Jossey-Bass directly call our Customer Care Department within the U.S. at 800-956-7739, outside the U.S. at 317-572-3986, or fax 317-572-4002.

Jossey-Bass also publishes its books in a variety of electronic formats. Some content that appears in print may not be available in electronic books.

Library of Congress Cataloging-in-Publication Data
Kouzes, James M., 1945–
    Credibility : how leaders gain it and lose it, why people demand it / James M. Kouzes,
Barry Z. Posner.
      p. cm.—(The Jossey-Bass business & management series)
    Includes bibliographical references and index.
    ISBN 0-7879-6464-6 (alk. paper)
    1. Leadership.   2. Executive ability.   3.   Interpersonal relations.   I. Posner, Barry Z.   II. Title.   III. Series.

    HD57.7.K678 2003
    658.4'092—dc21   2002043855

Printed in the United States of America
FIRST EDITION
HB Printing   10 9 8 7 6 5 4
First PB Printing   10 9 8 7
Second PB Printing   10 9 8 7 6 5 4

The Jossey-Bass
Business & Management Series

Consulting Editors
Organizations and Management

WARREN BENNIS
University of Southern California

RICHARD O. MASON
Southern Methodist University

IAN I. MITROFF
University of Southern California

For

Donna, Jackie, and Amanda—

whose humor and hope

uplift our spirits

CONTENTS

What We Say: The Critical Difference • The Six
Disciplines

On Credibility and Character

Credibility is about how leaders earn the trust and confidence of their constituents. It's about what people demand of their leaders as a prerequisite to willingly contributing their hearts, minds, bodies, and souls. It's about the actions leaders must take in order to intensify their constituents' commitment to a common cause.

Our intense interest in managerial values and leadership motivated us to write *Credibility* ten years ago. In fact, many years before we wrote this book, our first joint article was entitled "Shared Values Make a Difference." That research clearly showed that commitment, satisfaction, productivity, and other positive workplace outcomes were significantly higher when people shared the values of their organizations.

As our research evolved we discovered that unless *personal* values were clear it really didn't matter how clear the organization's values were. People don't get more committed to a company or to a cause because the organization nails its credo to the door. They get more committed because it matters to them.

During the past two decades, we continued to ask another question: "What do you look for and admire in a leader, someone whose direction you would *willingly* follow?" You might expect we'd get a different set of responses over this period of time. After all, people keep telling us that the world is *radically* different today than it was in 1983.

But we didn't get different answers. We've asked the question in large and small businesses, professional service firms and manufacturing companies, public and private sector organizations, educational, healthcare, and governmental institutions. We've asked it of men and women, young and old, and individual contributors and executives. We've asked around the world—on six continents, in fact. What's been most striking to us is that people keep on sending the same message. They want leaders who are honest, forward-looking, competent, and inspiring. What this adds up to, as we explain in depth in this book, is personal *credibility*. No matter whom we've asked and no matter where we've asked it, what we first reported in 1983 is just as valid today as it was then. *Credibility* is still the foundation of leadership. In fact, given what we're going through at the start of this century, this lesson is even *more* relevant today.

Let's put these two things together—personal credibility and personal values—and think about the implications for leaders. There are many important lessons, but the meta-message is this: *leadership is personal.* It's not about the corporation, the community, or the country.

It's about *you*. If people don't believe in the *messenger,* they won't believe the message. If people don't believe in *you,* they won't believe in what *you* say. And if it's about you, then it's about your beliefs, your values, your principles. It's also about how true you are to your values and beliefs.

But somewhere along the way to the New Millennium notions of ethics, morality, honesty, character, and personal discipline came to be viewed as quaint—at least by those from the me-first, free agent school of corporate strategy. People got sucked into the idea that leadership was all about extrinsic rewards, and they started offering very creative ways to attract talent to the good life. The intrinsic reasons for doing something important—really *caring* about the people and the purpose—too often got lost in the hyperbole. Certainly the context of leadership has changed, but given what we've all experienced, we've come to see how necessary it is to be reminded of some fundamentals that do *not* change.

Fundamental No. 1: Character Counts

At a recent character education conference at Santa Clara University's Markkula Center for Applied Ethics, Thomas Likona, author of *Educating for Character,* began his talk with this anonymous poem:

> Be careful of your thoughts, for your thoughts
>   become your words;
> Be careful of your words, for your words become
>   your deeds;
> Be careful of your deeds, for your deeds become
>   your habits;
> Be careful of your habits; for your habits become
>   your character;
> Be careful of your character, for your character
>   becomes your destiny.

Strategy is not a biological imperative. It begins in our minds, gets expressed in words, and then gets translated into action. Over time those actions become who we are, and what you do repeatedly will determine the legacy you leave.

Teaching people to use the tools of commerce is necessary but insufficient for creating a healthy and prosperous society. The right tools in the wrong hands invite evil ends. The more we study leadership, the more we're persuaded that leadership development is not simply about "how to's." It's also about character development.

Fundamental No. 2: Individuals Act; Organizations Create Cultures

Organizations don't act; individuals do. Organizations don't save lives; individuals do. Organizations don't create breakthrough products; individuals do. Organizations don't defraud; individuals do. It's important to make this distinction, because ultimately every one of us must take personal responsibility for what we do. Actions have consequences, and we all have to account for our own.

What organizations do is create *cultures*. Culture is the organizational equivalent of a person's character. The behavior that is modeled becomes the behavior that is followed. This is good news and bad news. Good news because solid cultures *can* be built around ethical behavior. The bad news is that cultures can also be built around the opposite, at least for a while. It really does matter what you choose to believe in.

Fundamental No. 3: Our System Is Based on Trust

As a result of the corporate malfeasance, fraud, and deceptions that were uncovered in 2001 and 2002, the outrage grew into a call for reform of the laws and rules that govern corporate accounting and stock options, along with demands to separate auditing and consulting. We've reached a point where an executive's word is no longer sufficient. Legislation has been passed requiring CEOs of the largest corporations to sign a document swearing their quarterly reports are correct. What was once implicit now has to be made explicit. Why has this become necessary? Where does it end?

Whether you like these changes or not, they just prove one thing: our entire capitalist system is based on trust. It's not based on an investment model that's taught in business school. It's not based on the price earnings ratio. It's not based on an income statement or a balance sheet. It's not based on any of these rational concepts, and it's not based on the numbers. It's based on whether people *believe* in the numbers and in the people who are supplying them. If people don't trust those who handle their money, their livelihoods, and their lives, they'll just refuse to participate.

We're all asking ourselves, "When will this market slide end? When will the bear go back into hibernation and the bull start to roam the Street? When will my retirement account start growing? When will I start to feel more economically secure?" We can't give you a date that's certain, but we can tell you that it'll only come when people *feel* they can once again trust the system and the people in it.

Fundamental No. 4: Leadership Is a Dialogue, Not a Monologue

Among the most positive outcomes of this very painful economic period is the initiation of a national dialogue. People are talking about ethics, values, corporate accountability, and social responsibility. There've been summits, editorials, conferences, town forums, legislation, protests, letters, TV specials, and online exchanges. Who'd have thought that honesty and ethics would ever become the topic of cocktail parties and golf games? But they have.

Talk is healthy. We should not shut up, and we should not shut others down for wanting to discuss matters of character. Leaders should encourage it. Leaders really can't impose values from the top, as you will read in this book. The more people are permitted to express and to explore, the sooner we'll discover our common values and our common vision. And, if your experience is similar to ours, you'll discover that one of our shared values is to live and work in a world with integrity.

Our Research into Credibility

Much has been written about what leaders do to get extraordinary things done, but little has been written about leadership from the constituent's point of view. There are a few books and articles about being a good follower, but we have not been satisfied with the perspective they present. The notion of being a good follower is too passive. What we need in these turbulent times are energized *constituents* who enthusiastically participate in the process and take up the call for more leadership at all levels. So it was essential to look into the specific behaviors constituents need from a leader if they are to become fully engaged in and committed to a leader's call to action.

Credibility is the result of an intensive, ongoing investigation. In writing this book, we have relied on our own surveys, which to date have been administered to over 75,000 people from around the world. The data reported in *Credibility* are from our study for this book, but, as we noted earlier, the results have not varied since we began our research in the early 1980s, and we update the findings continuously.

In addition, for our original study we collected over 400 written case studies, and we continue today to collect new case examples of credible leadership. We also conducted more than 40 in-depth interviews with managers in order to deepen our understanding and provide personal stories that would enrich our study. Unless otherwise noted, quotations in the text are from these sources. All titles and affiliations were current at the time the manuscript was submitted for the original publication.

From the surveys, we identified the qualities people *most* looked for in those individuals they would be willing to follow; from the case studies we identified specific actions that give leaders credibility. Focus groups and subject-matter experts helped us to define the most significant behaviors. Further survey research projects, both within and across organizations, enabled us to validate the importance of these leadership actions and to determine conclusively that credibility makes a difference in work attitudes and performance.

Who Should Read This Book?

With *Credibility* we continue our commitment to assist people at all levels and in all types of organizations—public, private, educational, religious, voluntary, governmental, military, and not-for-profit settings—in furthering their abilities to lead others to get extraordinary things done. Since aspiring or working managers and human resource professionals are the people with whom we interact most often, the majority of examples in this book are from managerial leadership cases.

But managers and human resource professionals are not our only inspiration or audience. In the course of writing this book we have also collected data from community leaders, volunteer leaders, political leaders, labor leaders, and student leaders, as well as those from all functional areas. Our research and practice have convinced us that each of us is a leader in one or another aspect of our lives. Consequently, we believe *Credibility* will be of interest to anyone—whether at work, at home, or in social and volunteer activities—who wishes to step forward and guide people to new personal, organizational, and social futures.

As a result of reading this book, you will learn:

- The qualities that constituents look for and admire in leaders
- The foundation of leadership and of all working relationships
- The principles and disciplines that strengthen leadership credibility
- The actions you can take to apply the practices to your own leadership initiatives
- The struggles leaders face in living up to their constituents' expectations

You will see that credibility is the foundation of leadership and all relationships that work. And you will see that credibility is essentially determined by our constituents.

Overview of the Contents

In Chapter One, we present our point of view that leadership is a relationship and a service. We use the results of our long-term research projects to identify the qualities people most look for and admire in their leaders. The data clearly indicate that credibility is the foundation of leadership.

In Chapter Two, we discuss the positive influence credible leaders have on people and organizations and the negative impact that low-credibility leaders have on morale and performance. In this chapter, we use anecdotes and examples from the leaders and constituents in our studies to bring to life the findings from our research.

In Chapters Three through Eight, we explore each of the six disciplines of credibility, which we developed as a result of our case studies and interviews. Although the discussions are built upon our research, we also draw on the work of other scholars. We illustrate each discipline with case examples and describe how practicing leaders strengthen their credibility by developing the discipline. Each of these chapters concludes with practical tips and techniques to help you apply the disciplines in your own leadership roles.

In Chapter Three, we see how the credibility journey begins with the process of self-discovery—with an inner exploration of credos, competence, confidence, and character. Credos are our guides, competence endows us with the skills to enact our credos, and self-confidence gives us the will to behave in a way that is consistent with our beliefs. The sum of it all is character.

In Chapter Four, we learn that leaders who are seen as trustworthy are those who are believed to have their constituents' best interests at heart. In order to strengthen credibility, leaders explore others' aims and aspirations. Credible leaders learn to listen and to listen well. They appreciate the hopes and dreams of their diverse constituencies.

But if leaders cannot integrate diverse viewpoints and affirm unifying themes, diversity can lead to fragmentation. In Chapter Five, we discuss our findings that shared values make a significant difference in the health of persons, organizations, and communities. We talk about how leaders can find common ground, build community, and resolve conflicts on the basis of principles, not positions.

In Chapter Six, we see that people cannot do what they do not know how to do. Organizations cannot provide consistently high levels of service, quality, innovation, or respect unless members have the skills and abilities to do so. Competent organizational leaders continuously develop the capacity of their organizations to put values into practice. They educate, offer choices, inform, foster self-confidence, and create a climate for lifelong learning. Credible leaders also liberate the leader in everyone, believing that all constituents can learn to take responsibility for continuous improvement.

Constituents do not serve leaders; leaders serve constituents. Both serve a common purpose. In Chapter Seven, we examine ways that credible leaders demonstrate their personal commitment to the shared values and visions of the organization. We see how leaders stay in touch with constituents, are the first to accept responsibility, spend time on the important values, teach others, and hold themselves accountable for the promises they make.

With cynicism rising and with the pace of change continuing unabated, the only leaders who will be able to attract constituents will be those who can lift people's spirits and restore belief in the future. In Chapter Eight, we examine how credible leaders sustain hope by taking charge and demonstrating the courage of their convictions, by arousing positive thoughts and images, and by seeking and giving support. Credible leaders keep hope alive for others—a critical task since, in the end, only people with hope will achieve greatness.

And finally, in Chapter Nine, we discuss the struggles leaders experience as they try to respond to constituents while remaining true to their own beliefs. We also identify some excesses of leadership and of expectation. Leaders are human. They make mistakes. Perfection should not be the ideal; rather, we should strive for an attitude of humility and continuous learning.

The Appendix provides a technical report that describes our studies of credibility, identifies key actions and behaviors of leaders, and analyzes the impact of those actions on work attitudes and performance. We included it for those who would like to know more about our research, including how we measured leader credibility, sample and respondent characteristics, methodology, and statistical relationships with important outcome variables.

You Can Make a Difference

Despite everything that has happened, people still want and need leadership. They just want leaders who hold an ethic of service and are genuinely respectful of the intelligence and contributions of their constituents. They want leaders who will put principles ahead of politics or profits and other people before self-interests.

Leadership matters. And it matters more in times of uncertainty than in times of stability. We certainly have our share of that right now. We can all expect many more massive and wrenching changes in the years to come.

Success in initiating or responding to change, however, is inextricably linked to the credibility of those leading the efforts. Constituents will become willingly involved to the extent that they believe in those sponsoring the change. It is wise, therefore, for leaders to begin every significant change with a "credit check." It's not just "Do my constituents believe that the new system will improve our performance?" Or "Do they believe that this risky policy is for the greater good?" It's also "Do they believe in me and my ability to lead this effort?"

Even so, unquestioned integrity is not enough. Leaders can't do it alone. Neither can companies, communities, or countries. Everyone—leaders and constituents alike—shares responsibility for getting extraordinary things done. Leaders need constituents' energetic involvement as much as the constituents need leaders' boldness of vision and courage of conviction. Leaders also need understanding. Responding to the demands of highly diverse populations is a social challenge and a personal struggle. Respect must run both ways.

Leadership should be everyone's business. By making leadership *our* business and not just *their* business, we all contribute to the renewal of mutual trust and understanding. By making leadership about *us* and not about *them*, we all take responsibility for the doing what we say we will do. In this process we all become more credible.

1

Leadership Is a Relationship

I don't think of leadership as a position.
I don't think of leadership as a skill.
I think of leadership as a relationship.
Phil Quigley
Pacific Bell

Leadership is a reciprocal relationship between those who choose to lead and those who decide to follow. Any discussion of leadership must attend to the dynamics of this relationship. Strategies, tactics, skills, and practices are empty unless we understand the fundamental human aspirations that connect leaders and their constituents. If there is no underlying need for the relationship, then there is no need for leaders.

What do constituents expect from leaders? What do they expect from constituents? What purpose do leaders serve? Why do people believe in some but not in others? Why do some people choose to follow one leader while others reject that person? Which actions sustain the relationship? Which destroy it? What is the state of the current relationship between leaders and constituents?

We cannot expect to renew our companies and our communities until we answer these and related questions, until we understand what forms the foundation of the leader-constituent relationship. And we cannot hope to build the towering institutions of our dreams until that foundation is strong and solid.

Lately it has become apparent that the relationship between leaders and constituents has shifted. The foundation has decayed and crumbled. Until we all, constituents and leaders alike, grab our picks and shovels and work to repair our interpersonal infrastructure, style will continue to succeed over substance, and technique will continue to triumph over truth.

To understand better the leader-constituent relationship, we must look with fresh eyes at our images of organizations, leaders, and constituents. We must see how they are connected and how those connections might be improved.

BEING PART OF, NOT APART FROM

When we called to schedule an interview with Gayle Hamilton, division manager of the Coast Division for the Pacific Gas and Electric Company, we got our first clue that she means it when she says, "I have a strong willingness to be a part of what is going on, rather than apart from. I don't think people enjoy working for long stretches for someone who won't be part of what's happening."[1] We could hear trains in the background. Hamilton explained that after the downtown Santa Cruz, California, PG&E office building had been severely damaged in the 1989 Loma Prieta earthquake, the company gave her a choice. She could move north to a more corporate setting or remain near her crew, taking up quarters in a trailer next to the railroad tracks that ran through Santa Cruz. Hamilton chose the trailer and the noise rather than lose the connection with her constituents.

Hamilton's connection to those she leads was apparent again the day we arrived to interview her for this book. She had been up since 4:30 A.M. to be at work by 5:30 A.M. That morning, all employees—over three hundred of them—had gotten together for a breakfast and communication meetings to celebrate the first time that performance recognition checks (based on earnings per share for the company) had ever been distributed to bargaining-unit employees. Hamilton's division had done extremely well, and that morning was the opportunity to say thanks.

We hear about celebrations all the time, so perhaps there's nothing unusual about a celebration breakfast. But in this case, Hamilton and her division council—those who report to her directly—did all the decorating, setting up, cooking, serving, and cleaning up. That breakfast was in many ways a microcosm of a new approach to leadership, one characterized by serving others rather than being served, based on giving rather than receiving.

Yet this approach contrasts sharply with how most of us conceive of the role of leaders in organizations. The dominant organizational metaphor of our time is still the hierarchy, organized by rank and authority. A *hierarchy* is at its roots a government by ecclesiastics: the word itself comes from the Greek for *holy* or *sacred*. In a sense, the modern-day manager has inherited the status of a priest.

This message is reinforced whenever people refer to each other as bosses and subordinates. Or when people say that employees are on "top," in the "middle," or on the "bottom." Or when those who deliver services and make products are referred to as being the "rank and file."

These are not trivial distinctions. Word choices reveal our most basic assumptions and color our most important attitudes about human relationships. Consider the word *subordinate*. It's a combination of *sub* (for under or, derivatively, less than, inferior to) and *order* (for row, rank). A subordinate, at least by root definition, is someone who is considered inferior in rank and perhaps by implication inferior in character. The word *boss* comes from a word meaning master. A boss is someone who is considered superior in rank and status. Using the terms *boss* and *subordinate* daily continuously reinforces a top-down, rank-ordered, superior-inferior, us versus them, management versus labor relationship.

Gary McBee, executive vice president at Pacific Bell, got us thinking about how vivid and powerful our images are of these words and what they imply. We also thought about how early in our lives we form these images. In talking with a group of senior executives about leadership, the conversation turned to empowerment. We talked for a few minutes about fostering collaboration and strengthening others, and then McBee jumped in with the following story: "When my son was seven years old," he said, "I thought it was time to bring him to the place where I worked and show him my office. I sat him down in that big chair behind my desk. He peeked up over the top and said, 'Dad, call somebody in here and fire him.'"

We all laughed. It was that kind of laughter that appreciates the story's irony but also recognizes its bittersweet truth. We would expect that McBee's son was not alone in the image he had of what managers do at work. This idea of what *managers* and *leaders* do has been with us for at least two thousand years. So common and pervasive is our use of these terms, that we assume them to be the natural order of things. But they are really not so innocent.

At about age seven, or perhaps even earlier, we begin to get a picture of a pyramidal structure with high priests at the top who issue orders and others down the "chain of command" who carry them out. These early images persist, reinforced by our experiences with our teachers, principals, coaches, and employers — even with our parents. Is it any wonder that as we begin our careers, empowerment is not exactly the feeling that overwhelms us? Is it any wonder that we have paid such reverence to those on the "top" and granted them so much power and control? Challenging the authority of the ecclesiastics is enough to deter anyone. Somewhere hidden in the dark recesses of our minds is a little voice saying, "Mommy, Daddy, call some people in here and fire them."

For centuries, the hierarchical relationship served us quite well when conquering foes, creating towns and cities, populating the planet, feeding the masses, building businesses. But the dominant organizational metaphor we have carried forward in history, myth, legend, and management textbook will not serve us well for much longer—in part because, as we will describe, the cynics are winning. The regard for leaders from all organized groups—politics, government, business, education, labor, and the church—is so low that they are no longer paid much heed. And lack of confidence has led people to be less willing to participate in the struggle to improve.

It is virtually impossible to conceptualize a different connection between people at work if our language forces us into top-down, boss-subordinate images, if we must accept the status of being superior or inferior. Jim Autry, retired president of the magazine group of Meredith Corporation, puts it this way: "Becoming a manager has much to do with learning the metaphors; becoming a good manager has much to do with using the metaphors; and becoming a leader has much to do with changing the metaphors."[2] To renew ourselves as leaders and to revitalize our organizations, we must change these metaphors.

Are there compelling business reasons to change them for organizations? We think so. Take the case of Xerox. In the 1980s, this company reduced the number of suppliers from five thousand to five hundred. Is the relationship between the Xerox people and their suppliers fundamentally different as a result? You bet it is. In its quality handbook, Xerox states, "The objective is to build long-term relationships with the best vendors and to involve them in the earliest phases. . . . Xerox treats the vendors as part of the extended family."[3] Take note of "extended family." You will be hearing it much more often in reference to relationships at work.

And listen to Bob Haas, chairman and chief executive officer of Levi Strauss and Company. When talking about the impact of LeviLink (Levi's electronic data-interchange system) on relationships with retailers and suppliers, Haas said, "We are at the center of a seamless web of mutual responsibility and collaboration. . . . There is a seamless partnership with interrelationships and mutual commitments, straight through the chain that would've been unimaginable ten years ago."[4]

"Seamless partnerships," "web of mutual responsibility and collaboration," "mutual commitments"—these are new phrases in the business lexicon. The evolving nature of relationships with vendors and distributors is changing how companies do business. It is inevitable that the way people relate inside the boundaries of the organization will have to change as well.

As Harvard professor Shoshana Zuboff has observed,

> We remain, in the final years of the twentieth century, prisoners of a vocabulary in which managers require employees; superiors have subordinates; jobs are defined to be specific, detailed, narrow and task-related; and organizations have levels that in turn make possible chains of command and spans of control. The guiding metaphors are military; relationships are thought of as contractual and often adversarial. The foundational image of work is still one of a manufacturing enterprise where raw materials are transformed by physical labor and machine power into finished goods. However, the images associated with physical labor can no longer guide our conception of work.[5]

What images should guide us in the final years of the twentieth century? Which should shape the conception of work relationships if not superior-subordinate?

In place of hierarchy, the metaphor should now be the "community." Here's what Paul Allaire, chairman and chief executive officer of Xerox, has to say about the new working relationships at that company: "Our objective is to create natural work groups, organized around natural units of work, which develop as work communities—communities of practice, communities of work, and communities of learning—communities that have communities within them."[6] Think community when imagining the possibilities of how organizations might function.

In a productive work community, one that is constantly learning and growing, people are contributing members and

professionals. Even in our most basic manufacturing industries, the knowledge required of employees is now greater than
when the work was performed solely by hand. As more and
more people become professionals in organizations whose
competitive advantage is knowledge and not brute force, there
will be increased resistance to being treated as "inferiors."
When people do things with their heads rather than by hand,
they rebel at being controlled and demand to be in control
themselves.

In the traditional hierarchy, managers boss subordinates.
In a productive work community, where we are all informed
and responsible professionals, who is going to willingly accept
another as "master"? In democratic societies, people do not
talk about themselves as being subordinate to their leaders.
Why should it be any different in our offices and factories? In
democratic societies, leaders serve the people's needs and
interests. Leaders serve their constituents.

Constituents are not ordered in rank; everyone has a
voice, regardless of job and social status. Constituents play a
significant part in the success of the enterprise. They are more
than just followers of someone else's vision and values. They
are participants in creating them.

And in today's borderless world where contact is a cellular
phone, a fax, or a modem away, leaders must realize that their
potential for influencing others extends far beyond those
seven, ten, or twenty people they "supervise." Constituents
extend beyond direct reports, the formal boundaries, and the
company phone directory. Leaders' constituencies are multiple and may be suppliers, distributors, customers, clients,
peers, and other leaders, as well as employed associates. Now
leaders must consider the diverse opinions, backgrounds,
cultures, and styles of the many different people they lead.

In a productive work community, leaders are not com-
manders and controllers, bosses and big shots. They are servers and supporters, partners and providers. We recognize that
it is not common for managers, whether in the public or
private sector, to talk about their employees as constituents
and themselves as servers and supporters. Think for a moment
about how you describe your relationships with others at work.

Then try going through a day at work without using the term *boss* or *subordinate*, for example. You may see how automatic your responses are. You are not alone: the hierarchical system and its language have conditioned us all to act and speak habitually in ways that are consistent with a top-down, superior-subordinate view.

We are not naive, of course. We recognize that the positions people hold in organizations do make a difference: rank does have its privileges. But should our automatic responses be to rely upon status, power, and privilege to get things done? Is this the way to optimize the potential of our capital and human resources? Is leadership a divine right, conferred by rank and position? Should modern-day managers expect quality to emerge from people treated as inferiors?

Quite the contrary. We believe that the old organizational hierarchy is hollow. And enlightened managers know that serving and supporting unleashes much more energy, talent, and commitment than commanding and controlling.

As we share this perspective with audiences, we often hear resistance, however. Sometimes we are challenged by someone saying something like this: "My subordinates do not elect me. My superiors do. And what a disastrous step it would be if employees were given a vote. Can you imagine how politicized organizations would become? Can you imagine people campaigning for office, complete with political action committees and conventions?"

Although we are not advocating open elections inside organizations, we suggest that managers not kid themselves. People do vote—with their energy, their dedication, their loyalty, their talent, their actions. Do you not put forth higher-quality effort when you believe that the people leading you are there to serve your needs and not just their own?

LINKING LEADERSHIP, SERVICE, AND QUALITY TO RELATIONSHIPS

To understand the importance of the leader-constituent, member-community metaphors in realizing the exciting possibilities of organizational life, read what John Gardner (former secretary of Health, Education and Welfare, founder of Common Cause, adviser to six U.S. presidents, and respected author and scholar) has to say: "A loyal constituency is won when the people, consciously or unconsciously, judge the leader to be capable of solving their problems and meeting their needs, when the leader is seen as symbolizing their norms, and when their image of the leader (whether or not it corresponds to reality) is congruent with their inner environment of myth and legend."[7] By this statement, Gardner does not mean that the leader will personally fix the problem. There is not an expectation that a leader should be a superhuman, all-seeing, all-knowing wizard. Rather, Gardner is suggesting that people willingly follow the direction of someone who is attuned to their aims and aspirations, worries and fears, ideals and images. He is also reminding us that the constituents are ultimately the arbiters of the quality of leadership they receive.

Loyalty is not something a boss can demand. It is something the people — the constituency — choose to grant to a leader who has earned it. The people's choice is based not upon authority, but upon the leader's perceived capacity to serve a need.

Perhaps we can better understand the importance of the constituent perspective by rephrasing Gardner's comment. Try reading it this way: "Loyal *customers* are won when the *customers*, consciously or unconsciously, judge the *company* to be capable of solving their problems and meeting their needs."

Isn't that exactly how organizations win customer loyalty? By solving their problems and meeting their needs? Books on service quality invariably list the first step in the quality-planning process as identifying customers and finding out what their needs are. The customer decides what quality is. If we want the customer's loyalty, it is our job to be responsive. There may have been a time when the company could dictate what the customer should accept as quality, but those days are gone forever. Companies that do not take this message seriously will disappear.

Much as the quality-improvement gurus — whether in service or product quality — have focused our attention on the importance of the customer, somehow the traditional view of employee relations continues to dominate inside the walls of organizations. We seem to have exempted managers from thinking about employees as internal customers or constituents. For quality to improve, this thinking must change. Ron Skeddle, president of Libbey-Owens-Ford, brought this point home at a recent quarterly managers meeting: "Our customers are not just those people at GM and Craftline and Walt's Auto Glass who buy our glass products. Our customers are found here in this room today, as well, and they are found among the seven thousand–plus employees throughout this company. . . . These are the people we are here to serve."

By reversing the traditional relationship, Skeddle has placed the manager in the role of service provider and the employee in the role of customer. If you can accept this perspective, even if only for the sake of learning, then we offer you this proposition: *there is greater connection between leadership and customer service than there is between leadership and traditional management.* We further assert that there is much more to be learned about leadership from reading the customer service and the quality literature than from reading most management texts.

Leadership is obviously not about manufacturing goods and selling them to customers. Then what is it about? Just make a comparison between the leadership relationship and the service relationship. Customer service researchers Valarie Zeithaml, A. Parasuraman, and Leonard Berry observe in their book, *Delivering Quality Service,* that services differ from goods in three fundamental ways: "First, services are basically *intangible.* Because they are performances and experiences rather than objects, precise manufacturing specifications concerning uniform quality can rarely be set. . . . Second, services — especially those with a high labor content — are *heterogeneous*: their performance often varies from producer to producer, from customer to customer, and from day to day. . . . Third, production and consumption of many services are *inseparable.* Quality in services often occurs during service delivery, usually in an interaction between the customer and the provider, rather than being engineered at the manufacturing plant and delivered intact to the customer."[8]

Leadership, too, is intangible. It is a performing art. It is an encounter. Leadership is something we experience in an interaction with another human being.

Leadership is high in labor content; in fact, that is all that it is. And it is performed in many ways. Performance varies from leader to leader, from constituent to constituent, and from day to day. No two leaders, no two constituent groups, and no two days in the life of leader and constituents are exactly alike. Although the practices of leadership, like those of service, may be definable and can be generalized about at some level, they are distinct and unique at the moment of the encounter.

Leadership acts (producing the behaviors) and the reception of those acts are inseparable. Constituents most often experience their needs being met or not met at the moment of the encounter. They are not engineered into a tangible good and delivered in a package whole to the constituent. What the constituent experiences is an interaction—at least when the leader comes in direct contact with constituents. Unfortunately, in this media age, direct contact is diminishing; as we will discuss, this change is the source of many of the leadership problems that we are experiencing.

As you read this book, remember to think "relationship." Leadership is a relationship, one between constituent and leader that is based on mutual needs and interests. The key to unlocking greater leadership potential can be found only when you seek to understand the service relationship.

LEARNING WHAT CONSTITUENTS EXPECT

As we discussed in *The Leadership Challenge*, the place to begin a new appreciation of the leader-constituent relationship is by asking, "What do we, as constituents, expect of our leaders?"[9] We began our investigation in the early 1980s with Warren Schmidt of the University of Southern California in a study sponsored by the American Management Association. We asked an open-ended question: "What values (personal traits or characteristics) do you look for in your superiors?"[10] (As you can see, we were stuck in the old metaphors a decade ago. It's not easy to shed familiar and comfortable perspectives.)

More than fifteen hundred managers nationwide provided 225 values, characteristics, and attitudes that they believed crucial to leadership. A panel of researchers and managers subsequently analyzed the factors and reduced them to fifteen categories. The most frequent responses, in order of mention, were (1) integrity (leaders are truthful, are trustworthy, have character, have convictions); (2) competence (leaders are capable, productive, efficient); and (3) leadership (leaders are inspiring, are decisive, provide direction). A follow-up study sponsored by the Federal Executive Institute Alumni Association, involving eight hundred senior public sector administrators, replicated these findings.[11]

In subsequent studies, we broadened the categories, elaborated on our earlier findings, and improved the research methodology. We eventually produced a twenty-item survey instrument, which became one part of the research protocol for the study discussed in this book. In an eight-year series of executive seminars conducted by Santa Clara University and TPG/Learning Systems, a company in The Tom Peters Group, over fifteen thousand managers completed our checklist of admired leadership characteristics. We asked the respondents to select from the twenty qualities (listed in Table 1.1) the seven that they "most looked for and admired in a leader, someone whose direction they would willingly follow."

In 1991, we expanded our study to include the collection of over four hundred written case studies of most admired leaders in which people responded to questions about leaders with whom they had personal experience and for whom they had great admiration and respect. From these case studies, we collected specific examples of actions of respected leaders, information on the affective nature of admired leader-constituent relationships, and the identification of the types of projects or programs involved. These data came from sources in North America, Mexico, Western Europe, Asia, and Australia. Focus groups conducted subsequent to the collection of early cases further enabled us to determine the behaviors of admired leaders. A series of empirical studies (described in the Appendix) provided further insights into the leadership actions that influence people's assessments of credibility.

Additionally, we conducted in-depth interviews with more than forty managers about qualities they looked for and admired in leaders and why. Their richly detailed, colorful anecdotes and specific examples brought the survey data to life. From all of these data, we were then able to develop a framework for describing the actions that admired leaders take to build a special kind of leader-constituent relationship, one that not only leaves a lifelong impression but also makes a significant difference in performance.

IDENTIFYING KEY CHARACTERISTICS OF ADMIRED LEADERS

The results of our surveys over the last decade have been strikingly consistent. Time and again, people sent a clear message about the qualities leaders must demonstrate if they want others to enlist voluntarily in a common cause and to commit themselves to action freely.

What are these crucial attributes? According to our research, the majority of us look for and admire leaders who are honest, forward-looking, inspiring, and competent. Take a moment to examine the data from our surveys. The results from our most current sample are displayed in Table 1.1, in the column for 1993.

As you can see, these four characteristics—being *honest,*

Table 1.1. Characteristics of Admired Leaders.

Characteristic	1993 U.S. Respondents Percentage of People Selecting	1987 U.S. Respondents Percentage of People Selecting
Honest	87	83
Forward-looking	71	62
Inspiring	68	58
Competent	58	67
Fair-minded	49	40
Supportive	46	32
Broad-minded	41	37
Intelligent	38	43
Straightforward	34	34
Courageous	33	27
Dependable	32	32
Cooperative	30	25
Imaginative	28	34
Caring	27	26
Mature	14	23
Determined	13	20
Ambitious	10	21
Loyal	10	11
Self-controlled	5	13
Independent	5	10

forward-looking, inspiring, and *competent* — rank well above the rest. If the qualities alone were running for office, these are the ones that would achieve consensus and victory. Let's examine each of them.

Honest

In virtually every survey we conducted, honesty was selected more often than any other leadership characteristic. Honesty is absolutely essential to leadership. If people are going to follow someone willingly, whether it be into battle or into the boardroom, they first want to assure themselves that the person is worthy of their trust. They want to know that the would-be leader is truthful and ethical. No matter where we have conducted our studies—regardless of country, geographical region, or type of organization—the most important leadership attribute since we began our research in 1981 has always been honesty.

This finding is reinforced by a study done jointly by Korn/Ferry International, the highly respected and successful search firm, and the Columbia University Graduate School of Business. Surveying over 1,500 top executives in twenty countries (from the United States, Japan, Western Europe, and Latin America), the study looked into external threats, strategies for growth, areas of expertise, and personal characteristics of the CEO and the importance of these related topics now and in the year 2000.

The joint survey reports that "[e]thics are rated most highly among the personal characteristics needed by the ideal CEO in the year 2000. Respondents expect their chief executive to be above reproach."[12] In 1988, 88 percent of executives believed ethics to be essential. The exact figures did vary somewhat by country and region, but the importance of being ethical was consistently ranked highly.[13] Similarly, office workers value honesty highly. In the most recent *Worldwide Office Environment Index*, sponsored by Steelcase and conducted by Louis Harris and Associates, significant numbers of office workers (for example, 85 percent in the United States) said it was very important for their management to be honest, upright, and ethical.[14]

No matter the country, the benefits of honesty cannot be overstated. Employees must know where they stand—as they only can with someone who is honest with them. Irene Prazak, vice president of Norstar Bank of Upstate New York, addressed this point in emphasizing her manager's honesty and explaining its importance to her: "You know exactly where you stand, and I have known exactly where I have stood, from day one. Now that's important to someone like me, because then I become a good follower."[15]

Forward-Looking

Janice Lindsay, director of internal communications and editorial services for the Norton Company, defines her ideal leader as "somebody who sets and defines the vision and encourages you to follow that vision, and then is there when you need them."[16] We expect our leaders to have a sense of direction and a concern for the future of the organization. Leaders must know where they are going. They must have a destination in mind when asking us to join them on a journey into the unknown.

In the joint Korn/Ferry–Columbia University study, 75 percent of respondents ranked "conveys a strong vision of the future" as a very important quality for CEOs to have now; it was so ranked by an almost unanimous 98 percent for the year 2000.[17] The desirability of this management style did not vary by more than three percentage points across the regions studied. This finding suggests that, especially for senior executives, being forward-looking is the most essential of the leadership attributes.

Our study indicates that being forward-looking is also very important for front-line supervisors and middle managers. If leaders are to be admired and respected, they must have the ability to see across the horizon of time and imagine what might be. We are not inclined to follow those who are directionless. Honest or not, leaders who don't know where they are going are likely to be joined by the rest of us for only as far as we ourselves can see.

Constituents ask that a leader have a well-defined orientation toward the future. We want to know what the organization will look like, feel like, be like when it arrives at its goal in six months or six years. We want to have it described to us in rich detail so that we will know when we have arrived and so that we can select the proper route for getting there.

Inspiring

We admire and respect leaders who are dynamic, uplifting, enthusiastic, positive, and optimistic. We expect them to be inspiring. Yet it is not enough for leaders to have dreams of the future. They must be able to communicate these in ways that encourage us to sign on for the duration and to work hard toward the objective.

Once again, confirmation comes from around the globe for the need to be inspiring. Of executives surveyed, 91 percent said that by the year 2000 it will be very important that CEOs be inspiring. This quality is rated as more important than "analytic," "organized," and "tough."[18] If you're planning to be leading in the year 2000, you'd better start looking on the bright side.

Joseph Gagliardi, vice president of marketing for Hertz Equipment Rental Corporation, testifies to the importance of uplifting people's spirits: "I think you've got to come to the work station day to day feeling that you can make a difference and just getting that enthusiasm throughout your department, because no one does it alone. I think enthusiasm becomes contagious, and the task becomes almost a fun pursuit."[19]

Competent

The fourth most admired leadership attribute is competence. If we are to enlist in another's cause, we must see the person as capable and effective. The universal expectation is that the person be able to get things done for the business unit. In this sense, having a winning track record is the surest way to be considered competent.

The type of competence that constituents look for seems to vary with the leader's role. For example, those who hold officer positions are expected to demonstrate abilities in strategic planning and policy making. If a new technology challenges the organization, a person more knowledgeable about that technology may be perceived to be a more appropriate leader. A leader on the line or at the point of customer contact will typically have to be more technically competent than someone more removed. Yet it is not necessary that the leader have the same level of technical competence as constituents do. Much more significant is that he or she takes the time to learn the business, to know the current operation before making changes and decisions that affect everyone in the organization.

We are, however, noticing a trend toward requiring more

technical competence of leaders. The age of the generalist manager may be coming to a close. This situation is especially true in the knowledge industries. Although an effective leader in a high-technology company may not need to be a master programmer, he or she must understand the business implications of electronic data interchange and networking. A good leader in a professional services firm may have little direct client responsibility but must have towering competence as a consultant.

Expertise in leadership skills per se is another dimension of competence. The abilities to challenge, inspire, enable, act as a model, and encourage—the practices identified in our prior study of leadership bests and published in our book, *The Leadership Challenge*—must be demonstrated if leaders are to be seen as capable.[20]

Consistency and Change over Time

Honest, forward-looking, inspiring, competent: these characteristics have, over the last decade, been consistently selected by all respondent groups as the four most admired leadership characteristics. Ten-year follow-up surveys of American Management Association and Federal Executive Institute Alumni Association members confirm the continuity in what we want from our leaders.[21]

Yet though these leadership attributes have remained remarkably stable, we have observed some recent changes in emphasis. In the years since we published *The Leadership Challenge*, both the quality of being forward-looking and that of being inspiring have increased in their importance. More people want their leaders to provide future direction and show enthusiasm than in years past. These times of transition require leaders with the vision and the energy to sustain hope.

Competence remains one of the four most admired characteristics, but it has been assigned less value than in the past. Some constituents appear to be looking for more vision and direction, more inspiration and excitement in these times of turmoil, than for a track record of getting things done. This shift causes us great concern because it runs counter to the need for greater expertise among leaders—and all organizational members for that matter. Given the increasing complexity of organizations and their environments, it is doubtful that any leader could navigate the white waters of today's organization without clear competence. We must acknowledge that, relative to our original study, fewer people have elected to choose competence, but we should all pause to consider the implications of being led by foward-looking and inspirational individuals who lack the capacity to implement their visions of the future.

The quality that has changed most in relation to the others is supportiveness. When we first reported our findings in 1987, supportiveness ranked eleventh, having been selected by 32 percent of the respondents. It now ranks sixth overall, with 46 percent of respondents identifying being supportive as an admired leadership characteristic.

Perhaps because of wrenching global economic and political changes, people require more understanding and help from their leaders. Perhaps the increase in diversity in the workplace has created a need for more affirmation and assistance. Perhaps the reason is the empowerment movement, which is enabling more and more to realize their potential in self-managing teams and self-directed work environments. Whatever the cause, more people today expect leaders to be supportive than just a few years ago.

Another significant change is in the value of being ambitious. In 1987, 21 percent selected it as an admired leadership quality; in our most recent study, only 10 percent did. Maybe the message is finally getting through that a self-serving style is no longer so beneficial to success in organizations as once thought.

These modest changes in preference suggest that our expectations of leaders can be somewhat dynamic. The external environment may influence what we look for and admire in a leader at any given moment in time. However, the shifting winds still do not steer us away from seeking leaders who are at their core honest, forward-looking, inspiring, and competent. This collection of four qualities has endured over time and across organizations; they are required fundamentals of leadership.

Global and Local Expectations

Honest, forward-looking, inspiring, and competent: these remain the prerequisites to developing ourselves globally as leaders. Yet to be leaders, we must also learn to adapt to and shape our local surroundings. Expectations can vary from organization to organization, function to function, group to group, and level to level.

In one organization we studied, being supportive was selected as a most admired characteristic by significantly more people (56 percent of the overall organization) than in any other group we have studied. In this organization, being understanding and helpful were considered dramatically more important by all—whether exempt or nonexempt, male or female, young or old—than in other companies. Thus, to be successful there, one would have to develop the skills to be supportive along with the skills to demonstrate the other four attributes.

In comparison, another organization we surveyed selected the quality of courage significantly more often than the international norm. As you might imagine, the differences between the organization valuing supportiveness and that favoring courageousness were great. The organizations were as different as night and day, even though each was among the best in its respective industry.

These findings lend support to the concept of corporate culture. Organizations seek to differentiate themselves not just in terms of products, but also in the desired qualities of their leadership. In so doing, they send messages about what people should develop in themselves to become successful. In fact, if organizations do not develop a unique culture, they will have a difficult time persuading high-quality people to join and remain. Who wants to work in an organization that is just like any other?

People may also see the world a bit differently based on

their roles. Managers consistently look for a leader who is forward-looking; often fewer than 50 percent of nonmanagers do. More than 60 percent of exempt employees generally look for supportiveness; fewer than 40 percent of senior managers do. Professionals in the human resources function are more likely to value supportiveness than professionals in other areas. More women than men tend to appreciate supportive leaders. People in finance tend to value the quality of being inspiring less than those in sales. Quite understandably, ethnic minorities often look for more broad-minded leaders than do people from the majority population group. Understanding these local differences is important.

And if we are to be able to move about as leaders, serving one constituent group today and another tomorrow, it is critical to keep a global perspective. Much as specific attributes may vary from country to country, organization to organization, and function to function, some things remain constant and universal. We have come to refer to these as transportable leadership characteristics. As leaders, we are expected to carry at least four of these qualities with us wherever we go, from one organization to the next, one situation to the next, one constituency to the next.

Taken singularly, the characteristics of being honest, forward-looking, inspiring, and competent provide a consistently useful guide for leadership selection, action, and development. Taken together, they communicate a powerful message, one that offers a deeper understanding of the fundamentals of leadership. But they mean much more.

DISCOVERING CREDIBILITY AS THE FOUNDATION

The qualities of being honest, inspiring, and competent compose what communications researchers refer to as source credibility.[22] In assessing the believability of a source of information—whether it is the president of the company, the president of the country, a sales person, or a TV newscaster—researchers typically use the three criteria of trustworthiness, expertise, and dynamism. Those who rate highly in these areas are considered to be credible sources of information.

These three dimensions of source credibility are strikingly similar to three of the four most frequently selected items in our survey: honesty, competence, and inspiration. What we found quite unexpectedly in our initial research and have reaffirmed ever since is that, above all else, people want leaders who are credible. We want to believe in our leaders. We want to have faith and confidence in them as people. We want to believe that their word can be trusted, that they have the knowledge and skill to lead, and that they are personally excited and enthusiastic about the direction in which we are headed. Credibility is the foundation of leadership.

Given the significance of our discovery, we expected to find numerous references to credibility in the research on management and leadership during the last ten years. To our amazement and dismay, the shelves were bare. We were able to locate studies of credibility and cooperation, credibility and reception of feedback, and credibility and persuasiveness; but credibility and leadership was a topic largely ignored. Why the dearth of research on this subject? Isn't it important for executives to know that credibility is what makes their messages believable to others?

In the late 1970s and in the 1980s, self-help and management books boomed. But in large measure this was a triumph of image over character, style over substance. In the 1990s, there is growing recognition that gaining credibility is far more important than being dressed for success. Credibility is the foundation on which leaders and constituents will build the grand dreams of the future. Without credibility, visions will fade and relationships will wither.

Building Equity

Max De Pree, chairman of Herman Miller, one of America's most admired companies, has written, "The first responsibility of a leader is to define reality. The last is to say thank you. In between the two, the leader must become a servant and a debtor. That sums up the progress of an artful leader."[23]

Leaders typically do not conceive of themselves as servants and debtors, but De Pree's observation provides a very useful analogy to use when thinking about the importance of credibility in enlisting others in a common vision. Just think about a time when you might need to borrow money, when you might have to become indebted. Imagine that you are trying to get a mortgage to build the house of your dreams. You sit down across the desk from the loan officer at your local financial services company. After you've completed all the paperwork, the first thing that the loan officer is likely to do is check your credit.

Credit and credibility share the same root origin, *credo*, meaning "I trust or believe." A loan officer checking your credit is literally checking on your store of believability, searching to know whether you can make good on your word. The officer wants to know whether to believe you when you say that you will pay the loan back on time and with interest.

When it comes to leaders, in many respects constituents act like loan officers. When a leader makes promises (like signing a promissory note) about what he or she will do to guide the organization on a journey to an uplifting new future, people instinctively do a credit check. They ask themselves, "The last time this person made such a promise, was he being honest about it?" "Did she tell the truth, or was that just some campaign pledge to get our support?"

People also ask themselves, "Does he have the enthusiasm to keep people excited along the difficult road to the future?" "Does she inspire others to make the sacrifices necessary to make it to the end?" And they wonder, "Does she have the competence to get us from where we are now to where we'd like to be?" "Does he have a track record of accomplishment that would give us confidence in his abilities?"

If the answers to these essential questions are yes, then people are likely to willingly give their time, talent, and toil. If the answers are no, people are not likely to volunteer. When leaders ask others to follow their new strategic directions, their visions of exciting possibilities of a better tomorrow, people first decide, most often intuitively, whether those leaders are to be believed.

Fostering Trust

Of all the attributes of credibility, however, there is one that is unquestionably of greatest importance. The dimension of honesty accounts for more of the variance in believability than all of the other factors combined. Being seen as someone who can be trusted, who has high integrity, and who is honest and truthful is essential. You may know someone is clearly competent, dynamic, and inspirational. But if you have a sense that that person is not being honest, you will not accept the message, and you will not willingly follow. So the credibility check can reliably be simplified to just one question: "Do I trust this person?"

If your response is yes, then follow. Even if your endeavor is unsuccessful, you will still respect yourself. If your response is "I don't know," get more information, and fast. But if your answer is no, find another job or find another leader. Even if you are successful, you will not respect yourself. Every time we follow someone we do not trust, we erode our self-esteem. We are diminished in our own and in others' eyes, and we become less valuable to ourselves and to others.

We recently offered these recommendations to a group of managers. A young woman raised her hand. She said she was in no position to fire her leader or to get another job at the moment. Thus, for her, there had to be a third alternative. What did she advise? "Revolt!"

Revolt sounded to us like a much more radical solution than getting another job or getting another leader, but in the 1990s it has to be added to the list of alternatives. It was noteworthy to us that about a week after revolt was added to the list, the cover of *Business Week* boldly displayed the headline "GM: The Board Revolt."[24] It's not exactly what we'd expect on the cover of a conservative business publication, but it supports the manager's observation. From the boardroom to the factory floor, from Wall Street to Main Street, from south central Los Angeles to Eastern Europe, from voting booths in the United States to the squares of the former Soviet Union, revolt is in the air. Peaceful or bloody, discontent with leadership is extraordinarily high, and leaders had better take note.

EARNING CREDIBILITY

A credibility check is rooted in the past. It has to do with reputation. Reputation is human collateral, the security we pledge against the performance of our obligations as leaders, friends, colleagues, and constituents. It is what supports the natural human instinct to want to trust. Reputation is to be cherished and cared for. A damaged one lowers people's estimation of a leader's worth and their motivation to follow.

Credibility, like reputation, is something that is earned over time. It does not come automatically with the job or the title. It begins early in our lives and careers. People tend to assume initially that someone who has risen to a certain status in life, acquired degrees, or achieved significant goals is deserving of their confidence. But complete trust is granted (or not) only after people have had the chance to get to know more about the person. The credibility foundation is built brick by brick. And as each new fragment is secured, the basis on which we can erect the hopes of the future is gradually built.

We know from our research that being forward-looking is the quality that distinguishes leaders from other credible people. We also know that without a solid foundation of personal credibility, leaders can have no hope of enlisting others in a common vision. In this book, we will be talking about the sound base on which visions stand and are supported; we will not be talking much about the dreams themselves. Instead, we focus on the leader's foundation of credibility, knowing that only when it is strong can the dreams of the future be supported.

We recognize that the taller and more expansive a leader's dream, the deeper the foundation must be. The less stable the ground underneath, the more solid it must be. Especially in uncertain times, when boldness may be required, leadership credibility is essential in generating confidence among constituents. Without that, nothing can be built—at least nothing that can survive the test of time.

But does building the foundation warrant the effort? Does credibility really matter? Don't we hear almost daily of business, political, labor, and religious leaders who have become successful yet lack credibility? Besides, isn't business about getting results, and if people without credibility still get good results, then what difference does it make anyway?

It matters a great deal. Despite the evidence that some people can succeed, for a time, in ways that are devious and dishonest, credibility has a significantly positive outcome on individual and organizational performance. In the next chapter, we will examine what difference credibility makes, how leaders rate on the credibility scale these days, and what leaders—all of us—can do to strengthen our own credibility.

CHAPTER

2

Credibility Makes
a Difference

You can't follow someone who isn't credible,
who doesn't truly believe in what they're doing—
and how they're doing it.
Gayle Hamilton
Pacific Gas and Electric

It is meaningless to talk about leadership unless we believe that individuals can make a difference in the lives of others. And unless each of us believes that *we* can make a difference. If we think that people are powerless to influence events and that only history shapes behavior, then this book has no purpose. Reading it will be of absolutely no help to anyone.

Your personal experiences with individuals you consider to be leaders have much to teach you about the difference that people can make in your life.[1] Take a moment now to think of a time when you willingly followed the direction of someone you admired and respected as a leader. Answer the following questions, making some mental or written notes:

◆ What was the situation—the project, program, or activity—in which you were involved with this person?

Was it at work or outside of work? What was the project or activity expected to accomplish? What results were you expected to produce?

♦ What three or four words would you use to describe how you felt when you were involved with this person? How did you feel when you were around him or her? How did this leader make you feel about yourself?

♦ What leadership actions did this person take to get you and others to want to perform at your best? What did this individual do as a leader that you admire and respect?

We have asked these questions of thousands of people. In responding, Kathy Lacoy, now director of operations for Hillhaven Corporation, an affiliation of convalescent hospitals, spoke with us of the time when she was director of nursing, just getting started in her career. Her experience is representative of what we heard.

As she told us, her hospital administrator was a progressive thinker who continually challenged those around him to expand:

> He always had some kind of new project to work on. He could see what was coming next, something new, something interesting, something different to do. He taught all the time, *all* the time. Just in general conversation, he was teaching you something, so there was always that opportunity to learn. . . .
>
> He was scrupulously honest so that I had this real trust in him, and I just knew that he would never cause me to be in a situation where I'd sacrifice my ethics or my own personal values or standards. . . . He worked very hard, very long hours. . . . I worked probably the hardest I've worked in my whole life, but I never felt used or abused. . . He totally trusted me to do my job, wanted to hear feedback, was always available to help problem solve. . . .

And one method of communication — two-way communication — he used was to call floor conferences. These were little meetings . . . a time for people to be able to ask questions or make suggestions or share their little gripes. . . . He'd take notes while he was doing it, and then get the notes typed up with a response within twenty-four hours. . . . He was able to take complex issues and synthesize them in terms that people could understand so that everybody shared in the common goal. . . . He set a very high standard.

Lacoy continued, saying that this administrator taught her every day and increased her confidence, often with compliments. One notable way was to introduce her by remarking to the visitor — or president of the company — "You're going to have a real treat today. You're going to meet the best damn nurse that ever was." He made it clear that he took a genuine personal interest in Lacoy and in all the employees.

And then Lacoy related a most dramatic and memorable story of absolute trust:

I bet nobody ever had a boss that did anything like this. My husband and I had been married for about eight years, had three little kids, and had never had an opportunity to go away for what we call a real vacation. . . . We saved our money — it took a little over six months — and we were going to Acapulco. . . . The day I left, my boss called me into his office, and he said, "Now, I don't want to insult you, but I want you to do something. When you go on vacation sometimes, every once in a while, there's something you just really want but that you know maybe you can't afford, and you feel you shouldn't buy it because you've got three kids that want something else. I'm going to insist that you take with you my American Express card just in case there's anything you really want." Now that's awesome. People asked me so many times, "How come you have such tremendous loyalty to this company?" It's because of things like that. I mean, I never used that card . . . He just believed in the inherent self-worth of everyone.

THE SPIRITED INDIVIDUAL

Over and over again, we heard similar examples of how people were made to feel more worthy as a result of the interactions with leaders they admired and respected, people whose direction they would willingly follow. Irwin Federman, venture capitalist and former president of Monolithic Memories (acquired by Advanced Micro Devices), was onto something in saying, "You don't love someone because of who they are; you love them because of the way they make you feel.

"This axiom," Federman points out, "applies equally in a company setting. It may seem inappropriate to use words such as *love* and *affection* in relation to business. Conventional wisdom has it that management is not a popularity contest. . . . I contend, however, that all things being equal, we will work harder and more effectively for people we like. And we will like them in direct proportion to how they make us feel."[2]

In sorting out how people felt when working with leaders they admired, we analyzed the themes that were expressed in over four hundred case examples of admired leaders. The ten words most frequently used were

- *valued*
- *motivated*
- *enthusiastic*
- *challenged*
- *inspired*
- *capable*
- *supported*
- *powerful*
- *respected*
- *proud*

The rest of the words used to describe how people felt are similar. And they are all positive. No one mentioned *fearful* or *intimidated* or *stupid* or *sad.* Every case was about a leader who uplifted the spirit. Every story was one of enhanced self-worth. Every example was about how admired leaders strengthened the people around them and made others feel more important. The conclusion is inescapable: when people work with leaders they admire and respect, they feel better about themselves. Credible leaders raise self-esteem. Leaders who make a difference to others cause people to feel that they too can make a difference. They set people's spirits free and enable them to become more than they might have thought possible.

The case study evidence we have gathered is supported by organizational research, as we discuss further in the Appendix. The conclusions are consistent, and it is extremely important to grasp their significance. Leaders we admire do not place themselves at the center; they place others there. They do not seek the attention of people; they give it to others. They do not focus on satisfying their own aims and desires; they look for ways to respond to the needs and interests of their constituents. They are not self-centered; they concentrate on the constituent.

In our later research, we expanded on the initial investigation, this time using a behavioral measure of credibility based on the dimensions of being honest, competent, and inspiring. We asked respondents to think about the extent to which their immediate manager exhibited credibility-enhancing behaviors.[3] We found that when people perceive their managers to have high credibility, they are significantly more likely to

- Be proud to tell others they are part of the organization
- Feel a strong sense of team spirit
- See their own personal values as consistent with those of the organization
- Feel attached and committed to the organization
- Have a sense of ownership for the organization

But when people perceive their managers to have low credibility, they are significantly more likely to believe that other organization members

- Produce only if they are watched carefully
- Are motivated primarily by money
- Say good things about the organization publicly but feel differently in private
- Would consider looking for another job if the organization started experiencing problems

They are also significantly less likely to be proud of the organization, to see their own values as similar to the company's, to feel a strong sense of team spirit, to feel attached to the organization, or to have a sense of ownership.

Does credibility make a difference? If employee loyalty and commitment matter, then it obviously does. But if managers are content to pay more money to increase productivity, to watch over people carefully, to know employees are talking behind their backs, and to live with high rates of turnover, then credibility be damned.

The difference is an increase in people's willingness to exert themselves more on behalf of the shared values and visions. The credibility of leadership is what determines whether people will want to give a little more of their time, talent, energy, experience, intelligence, creativity, and support. Rather than sheepishly following orders, constituents of credible leaders act with moral commitment in following a common purpose. Managers with little or no credibility could threaten to fire people who balk at actively participating in the program. Or they could entice constituents with more money. But threat, power, position, and money do not earn commitment; they earn compliance. And compliance produces adequacy, not greatness. Only high credibility earns intense commitment. And commitment will ultimately enable people to regenerate great businesses, communities, and economies.

The credibility difference is critically important in this era of wrenching organizational change and global competition. Business leaders worldwide have pushed product quality and service quality improvement efforts to the top of their agendas. Thousands of applications for the Baldrige Award go out every year to American corporations, and nearly four hundred companies have gone through the rigorous application process. The American Society for Quality Control estimates that fifty thousand organizations have instituted some form of a quality-improvement program. Every day across the corporate landscape, new initiatives sprout up to shorten time to market, reduce layers, enhance service productivity, eliminate steps from the work process, shrink the staff, break the organization into smaller units, and make other improvements.

If credibility is the foundation of leadership and makes such a significant difference, how are leaders doing on the credibility scale? Unfortunately, not well. We have seen a large-scale erosion of employee confidence in management over the last decade.

GAINS FOR THE CYNICS

Substantially fewer of us believe that the leaders and managers of our business and governmental institutions are capable enough or trustworthy enough to guide us to the top in this intensely competitive global marketplace. There is a growing sense among employees that management is not competent to handle these tough challenges, that they are not quite telling us the truth, and that they are motivated more by greed than by concern for the customer, the employees, or the country.

At a time when executives are appealing to their employees to boost productivity, to improve the quality of products and services, and to be more committed to winning competitive global battles, more and more doubt the sincerity of these calls to action. Workers are responding with a noticeable shrug and sighing, "Why should I put out? They are just in it for themselves, anyway."

For example, according to research by professors Donald Kanter and Philip Mirvis, in the late 1980s 43 percent of

American workers were "cynical," 41 percent were "upbeat," and 16 percent were "wary."[4] By the early 1990s, the percentage of cynical workers had increased to 48 percent—that is, nearly one in every two workers. Fewer people are upbeat today than they were at the close of the last decade.[5]

Cynics have significantly less trust in their managements than those who are upbeat. Nearly half of the cynics doubt the truth of what management tells them, and only a third believes management has integrity. Three-quarters believe that top executives do pretty much what they want to no matter what people think.[6] When listening to management's latest organizational improvement initiative, the cynic is likely to say, "Yeah, sure. I know who that will benefit. Besides, the last time you guys said things were going to get better, the only thing that happened was more of my friends got laid off."

A survey by Lou Harris and Associates for Steelcase revealed that only 40 percent of U.S. office workers believe it is "very true" that management is "honest, upright, and ethical," though 85 percent of office workers said it was "very important" for management to be so.[7] Steelcase extended its survey to include countries other than the United States, and found that there is a desire for ethical management worldwide.[8] But, as in the United States, what we expect and what we believe we get are not the same (see Table 2.1). It would appear that the credibility gap is found around the globe.

Consider the question: "Is the company treating you with dignity and respect?" In a recent survey by the Opinion Research Corporation, only 37 percent of hourly employees and 44 percent of professionals responded positively to that question. And just 45 percent of hourly workers and 53 percent of professionals have confidence in the abilities of their top managements. Managers, quite understandably, are inclined to feel differently; but still only 65 percent of them feel treated with respect, and only 66 percent have positive feelings about top management's ability. These figures are not exactly a vote of confidence from those in the middle.[9]

The Harris Poll 1992 survey of public confidence in major institutions found that there was a significant decline in

Table 2.1. Ethical Management.
Statement: *"Management is honest, upright, and ethical."*

Office workers	Percentage of office workers who rank this statement as	
	Very important	Very true
Canada	87	36
United States	85	40
European Economic Community	80	26
Japan	72	16

Source: Steelcase *Worldwide Office Environment Index Summary Report* (Grand Rapids, Mich.: Steelcase, 1991): 7.

the confidence in major companies. Only 11 percent had great confidence in major businesses. That finding is the lowest in the twenty-six years of the survey. Compare this with the 55 percent who had great confidence in 1966.[10]

These attitudes are not confined to business. Politicians score even lower on the confidence scale. The overall rating for political cynicism, according to Kanter and Mirvis, is 59 percent.[11] More than half of those surveyed by the researchers believe politicians will say or do anything to stay in office and make promises they don't intend to keep. The Harris Poll shows that only 10 percent of the public have great confidence in Congress.[12] An April 1992 survey by the *New York Times*/CBS News found that 71 percent of the people agreed with the statement "there is practically no connection between what a politician says and what he will do once he gets elected."[13]

We recently observed firsthand the manifestation of this lack of confidence in political leadership. We had the opportunity to be part of a panel discussion of regional problems in the San Francisco Bay Area. Two highly respected regional economic and planning experts articulately presented the serious transportation problems facing the region. After they spoke, we asked the well-educated and concerned members of the audience, "How many of you have confidence that our elected and appointed officials will solve these problems by the year 2000?" No one raised a hand. "By the year 2020?" we asked. Again, no hands went up.

Increasing cynicism is a threat to both democracy and the world economy. Cynics, for example, are more likely to believe that they do not count for much, that politicians don't care about them and are just out for themselves. They translate these beliefs into apathy; thus, they are less inclined to vote in political elections.[14] If more and more people come to believe that most people are just out for themselves, imagine what will happen to democratic societies. The cynics' view will indeed become reality. Only the elite special interests will control nations.

At this moment in world history, when we desperately need all citizens to take part in learning, creating, and improving, we find that fewer and fewer are inclined to do so. Even when the evidence of impending crisis is clear (whether in the global market or in the local workplace) we have little faith that our leaders have the ability to get us out of the mess.

Now you may think that you don't want cynics to participate. You may not want all that negativism and suspicion. But just consider all that wasted talent and energy. Just think what communities and organizations could do if they had 100 percent, enthusiastic participation. Just think what they could do if cynicism was transformed into hope!

THE REASONS
FOR CYNICISM

In order to find solutions to this crisis of confidence, we must first understand what is creating this increased cynicism and alienation. What is the root cause of declining confidence in our leaders and institutions? The major explanations we heard when we asked why cynicism has increased and credibility declined range from current scandals to overall suspicion.

Scandals, Betrayals, and Disillusionment

The most common reasons for the decline of credibility are the most visible. We have seen the S&L and Wall Street scandals in the United States—and the BCCI rip-off, which makes the others look like child's play. There have been the Iran-Contra affair, the sexploits of politicians, the check bouncing of congressional representatives, and the abuse of White House perks. In England, Robert Maxwell proved to be a rogue of proportions larger than his own larger-than-life size. Religious evangelists have been caught with their pants down, their hands in the collection box, and worse. The most sacred and spiritual traditions have been violated. Nations have had to painfully reexamine the character of some of their most beloved leaders in the light of reports on their personal lives. In Japan, prime ministers and government officials resigned in shame over fraud and abuse in the 1980s and early 1990s.

Each year, political campaign pledges are made—the "read my lips" statements—but people seldom believe them anymore. And the longer the list and the more appealing the promise, the less likely people are to believe it. There is growing disillusionment with the political process and a seething resentment of the powerful elites who control institutions.[15] By the spring of 1992, political cynicism had reached fever pitch. The *New York Times* interviewed hundreds of voters across the United States over a five-month period. They found voters were angered most by failed promises. Keith Ditmor, a worker in the General Motors chassis department in Ypsilanti, Michigan, was typical of the majority when he said, "The politicians say, 'I'll do this, I'll do that.' Then they get elected and do nothing. If I had my way, I'd throw out every politician. I would. They're liars."[16]

Similar attitudes extend to the business world. We all have friends or friends of friends who have suffered the unintended consequences of too much debt from leveraged buyouts. Downsizings, massive layoffs, restructurings, and market-share losses to foreign competitors have led some to attribute these failures to the incompetence of business leaders. With the squeeze on profits and the pressure to get "lean and mean," some of our most grand, even mythical, corporations have experienced employee disillusionment of unprecedented proportions.

As a consequence of all the scandal and broken promises, people feel betrayed. Although 93.8 percent of respondents to an *Industry Week* poll said that loyalty was an important factor in a company's success or failure, 75.6 percent said they thought their companies were less loyal to them than they were five years previously.[17] Bob Burak, a steel worker who lost his job after thirty-four years at Jones & Laughlin Steel, sums it up for many workers alienated by the actions of business during the last decade: "You really don't trust the company because you don't know what it's going to do."[18]

Many more now inquire if there is any leader who has the strength of character to sustain our faith. People openly wonder if their political and business leaders aren't just in it for themselves. What ever happened to those who serve for the good of the country or the good of the company? Can any leader be trusted?

Obscene Compensation for Executives

In America, top-executive pay has gone through the roof at the same time that corporate performance has declined. Real or imagined, it appears that the average workers are suffering while the bosses are luxuriating. Their indulgence, say some, is costing people their jobs and companies their markets.

One of America's leading compensation consultants, Graef Crystal, writes that things have gone too far:

> While the pay—in inflation-discounted dollars—of the average American worker has decreased by almost 13 percent during the past twenty years and by some 5 percent during the 1980s, the pay of the typical CEO of a major company—in those same inflation-discounted dollars—has risen more than three times.... Where that typical CEO earned total compensation (excluding perquisites and fringe benefits) that was around 35 times the pay of an average manufacturing worker in 1974, a typical

CEO today earns pay that is around 120 times that of an average manufacturing worker and about 150 times that of the average worker in both manufacturing and service industries.[19]

No other issue seems to anger employees, including managers, more than this one. *Industry Week* reports that 62 percent of managers believe that executive pay is too high. Reporter Joani Nelson-Horchler writes that because of exorbitant executive pay, morale is low and cynicism high throughout industry.[20] Executive pay, the magazine's poll shows, is actually having a demotivating effect on people in organizations.

There is increasing recognition among executives that pay is a hot potato and a topic that provokes tension. Particularly in today's economy, as "American companies lose ground to foreign rivals, whose chiefs are often paid pittances by U. S. standards, the debate over executive pay is reaching fever pitch."[21] And CEOs are on the defensive.

Not only is there a perception that CEO pay is too high, scholars who have studied the subject conclude that "there are few, if any, meritocratic elements in the formulation of American CEOs' compensation."[22] In other words, for all the rhetoric about "pay for performance," there isn't much evidence to support a link between CEO salaries and their achievements. Recovery from the credibility recession may have to be linked to self-initiated reforms in executive pay.

Quality Illusions

A majority of line employees and managers believe that quality is very important. Espoused commitment to quality is understood as the first step in the improvement process. But embedded in the quality movement is a somewhat surprising issue. "Quality, quality, quality!" may be the new competitive war cry, but worker opinion suggests that companies aren't heeding it. In one survey of employee attitudes toward quality-improvement programs (conducted for the American Society for Quality Control by the Gallup Organization), 55 percent of employees reported that their companies said that it was extremely important to "show our customers we're committed to quality." However, only 36 percent stated that the company followed through extremely well on this commitment. Fifty-three percent stated that their companies considered "making quality everyone's top priority" extremely important. But only 35 percent said that the company was doing very well in that area.[23]

Actions, say employees, are falling short in the quality-improvement game. But how can this be when so many dollars are being spent and so much effort expended to train every worker in statistical process control and Pareto charts? How can this be when companies are competing vigorously to win the Baldrige Award or the Deming Prize? How can this happen when quality is at the top of nearly every organization's strategic agenda?

Perhaps the money, the training, and the prizes play a role. You can't pick up a local newspaper or a company newsletter without reading about the importance of quality. You can't miss the "quality is job one" ads on television. Expectations are raised. People come to believe that quality is the source of wealth and advantage. They expect the intensity of the actions at a minimum to match the force of the rhetoric. But when it comes to quality, apparently people have heard the talk but not seen the results.

And, as is often the case with rising expectations, even though more is accomplished, it is not enough. People believe that what is being done is not enough to close the gap. Evidence supports this observation. For example, American automobiles have significantly improved in the last decade, yet relative to the Japanese competition they still lag behind. Perhaps American automobile industry leaders assumed that the competition would stand still while they caught up.

When the perception is that leadership actions fall behind leadership promises, the credibility gap invariably widens. The message the work force is sending, however, is a healthy one, one that enlightened leaders are heeding: "Good is not enough when you dream of being great."

Suspicion of Power

Taking a historical view of the issue, we can see that there is more to the credibility-gap story. Political scientists Lipset and Schneider astutely observe that one of the reasons for the legitimacy crisis among American institutions is the tradition of suspicion of people and groups in power:

> A related consequence of this country's egalitarianism and democratic values is the absence of deference for elites and the recurrent waves of populist attacks on various leadership groups. Although most Americans hold the country's basic institutions in high regard, they have almost always found much to object to in the way these institutions operate and in the performance of their leaders. . . . [Americans] assume the worst, or the possibility of the worst, from the leaders of all powerful institutions, whether public or private. Indeed, the public has shown a tendency to personalize social problems, that is, to attribute them to inept leaders and corrupt power-holders.[24]

Strong evidence for the American's populist bent could be seen in the 1992 presidential and congressional election campaigns. Establishment candidates were attacked from all sides. The anti-incumbent mood enabled term-limit initiatives to pass in fourteen states. The Republican party faithful voted for Pat Buchanan not because they believed he would win, but because they wanted to send a message to the White House about failed promises. Jerry Brown rode the wave of populism in the Democratic primaries.

And then along came Ross Perot. A ground swell of support lifted him into the running. He emerged literally overnight—after a talk-show interview with Larry King—and gained extraordinary momentum. The fuel for his campaign was voters' extreme alienation and cynicism. The Ross Perot candidacy is direct evidence that frustration can be turned into action if a person emerges that the people perceive to be credible. In commenting on the Perot candidacy, William Schneider, political analyst with the American Enterprise Institute, said: "It's credibility. I ask Perot signers, 'Where does he stand?' They say, 'It doesn't matter to me that he has no position, because then he's not going to lie to me.'"[25]

Then Perot suddenly dropped out of the race. His constituents were devastated. His favorable ratings dropped into the teens. It seemed as if his initial credibility had been destroyed. But he returned, regaining most of his lost ground with his straight talk about the economy, his thirty-minute "infomercials" on the state of the economy, and his no-nonsense appeal to the disaffection that many voters felt with politics as usual. Despite his sometimes seemingly paranoid explanations for his earlier withdrawal, Perot amazed the pundits and garnered 19 percent of the popular vote. Nineteen million voters testified that populism was alive and well.

Perhaps no one suffered more from the people's questions about a politician's credibility than candidate Bill Clinton. George Bush and the Republicans made trust *the* issue in the final weeks of the campaign. Their constant questioning of Clinton's fitness to hold the office of the president caused his credibility rating to drop from a high of 70 percent in August 1992 to a low of 52 percent two weeks before the election.[26] This issue may explain why Clinton did not earn a popular majority in the election. His final tally was 43 percent. Only time will tell whether the trust issue will follow him during his tenure as president.

But the numbers also teach us another important lesson about credibility. Those same polls that showed Clinton lagging on the honesty and integrity scale also indicated that on the two most important issues to the voters (creating jobs and curing the economic ills), Clinton was consistently rated most able. Credibility is not an isolated phenomenon, independent of the context, but is linked to the issues that are most important to people at the time they are deciding whom they will follow. On this balance sheet, Clinton won. He and his campaign strategists stayed absolutely focused on jobs and the economy. That focus kept the trust issue from sinking the aspirations of Bill Clinton.

A similar "I-won't-take-it-anymore" attitude can be seen in business. People are exercising their votes and exorcising their resentment in the form of shareholder movements. Boards and officers are now taking a much more serious view of what one of their important "constituencies" expects. *Business Week* reported it this way: "This proxy season, investors, like fed-up voters, are raring to send a message. Where corporate performance is poor, pay excessive, or management unresponsive, they want change, even to the point of throwing out the bums—not just insiders, but independent directors, too. . . . Protest is the point this mean proxy season. Colorado's Public Employees' Retirement Assn., for example, is hardly an activist investor, never even having sponsored a resolution. But this year, the $11.5 billion fund is withholding votes from directors at American Express, Occidental Petroleum, Travelers, Westinghouse, and Unisys—thus far."[27]

The low ratings of management's integrity by office workers in Canada, the European Economic Community countries, and Japan suggest that suspicion of power is not exclusively an American phenomenon.[28] In the early 1990s, there were strikes in Germany; upheavals in the Baltic states; displays of voter discontent in Denmark, France, and England; and unrest in many other parts of the world. It is certainly not business as usual.

The empowerment movement is also a form of populism. It is an effort to create more sociological and psychological equity in organizations and in many cases (such as gainsharing programs) to produce greater financial equity as well. Empowerment, whether in the form of self-managed teams or flexible work schedules or telecommuting, is a redistribution of wealth and power from the managerial elites to the line workers. It can only occur in a society that is positively oriented to the value of more local control and is suspicious of centralized authority.

Somewhat paradoxically, however, suspicion of power

also enables people to maintain confidence in their institutions. They blame the leaders, but not the institutions of government or business or labor. It also fuels the belief that individuals can make a difference. A strong heritage of not accepting a powerless condition and a passionate desire to assert control over one's own life are powerful forces in creating viable economic and political institutions. This healthy skepticism has been one of the major inhibitors to fascism. Strong individualism and free choice are great protectors of liberty.

Opinions of the people in leadership positions also tend to rise and fall with events.[29] When times are good, people exhibit more confidence in their leaders; when times are bad, they show less. The more severe the events and the more compressed the time frame, the more cynical people are likely to become. It is thus understandable that in a prolonged recession, with attendant layoffs and shrinking family incomes, the credibility of business, labor, and government leaders will decline. A natural suspicion of power and the confluence of events (such as the scandals of the 1980s and 1990s) certainly can explain a great deal about why leaders have lost credibility. We are seeing that bad timing can often ruin credibility as much as bad actions.

Yet dismissing credibility problems as simply a function of the times permits leaders to escape responsibility for their own actions. Suspicion of power may help in understanding why people sometimes get the urge to "throw the bums out," but it does not explain why some in power are more trusted than others. These explanations fail to suggest the real cause and positive actions that the people or their leaders might take to strengthen credibility over time.

What's a constituent to do? What's a leader to do?

THE VISIBLE LEADER

To understand the underlying cause of lost credibility and the solution for strengthening it, we need to understand the human dynamics of trust. Let's look again at the finding that only about a third of office workers consider executives to be very honest. Consider that finding the next time you are in a meeting at your organization. Look to your left, look to your right. Then, given that statistic, decide which two of the three of you are dishonest.

The fact is that we do not believe that statistic. We do not believe that only a third of our business — or political or labor or community — leaders are honest. The perception is that the invisible "they" are dishonest. Rarely do we view the folks we sit next to at work as not trustworthy. It is always the other people, not the ones we know.

Kanter and Mirvis's studies show that people have more trust in members of their own work groups than they do in management, that they are less cynical in dealing with their co-workers. Why? "For one thing, it is simply harder to hold cynical stereotypes about people you work with every day. Research on prejudice also shows that people can hold stereotypes about general groups of others (say, management) but often modify or abandon them when dealing with individual members of the stereotyped group."[30]

Ask yourself this question: "Whom do you trust more — the people you know or the people you do not know?" Your answer is likely to be those you know. Admittedly, you may not trust some people you know well, but that is much less often the case.

There is a telling scene in a video with Pat Carrigan, a General Motors plant manager at the time (now retired). This scene reveals the essence of how we earn credibility and how we lose it. A group of UAW members are sitting around talking about Carrigan's leadership. A veteran of the plant observes that if the plant manager who had preceded Carrigan at the facility were to enter the room, he wouldn't know who he was. Carrigan, he says, is the first plant manager ever to walk around and shake everybody's hand. Later in the tape, Jack White, then UAW local president, says, "Pat Carrigan ain't got a phony bone in her body."[31]

We have viewed this video with thousands of people. In

recalling the scene, one participant remarked, "She had to get awfully close to them for them to know her bones!" Exactly. It was Carrigan's physical presence that earned her the respect and trust of the workers. It was her closeness and her visibility that enabled her to overcome the years of cynicism and distrust.

What lesson can we take away from this insightful observation? The lesson for all leaders is this: earning credibility is a retail activity, a factory floor activity, a person-to-person one. It is gained in small quantities through physical presence. Leaders who are inaccessible cannot possibly expect to be trusted just because they have a title. Credibility is earned via the physical acts of shaking a hand, touching a shoulder, leaning forward to listen. By sharing personal experiences, telling their own stories, and joining in dialogue, leaders become people, not just holders of positions.

Too many leaders have become remote and insulated. We, the people, have come to see business, government, and labor leaders as not a part of, but apart from, us. Washington, D.C., is talked about as if it were on another planet, and corporate headquarters might as well be on a distant star. Leaders have not been close enough to get to know.

Too many leaders are not real people anymore. Technology, for all its wonders and potential, has actually made them less accessible and more distant. Though you may see more of their electronic images and hear more of their Teleprompted words, you really know less about the person. You do not know what is real and what is hype. You don't know them, and they don't know you. That's no relationship.

The secret to closing the credibility gap lies in a collective willingness to get closer, to become known, and to get to know others—as human beings, not as voting statistics or employee numbers. By getting closer to their constituents and by letting their constituents get to know them, leaders can strengthen their foundation of credibility.

What people want in a leader is someone who is trustworthy, is competent, has a vision of the future, and is dynamic and inspiring. People are more cynical today in part because they believe their leaders do not live up to these expectations. The gap between what people want from their leaders and what they believe they are getting has grown to Grand Canyon proportions. This canyon is not likely to be bridged until leaders are able to realign their own principles with those of the people they wish to lead. Admittedly, leadership credibility is not the cure for all the ills of cynicism, but by renewing it leaders can begin to close this gap and restore faith in the power of persons.

DOING WHAT WE SAY: THE CRITICAL DIFFERENCE

We asked people to define *credibility* in behavioral terms, to tell us the behavioral evidence they would use to judge whether or not a leader was believable. The most frequent response was "they do what they say they will do." Similarly, people would say, "They practice what they preach." "They walk the talk." "Their actions are consistent with their words."

This simple definition leads to a simple prescription for strengthening credibility: DWYSYWD — do what you say you will do. DWYSYWD has two essential parts: the first is "say" and the second is "do."

Credibility is mostly about consistency between words and deeds. People listen to the words and look at the deeds. Then they measure the congruence. A judgment of "credible" is handed down when the two are consonant.

In the domain of leadership, however, DWYSYWD is necessary but insufficient. When you do what you say, it may make you credible, but it may not make you a credible leader. Your constituents also have needs and interests, values and visions. To earn and strengthen leadership credibility, leaders must do what *we* say *we* will do — DWWSWWD.

That *We* is crucial to leadership credibility. Certainly leaders are expected to do what they say. They are expected to keep their promises and follow through on their commitments. But what they say must also be what we, the constituents, believe. To take people to places they have never been before, leaders and constituents must be on the same path. And to get people to join the voyage of discovery voluntarily requires that the aims and aspirations of leaders and constituents are harmonious.

Forgetting the *we* has derailed many managers.[32] Their actions may have been consistent only with their own wishes, not with those of the people they wanted to lead. When managers resort to the use of power and position, to compliance and command to get things done, they are not leading. They are dictating.

The credible leader learns how to discover and communicate the shared values and visions that can form a common ground on which all can stand. Credible leaders find unity among the diverse interests, points of view, and beliefs. Upon a strong, unified foundation, leaders and constituents can act consistently with spirit and drive to build viable organizations and communities.

As we see it, then, strengthening leadership credibility has three phases—clarity, unity, and intensity—that are closely linked, as shown in Figure 2.1. By clarifying meaning, unifying constituents, and intensifying actions, leaders demonstrate their own commitment to a consistent set of expectations. This process, repeatedly followed, earns leadership credibility and sustains it over time.

Clarity

Commitment to credibility begins with the clarification of the leader's and the constituents' needs, interests, values, visions, aims, and aspirations. This phase of the process may require personal clarification of one's own values and capabilities. It also requires attending to others. Clarity exists when people can state, "I have a clear idea of what others value and what they can do." When clarity exists, everyone knows the guiding principles and core competencies that most directly contribute to organizational and individual vitality and success.

Figure 2.1. The Credibility-Building Process Model.

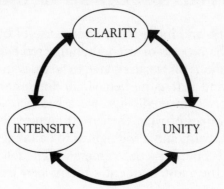

Unity

To build a strong and viable organization, people must be united in a common cause—united on where they are going, on why they are headed in that direction, and on which principles will guide their journey. Credible leaders are able to build a community of shared vision and values. Unity exists when people widely share, support, and endorse the intent of the commonly understood set of aims and aspirations. Not only do constituents know what these are, they are in agreement that shared vision and values are important to the future success of the organization. They also have a common interpretation of how the values will be put into practice.

Intensity

Understanding and agreeing to aims and aspirations are essential to the process of strengthening credibility. But we have learned that actions speak louder than words, so people who feel strongly about the worth of values will act on them. Intensity exists when principles are taken seriously, when they reflect deeply felt standards and emotional bonds, and when they are the basis of critical organizational resource allocations. When values are intensely felt, there is greater consistency between words and actions, and there is an almost moral dimension to "keeping the faith."

THE SIX DISCIPLINES

Clarity, unity, and intensity provide a useful framework for looking at the process of strengthening credibility. But what about the actions that leaders need to take day in and day out? To understand better the behavioral dimension of how admired leaders earn credibility, we asked people to give us specific examples of what their most admired leaders did to gain respect, trust, and a willingness to be influenced.

Several common actions emerged. The following is a list of some of the most frequently mentioned behaviors. The leader

- Supported me
- Had the courage to do the right thing
- Challenged me
- Developed and acted as a mentor to others
- Listened
- Celebrated good work
- Followed through on commitments
- Trusted me
- Empowered others
- Made time for people
- Shared the vision
- Opened doors
- Overcame personal hardships
- Admitted mistakes
- Advised others
- Solved problems creatively
- Taught well

This list closely reflects the words people used in describing how they felt when working with leaders they admired. In fact, the vast majority of the actions mentioned were about making the constituent the center of attention. They were about serving others and making others feel important, not about making the leader look important. They were about empowering others, not about grabbing power. These actions were also about doing what you say you will do, being consistent, and working hard. And they have to do with optimism and overcoming personal hardships.

We conclude from our interviews and case analyses that credibility, respect, and loyalty are earned primarily when leaders demonstrate by their actions that they believe in the inherent self-worth of others. They are earned by appreciating others, affirming others, and developing others. Earning credibility does not necessarily mean lending a credit card, as Lacoy's hospital administrator did, but it does mean acting in ways that show trust in others.

Credibility is also earned and strengthened when the leader has a philosophy and acts in ways that are consistent with it. Maintaining credibility requires tenacity and persistence, especially in the face of adversity. Often the lessons are learned the hard way, and admired leaders are ones that admit mistakes and learn from their experiences. Admired leaders are also optimists. They face reality with conviction and a "can do" spirit.

From our analysis of common themes in the cases we collected, we derived six practices, which we have come to call the six disciplines of credibility. These are

1. Discovering your self
2. Appreciating constituents
3. Affirming shared values
4. Developing capacity
5. Serving a purpose
6. Sustaining hope

We have chosen the word *discipline* quite intentionally, in part because its root originates from a word meaning "to learn." Someone who follows a discipline is a *learner*. Learning and practicing these six disciplines can help you build and maintain your leadership credibility.

Let's now look at these in turn.

Discovering Your Self

The place to begin the enhancement of credibility is with an exploration of the inner territory. Who are you? What do you believe in? What do you stand for?

To be credible as a leader, you must first clarify your own values, the standards by which you choose to live your life. Values guide how you feel, what you say, what you think, how you make choices, and how you act. Once clear about your own values, translate them into a set of guiding principles, a credo, that you can communicate to the people you hope to lead.

But a leadership philosophy isn't enough. You must have the competence to deliver on your promises. You must know what you are doing and have the experience and training to do it. You also must have the confidence that you can deliver. You must really believe that you have the will and the skill to persist in the face of adversity. So assess your towering competencies. Determine if they are sufficient to meet the demands of the situation. Test your self-confidence against the realities of the challenge. Then seek the developmental experiences you need in order to improve your capacity to lead. To be a credible leader, you must have character, whose essential ingredients are credo, competence, and confidence.

Appreciating Constituents

Understanding your own leadership philosophy is only the beginning. To be a leader, you must also develop a deep understanding of the collective values and desires of your constituents. Leadership is a relationship, and strong relationships are built on mutual understanding. Leadership is a dialogue, not a monologue. Constituents come to believe in their leaders — to see them as worthy of their trust — when they believe that the leaders have their best interests at heart. Leaders who are clearly only interested in their own agendas, their own advancement, and their own well-being will not be followed willingly. Reach out and attend to others. Be present with them; listen to them. Go out and talk to your constituents, and find out what they value.

Understanding and appreciating constituents' needs and values is made more difficult in today's complex work environment. Leaders know that compassion for the struggles of others, for the diversity of cultures and beliefs, enriches everyone. So define your constituents broadly and seek diversity of views. By forcing yourself to look at a wide range of possibilities, you will make better decisions and produce more accurate results. You will be more adaptable and more resilient.

Affirming Shared Values

Credible leaders honor the diversity of their many constituencies. They also find a common ground for agreement on which everyone can stand. They bring people together and unite them in a cause. They know that shared values make a difference and give everyone a shared language for collaboration. Leaders show others how everyone's individual values and interests can be served by coming to consensus on a set of common values.

Inevitably, conflicts will arise among diverse constituencies. Yet shared values give everyone an internal compass that enables them to act independently and interdependently, responsibly and publicly. In a credible community dilemmas are resolved using principles not positions; the focus is on problems, not people.

Credible leaders build a strong sense of community. It's a good idea to get people together in forums to talk about their values. Find the common ground and build consensus around a core of shared values. Affirm these passionately and speak enthusiastically on behalf of your community. And renew your community. Do not allow it to decay into anomie and normlessness.

Developing Capacity

People cannot contribute to the aims and aspirations of an organization if they do not know what to do, and they cannot help if they do not know how to do it. Strategic initiatives to deliver "six sigma quality" or "world-class service" can actually make people feel weak and incompetent if they do not have the skills and abilities to perform. Therefore, it is essential for leaders to develop continuously the capacity of their members to keep their commitments.

You must educate, educate, educate. Bring the values and purposes to life, whether in one-on-one sessions or in large group forums, on video, in conversations, or in presentations. Assure that educational opportunities exist for individuals to build their knowledge and skill. Provide the resources and other organizational supports that enable constituents to put their abilities to good use.

Credible leaders are not afraid to liberate the leader in everyone. They liberate others by giving them the latitude to make choices, by constantly keeping people informed about what is going on, and by creating a climate that encourages risk taking, experimenting, and learning from mistakes. Out of this ethic of continuous learning and improvement comes increased self-confidence and personal responsibility. If everyone is a leader, then everyone is responsible for guiding the organization toward its future.

To strengthen your credibility as a leader, give people more discretion and keep them informed. Set them free to experiment and to learn. But also foster an "earning mentality"—engender the attitude that people benefit and get ahead based on merit and productivity, not status and entitlement. Stress that in this age of liberation, organizations will only become what all their constituents want them to become. Everyone takes initiative. No one waits.

Serving a Purpose

Leadership is a service. Leaders serve a purpose for the people who have made it possible for them to lead—their constituents. They are servant leaders — not self-serving, but other-serving. The relationship of leader and constituent has been turned upside down. Or rather it has been righted.

All credible leaders know that it is their visible actions that demonstrate their true commitment. When leaders affirm the shared values of an organization, they are also vowing that the promises will be kept consistently. Credible leaders are the first to do what has been agreed to and learned. They set the example by going first. They spend their time, the truest indicator of priorities, on core values. Leaders hold themselves accountable to the same standards as everyone else. When their leadership service is inadequate, they make amends for it, just as they would expect others to do.

When a key value is at stake or when someone's behavior is inconsistent with the stated values, leaders must step in and make decisions based on matters of principle. By taking a stand, leaders let others know that they are willing to put personal careers or safety on the line in service to the principles.

So show others what is important to you and the organization. Audit how you spend your time. Do the proportions relate to the importance of the shared values? Establish new routines and systems that reinforce these values, and when necessary take dramatic actions to confront critical inconsistencies. Take a stand based on principle.

Sustaining Hope

Credible leaders keep hope alive. An upbeat attitude is essential in these troubling times of transition. People need more energy and enthusiasm, more inspiration and optimism from their leaders than in times of stability and growth. Optimists are proactive and behave in ways that promote health and combat illness. People with high hope are also high achievers. They have higher aspirations and better levels of performance. Leaders foster the optimistic attitudes that lead to more challenging goals and achievements.

In times of challenge and difficulty, leaders are also available as a support and as a friend. They draw on their own knowledge and experience to offer advice and counsel. They are there to tell the team that it can succeed, that it can do it, that it has the will and the way to make it to the top. They act not as a Pollyanna, but as a cheerleader. And if necessary, credible leaders reassess the situation and find new ways to reach the goals or reset their original targets.

Credible leaders are compassionate. They understand how their constituents have suffered and know that they must suffer along with them. Cynicism is only reinforced when leaders appear exempt from paying the price for change. Only those who have felt the pain of loss and yearning for fulfillment can truly inspire. Situations arise that continuously test a leader's beliefs. During those times, credible leaders let shared values be their guide. This is the only way they can maintain the respect and trust of their constituents. Their courage is an inspiration to others to make sacrifices.

Credible leaders recognize and reward people for actions that strengthen shared aims and aspirations. Recognition reinforces the shared values and provides an opportunity to tell success stories. When people see that rewards are linked to values-oriented behavior, they are much more likely to strive to live by the principles.

To sustain hope, be there for the team in times of need. Tell the members that they can do it and that times will improve. Be flexible in plans to achieve shared goals, and set a new course or a new target if things aren't working out. And don't forget to turn to a friend when in need of a lift or a lesson.

Rebuilding lost leadership credibility will require daily attention. Leaders will have to nurture their relationships with constituents. They will have to show people that they care, every day. They will have to take the time to act consciously and consistently. Their actions must speak louder than their words. Leadership, after all, exists only in the eyes of the constituents.

We will examine each of these disciplines in turn in the following chapters. First, we turn to the place where every leadership journey begins—the inner quest to discover our core beliefs and capabilities. The leadership adventure is at the beginning a self-exploration.

3

Discovering Your Self

One key to being a successful leader is self-awareness.

James A. Autry
Magazine Group
Meredith Publishing

"I know who I was, who I am, and where I want to be," says Dan Kaplan, president of Hertz Equipment Rental Corporation. "So in other words, I know the level of commitment that I am prepared to make and why I am prepared to make that level of commitment personally. I know what it takes to achieve success for me. That success for me comes from paying a big price, putting a lot of work and a lot of sacrifice behind it."[1]

Kaplan's words reflect an ancient commandment that was carved over the entrance to the Delphic oracle of Apollo, the mythological Greek god of the sun, prophecy, music, medicine, and poetry.[2] This message—*Know Thyself*—remains true today. Today's leaders should seek self-knowledge if they mean to establish and enhance their credibility.

Leadership scholar Warren Bennis, in his study of how twenty-nine successful people learned to become leaders, notes that self-knowledge was an essential part of defining a leader's integrity. Bennis writes, "To become a leader, then, you must become yourself, become the maker of your own life."[3] He observes that knowing thyself is "the most difficult task any of us faces. But until you truly know yourself, strengths and weaknesses, know what you want to do and why you want to do it, you cannot succeed in any but the most superficial sense of the word."[4]

Your capacity to win the personal credibility jackpot—to align words and deeds—depends on how well you know yourself. The better you know yourself, the better you can make sense of the often incomprehensible and conflicting messages you receive daily. Do this, do that. Buy this, buy that. Support this, support that. Decide this, decide that. We need internal guidance to navigate the permanent white waters of today's environment.

Our research indicates that to know genuinely the level of commitment you are willing to make, you must discover three essential aspects of your self: your credo, your competencies, and your confidence. Your values, your personal *credo*, give you the right words to say. Your capabilities, your *competencies*, give you the skills to turn your words into actions. And your trust in your abilities to do what you believe, your *confidence*, gives you the will to make use of those skills.[5]

Seek, then, to discover your credo, your competence, and your confidence. They are the required deposits in your credibility bank account. As a first step, let us explore the process for discovering your leadership credo.

CLARIFYING YOUR CREDO: "THIS I BELIEVE"

In our studies, we have asked hundreds of people to list the historical leaders they most admired—leaders who, if alive today, they could imagine themselves following willingly. Although no single leader received a majority of the nominations, the two most frequently mentioned were Abraham

Lincoln and Martin Luther King, Jr. — two leaders who lived a century apart but in times of national struggle, two leaders with unwavering commitment to principles.

In reviewing the list of others nominated for most admired leader, we found that the entire list was composed of people with strong beliefs about matters of principle. From Eleanor Roosevelt to Franklin D. Roosevelt, from Mother Teresa to Jesus Christ, from Golda Meir to Mahatma Gandhi, all were passionate about what was right and just. The message is clear. We admire those who stand for something. We respect those who believe in something.

Constituents rightfully expect their leaders to have the courage of their convictions. They expect them to stand up for their beliefs. If leaders are not clear about what they believe in, they are much more likely to change their positions with every fad or opinion poll. Without core beliefs and with only shifting positions, would-be leaders will be judged as inconsistent and will be derided for being "political" in their behavior. The first stop on the credibility journey is thus clarification of values.

Defining Values

What does it mean to have beliefs? What does it mean to have values? According to the late Milton Rokeach, one of the leading researchers and scholars in the field of human values, "A value is an enduring belief that a specific mode of conduct or end-state of existence is personally or socially preferable to an opposite or converse mode of conduct or end-state of existence."[6] Values inform us of what to do and what not to do. They are the guiding principles in our lives with respect to the personal and social ends we desire — such as salvation or peace — and with respect to moral conduct and personal competence — such as honesty and imagination.

Values are directly relevant to credibility. To do what we say we will do (our respondents' behavioral definition of credibility) we must know what we want to do and how we wish to behave. That's what our values help us to define.

Using Values as Guides

Values serve a number of important functions. They are standards that guide our conduct in a variety of settings and situations. Through them, we can take positions on issues, actively choose our policies, and evaluate ours and others' actions, beliefs, and attitudes.

Values enable people to *know* in their own minds what to do and what not to do. When values are clear, they do not have to rely upon direction from someone in authority. By knowing what means and ends are most important, people can act independently, or at least they can recognize that they may have a conflict between their own values and those of business or society. In either case, people are in more control of their own lives than if the values are unclear and hidden. Values, in this sense, are empowering. Constituents know that at least some things — these values — will endure over time. The more volatile the environment, the greater the need for clear and abiding principles.

Values and value systems also serve as plans for resolving conflicts and making decisions. If you believe, for instance, that diversity enriches innovation and service, then you should know what to do if the women in the group keep getting cut off in conversation. By contrast, if you believe in the survival of the fittest, you would be unlikely to intervene. If you think independence and initiative are more important than conformity and obedience, you would be more likely to challenge something your manager said if you think it was wrong.

It is unlikely, however, that people can behave consistently with each one of their values all the time. For example, a person may believe strongly in the merit of customer responsiveness and responsibility to family. But when a customer request for a special order requires that she and her colleagues work more hours than normal, she is likely to be in conflict. If she works late and has to cancel a family engagement, she may be seen as insensitive to her loved ones. If she tells her colleagues that she cannot work late because she needs the time with her family, she may be seen as unresponsive to the customer or to her team members. Yet by being clear about personal values and by being willing to articulate them, people can engage in a meaningful dialogue about their priorities. It is not one specific incident that defines the importance that people give to values; it is how choices are made over time.

Values also serve a motivational function. They keep us focused on why we are doing what we are doing and the ends toward which we are striving. Values are the banners that fly as we persist, as we struggle, as we toil. We refer to them when we need to replenish our energy. Through them, we can answer the question "Was it worth it?"[7]

Values, then, are the beliefs about what means and ends are desirable or undesirable, preferable or not preferable. But how do you clarify your own values? There are hundreds of methods.[8] We offer several techniques at the conclusion of this chapter. But don't wait to get started. Here are two techniques — writing your leadership credo and engaging in meaningful dialogue — that you may find useful in discovering your guiding beliefs.

Writing Your Credo

We use the following exercise in our workshops to get people started on writing their leadership philosophy. We call it the credo memo.[9] Try doing it right now.

> Imagine that your organization has afforded you the chance to take a six-month sabbatical, all expenses paid. You will be going to a beautiful island where the average temperature is about eighty degrees Fahrenheit during the day. The sun shines in a brilliant sky, with a few wisps of clouds. A gentle breeze cools the island down in the evening, and a light rain clears the air. You wake up in the morning to the smell of tropical flowers.
>
> You may not take any work along on this sabbatical. And you will not be permitted to communicate to anyone at your office or plant — not by letter, phone, fax, e-mail, or other means. There will be just you, a few good books, some music, and your family or a friend.

But before you depart, those with whom you work need to know something. They need to know the principles that you believe should guide their actions in your absence. They need to understand the values and beliefs that you think should steer their decision making and action taking.

You are permitted no long reports, however. Just a one-page memorandum.

If given this opportunity, what would you write on your one-page credo memo? Take out one piece of paper, and write that memo.

It usually takes about five to ten minutes to write a credo memo. We do not pretend that this exercise is a substitute for more in-depth self-discovery, but it does provide a useful starting point for articulating your guiding principles. To deepen the clarification process, identify the values you listed in your memo (usually they appear as key words or phrases) and put them in order of priority. Or give them an importance rating from one (low) to ten (high). Or place them on a continuum. Forcing yourself to express preferences enables you to see the relative importance of each value.

For an idea of how others have expressed their beliefs about leadership, people and organizations, review Exhibits 3.1 and 3.2. These provide examples of credo memos.

Reflecting on one's values requires internal dialogue. But external dialogue with others about fundamental questions of values is also essential and is the basis of a second technique for clarifying your beliefs.

Engaging in Dialogue

As you articulate the principles you believe are important to live and to work by, others may ask, "Can you clarify what you mean by that?" "How does that apply to me?" Your internal search for a response and the resulting dialogue can increase your understanding of yourself and enable others to increase theirs of you.

Dialogue does not have to be only about well-formed

Exhibit 3.1. Sample Credo Memorandum.

Donna Goya
Vice President, Human Resources
Levi Strauss & Co.

To: Personnel Staff
Subject: Managing in My Absence

We all have agreed that our mission in Personnel is to "create an environment consistent with the Company's values that optimizes employee effectiveness." The environment must be one that is fair, motivating, provides growth, development, recognition, and fun! Therefore, <u>our Personnel programs and behavior must support the Company's Aspirations, not contradict them or give mixed messages.</u>

Remember, we are a service organization. Don't be up-ward serving. I want you to get out of your offices and listen to employees — they know what's needed.

It's not important that we have new state-of-the-art programs. Let's focus on improving what we have, and again, asking what our clients need.

Lastly, carry on in an Aspirational manner and everything will be fine.

- Operate as a team.
- Talk/listen to one another.
- Recognize your peers when deserved.
- Be empowered.
- TRUST YOUR JUDGMENT!
- CELEBRATE YOUR SUCCESSES!

You're all great!

---

beliefs. It is also exhilarating and educational to explore values with constituents openly. When we interviewed Cam Starrett, executive vice president of Nestlé U.S.A., we noticed on her desk an obviously well-read copy of Shelby Steele's book, *The Content of Our Character: A New Vision of Race in America*.[10] She told us that she used it to initiate some dialogue with African-American employees in the company: "I say, 'Do you know the book?' Some do and some don't. And then I say, 'Let

Exhibit 3.2. Sample Credo Memorandum.

Fred Fuller
Vice President, Operations
Ciba-Geigy Seed Division

CREDO

- Seize the initiative; do what you know needs to be done.

- Continually seek to understand your customers' needs, and remember to modify your objectives accordingly.

- Learn what your team members' goals may be, and find ways to help them succeed.

- Trust your instincts.

- Work hard, but take time to celebrate each other's accomplishments.

---

me read some to you. I want to know what you think of this.'"
Conversations like these help Starrett to clarify her own and others' values. The process of values clarification is at once reflective and interactive.

By engaging in discourse and dialogue, people develop a sense of their own and others' moral language. This discourse can be about anything, whether the selection criteria of suppliers or the conditions for termination of employees. It can be about the approach to serving customers or the appropriate return to stockholders. Whatever the topic, when seeking to understand values, don't pursue the solution. Listen instead for those principles that seem to be governing your responses, and bring them to the surface.

Discourse about values and ideas is sorely lacking in most organizations. It is often considered a waste of time to talk about ideas, as if business has nothing to do with them. Yet it can be enlightening and even joyful when the questions are provocative. In their book *Organizational Values in America*, William G. Scott and David K. Hart present a most challenging question: "What are the requisite conditions of a worthy life in modern organizations?"[11] Try discussing that question at your next staff meeting!

EVALUATING VALUES

In a recent seminar, participants were talking about leaders they admired. The vice president of a large petrochemical company challenged us with this question: "Was Charles Manson a leader?" In his opinion, Manson fit our definition of a credible leader: he had loyal followers and strong beliefs about what was appropriate conduct. He was dynamic and spoke passionately about what he believed. Others at the seminar suggested additional notorious villains who might be added to the list: Hitler, Saddam Hussein, Stalin, Jim Jones. How would you have answered this question? Was Charles Manson a leader? Was David Koresh a leader?

Here is where the role of values in leadership becomes most salient. Leadership is a process and a set of practices. As such, leadership is amoral. The process and practices admit no right or wrong. All processes can be used for good or evil. Nuclear science, biological science, social science: each can be used to heal or kill. Processes themselves are neither positive nor negative. People give processes their charge.

Leaders, however, are most decidedly moral or immoral. Manson may have been an insanely skillful practitioner of the art of leadership in the amoral sense of the term, but he was *not* a moral leader. To our way of thinking, Manson, and anyone who would do evil, has no legitimacy as a leader. Such legitimacy is determined not by the leader, but by the society that envelops the leader and the constituents. Manson and those like him who take others down paths that violate the shared and sacred values of the societies from which they come cannot be called credible moral leaders.

We wish we could also say that only moral people can develop the abilities to get others to want to follow them. But we cannot. Everyone of us should therefore be ever vigilant, watching for those who chose to lead others in immoral ways toward evil ends—or moral ways to evil ends, or immoral ways to good ends. This vigilance means that it is essential that you, as a constituent, demand to know what your leaders value. It is also why you, as a leader, must discover what you believe to be right conduct and right results.

The true test of moral legitimacy, says leadership scholar James MacGregor Burns, is "grounded in conscious choice among real alternatives."[12] Any leader who would impose his or her will upon others and allow them no choice is not morally legitimate. One way to recognize moral leaders and to guard against immoral ones is to observe if they engage in learning the true needs and values of their constituents. If they are more intent on telling than on listening, it is likely that they are up to no good.

A free society permits a wide variety of groups to form and disband on the assumption that those with undesirable social goals will be kept in check by competing groups and that organizations that do not serve a useful purpose and meet the needs of followers will in time fail to attract sufficient individuals who share their values.[13] To make an informed choice, constituents must be able to perceive, comprehend, evaluate, and experience alternatives offered by those who would be their representatives.

At first, this perspective about moral legitimacy may seem contrary to the notion that credible leaders are characterized by taking stands based on clearly defined personal principles. It is not. What it says is that leaders must first decide what they stand for, realizing that ultimately the constituents will choose their leaders based on moral judgments.

Our research gives us great confidence that in the end the constituents' choices will be for a moral society. Respondents in our studies consistently favor honesty, competence, dependability, support, fairness, and caring. Leaders should bear this in mind—and constituents should be more willing to take a stand against those who would undermine these principles.

This finding strongly reinforces our prescription urging dialogue and dissent in the values clarification process. Why? "Why?" is exactly the question. In a significant piece of research on the subject of moral education, Lawrence Kohlberg, the originator of the theory of stages of moral reasoning, and his colleagues looked at whether one could advance the ability of young people to think morally. They found that they could. Three factors contributed to raising the level of moral reasoning. First, controversial dilemmas were posed, and disagreement was encouraged. Second, the group of students was mixed in terms of their ability to reason morally. Third, the teacher's behavior was critical. Surprisingly, only one teacher behavior resulted in change in students' moral reasoning. That teacher behavior was the extensive use of "why?"[14] In related research, we have found that managers' level of moral reasoning was higher following a discussion with others than if the manager did not consult others and resolved the dilemma alone.[15]

The lessons for leaders are clear. To create high morality in your organization, it is important to hold the right values. It is also necessary to challenge constituents to confront controversial dilemmas and to encourage disagreement. And it is important to refrain from resolving disputes by imposing the will of authority. If ethics, high purpose, and high performance are important goals, then asking why is a better strategy than giving answers. And if personally confronted with an ethical dilemma yourself, the best strategy is to seek counsel. When the issues are ethically challenging, even the most moral people reason better in consultation with others.

But we must add a caveat. In responding to some of the criticisms of the neutral position historically taken by proponents of the values clarification process, one of the early developers, Merrill Harmin, confessed, "Our emphasis on value neutrality probably did undermine traditional morality, although that was never our intent. . . . It makes a good deal of sense to say that truthfulness is better than deception, caring is better than hurting, loyalty is better than betrayal, and sharing better than exploitation."[16] Harmin goes on to say, however, that fostering moral values and advancing the values-clarifying process are not mutually exclusive. Leaders, if they wish to be credible, have an obligation to their constituents both to promote the higher morality of society *and* to teach the skills of value-directed living.

ACQUIRING COMPETENCE

Of course, just having the right messages does not make a person credible; practicing them does. But before you can do the right things, you have to know how to do them.

Competence, we have learned, is one of the key elements of credibility. Unfortunately, it has not received adequate attention in recent discussions of leadership. In stressing the relationship-building aspects of leadership, the business-building aspects have too often been bypassed. People must have the knowledge and abilities to perform their tasks and live up to their promises.

To commit to doing something that you have no capacity to perform is either disingenuous or stupid. There is nothing courageous about boldly saying you will successfully launch a new product or turn around a factory if you know you have neither the skills nor the resources to do it. Leaders must be aware of the degree to which they actually have the capabilities to do what they say. And if they lack the competence, they must dedicate themselves constantly to learning and improving.

Acquiring competence is all about being genuine. People who boast unrealistically of being able to perform a task or achieve a goal or those who make exaggerated claims of possessing noble attributes or desirable material goods are called phonies. People who actually have the attributes or accomplish the results are called genuine. Genuineness is that quality of being authentic, of being free from hypocrisy and dishonesty. We have found that the response to the item "My manager is genuine" is crucial to whether constituents rate a manager as high or low on credibility.

People do not voluntarily follow the direction of someone they believe is disingenuous, someone who is blindly unaware of personal limitations or consciously lying to gain some favor or influence. If people follow someone's direction, only to discover later that they were influenced badly or deliberately deceived, they say they were misled. This is the inevitable result of swashbuckling overconfidence accompanied by lack of ability. (Think of those you consider genuine: chances are they never brag; they just perform.)

Even if there was no intent to do them wrong, people feel deceived or injured when they have been misled. Being mismanaged does not carry the same moral tone. Genuine leadership is definitely associated with something more than handling and controlling. There is supposed to be some moral force behind it. To lead, not mislead, you must have the knowledge, skills, and abilities to consistently exemplify the values you profess.

Building the Skills

In the previous chapter, we discussed Pat Carrigan and her credibility. She managed both the Lakewood plant outside Atlanta, Georgia, and the Bay City plant in Michigan; both plants' accomplishments during her tenure are renowned.[17] Under Carrigan's leadership at Lakewood, the plant achieved a record corporate quality standard. Grievances were reduced to zero (from a record high of 5,500 at the time of a long strike, some years before her arrival) and remained at or near zero; discipline incidents declined by 82 percent; and there were no cases of protested disciplinary action. Bay City provides a similar story. Productivity shot up 40 percent. The plant attained a reduced budget with savings in the millions, instituted voluntary self-managed teams, and was the first GM plant at which a "living agreement" was signed with the UAW.

All of this from the first (and to date only) woman to manage a GM car assembly plant. And what is Carrigan's background? She holds a doctorate in psychology from the University of Michigan and began her career as a school teacher in the Michigan public school system. When she switched to industry in the 1970s, she started out in human resources—then a typical career path for women interested in joining industry. She signed on with GM in 1976 and began consulting internally on human resource issues.

But it was not her background as an educator, psychologist, and human resources expert that earned Carrigan the job as plant manager. Her education and experience certainly played a big role, but she had to acquire competence in the car business before she could run a plant. And she had to develop those skills the hard way.

When he first interviewed her, the general manager of the GM Assembly Division had asked Carrigan if she would consider a plant management assignment. She told him, "I've never been in a car plant, so I can't answer that. But I like management; I think I'm pretty good at it. I wouldn't rule it out."

In a recent interview with us, she described her learning adventure:

> I spent about a year and a half doing what I'll call "establishing credibility," which included being sent on funny little missions whose real intent nobody tells you. Like being sent on my first plant visit, ostensibly to learn how cars get built. But the real mission was to get invited back to help with some plant problems. And when I came home able to say I was going back the next week, my immediate supervisor said, "I knew it! I knew you could do it!" That kind of thing happens to every new kid on the block, I expect—maybe with a special flavor if she's female.

At the end of these credibility-building assignments, Carrigan reports, people would report to her boss that "she knew her stuff, she was helpful." But, as Carrigan points out, "That, of course, did not establish credibility as a prospective plant manager; it simply established credibility for Pat Carrigan, human being and somebody who might do something useful in our midst."

Then the time came to decide. Would she go into plant management or not? Carrigan was very interested, had liked what she had done in the plants, and wanted to be in a plant. And GM management liked what it had seen of Carrigan. So she and three divisional executives designed a five-year plan to prepare her to become a plant manager.

During the next year and a half, Carrigan got involved in every aspect of car assembly, learning operations and replacing vacationing superintendents in various production departments. She was then appointed to a two-year stint as general superintendent, first helping the plant prepare for a major model change and then overseeing its implementation.

Along the way, she had expressed an interest in learning more about the financial end of the plant business. The plant manager Carrigan was working for at the time was creative and a risk taker. She reports, "He said, 'You know, our financial department could really use some human relations skills exposure, and there are some real good folks up there who could teach you what you need to know about plant financial operations. How would you like to be controller?' I spent a year and a half in that position. He was right: it was a good fit for me and for the organization. From there, I was promoted to plant manager."

Carrigan is quick to emphasize that "the promotion to plant manager wasn't an isolated event. It was the end point of a series of assignments, each of which I had performed well."

It is clear from Carrigan's account that there is more to running a plant than being credible as a person. When others got to know Carrigan as a person — to know her values and her personal history — they were indeed willing to trust her first as a consultant and then as a colleague, friend, and neighbor. But willingness to entrust her with an entire plant and its assets, with careers and livelihoods, was another matter. Carrigan concluded, "There has to be an opportunity for a nontraditional newcomer to demonstrate competence if that individual's going to be accepted."

Learning terminology and learning by watching are not enough. Carrigan's five-year journey was designed to add the experience and the knowledge necessary for her to earn credibility as a senior leader in the plant, credibility that went beyond her personal credibility.

Expanding the Skills — and Their Value

David Maister is a consultant — a good one. Previously on the faculty at the Harvard Business School, Maister had published articles that got the attention of business organizations. He decided to try it on his own: "At the end of my first full year as a management consultant, at the age of 39, I decided to take stock," he reports.[18] He had done well—at least that's what the bank account said. Yet Maister began to worry about his value to his clients.

Maister recalled that the health of a business is judged not only by the income statement, but also by the balance sheet. So he asked himself what assets he had as a professional consultant. First, he had his knowledge and skill, and, second, he had his client relationships.

Maister began to realize that these were interdependent. If he relied only upon what he already knew, then he would only acquire clients who needed what he knew at that time. That, he surmised, was a finite number. Worse yet, his existing clients had already been served by what he already knew, so they were not likely to hire him again unless he learned more. Then it hit him. He hadn't learned anything new in his first year on his own. Maister writes, "By definition, the unsolicited phone calls requesting my services had been for things that I was already known for. Even though each client project was customized (to a degree) I found myself doing basically very similar work for a variety of clients. I had not added to my abilities. What was even more shocking (and depressing) was the realization that not only had I not grown my asset, but its value on the market was going down—rapidly. Left untended, knowledge and skill, like all assets, depreciate in value—surprisingly quickly."[19]

Maister also realized that the value of his "client relationships was not to be measured by the number of clients, nor by their prestige, but by how deep the relationship was."[20] If he learned nothing new, then he would no longer be of use to his existing clients and would only be able to work with those he had never worked with before. For a consultant, this could be disastrous. By flying from client to client, he was not building the deeper relationships with any of them—so essential to success in consulting. And by having to fly from one to the other, eventually he would not have time to find that next one.

"In sum," Maister concludes, "I learned that unless I

actively worked at it, my career prospects would inevitably decline, even when (or perhaps especially when) I was making lots of money. Having a good current year financially was clearly a necessary condition for my success, but it was far from being a sufficient condition. Keeping my career moving forward, even staying level, was going to take conscious effort."[21]

Carrigan and Maister give testimony to the fact that if you want to be promoted, if you want to be hired, if you want to be followed, then you have to acquire new knowledge and skills constantly. You have to ask yourself repeatedly, "How valuable am I to my colleagues, to my customers, to my stockholders, to my partners in business?" Your value as a leader and as an individual contributor is determined not only by your guiding beliefs, but also by your abilities to act on them. To strengthen credibility, you must continuously improve your existing abilities and learn new ones. And that takes time and attention.

But competence alone does not determine the capacity to act on your values. You must also have the confidence that you can, in a given leadership situation, apply your skills and act on your beliefs. Yet another important aspect of self-knowledge is critical to leadership performance. It is perhaps the deepest belief of all: an honest trust and confidence in your own ability to meet competently the specific leadership challenges that confront your organization.

SELF-CONFIDENCE: BELIEVING YOU CAN DO IT

Self-confidence is not the same as competence, of course. Knowing that you have competence and believing that in a given situation you can use your skills to achieve your goals are different mental sets. Cognitive psychologists refer to this quality as self-efficacy. As Stanford University psychologist and cognitve researcher Albert Bandura writes, "Perceived self-efficacy is concerned with people's beliefs in their capabilities to mobilize the motivation, cognitive resources, and the courses of action needed to exercise control over task demands."[22]

Researchers have found that beliefs about capabilities partly govern the level of a person's performance. Bandura observes that "a capability is only as good as its execution. People often fail to perform optimally even though they know full well what to do and possess the requisite skills."[23] They fail to perform optimally because they doubt their ability to put those skills to use in a particular situation. It is thus not only competence that determines execution and outcome. Belief in one's abilities counts. Remember what Carrigan said about her leadership abilities: "I think I'm pretty good at it."

Beliefs about one's capabilities influence personal motivation. They determine how much effort a person is likely to exert and how long the individual will persevere when the task gets difficult. The greater the self-efficacy, the less stress and depression people feel in taxing and threatening situations. The greater the belief in their own capabilities the higher the goals people set for themselves and the firmer they are in their commitment to them. And self-efficacy even has the power to influence career choices. Bandura explains, "The more efficacious people judge themselves to be, the wider the range of career options they consider appropriate and the better they prepare themselves educationally for different occupational pursuits."[24]

From this research, you can see that self-belief in efficacy influences the leadership roles you might select. If you believe a particular leadership task is outside of your control or will require more time and energy than you can muster, you are unlikely to pursue that task—even if you know that it is essential to your group's success. Belief in your own efficacy influences the level of challenge you will seek.

We often see this in outdoor initiatives we use in some of our leadership development programs. One activity requires people to walk across a six-inch-wide beam. When the beam is placed on the ground everyone confidently scampers across.

No problem. But when asked to climb a rope ladder and then walk another six-inch-wide beam that is thirty feet off the ground, people react quite differently. Some say, "No way!" or "You've got to be kidding." And then there are those who race across like cats.

The point of this exercise is not to see who is athletic or who is afraid of heights or who is brave. The point is that execution of a simple skill often depends on the situation. We *can do* it in some situations, yet in others we may not believe we can mobilize the motivation, the cognitive resources, and the appropriate actions to control the demands of the task.

This is an especially important lesson for leaders. If they do not believe that they can meet the challenges of a particular task, even when they have the requisite skills to do so, they have no business trying to lead a group under those circumstances. It is not a display of courage to lead people when one has low self-belief. It is foolhardy. The consequences could be disastrous for leaders and, more significantly, for constituents.

Leaders need to understand their limitations as well as their strengths. Of course, leaders do not have to give in to their limitations; they do not have to accept them as permanent. In fact, there is no way anyone can overcome a doubt unless it is confronted and unless the competence and confidence are developed to handle a similar encounter in the future. But leaders must not experiment with constituents as subjects. They should have well-founded confidence in their skills before involving others.

A leader should also recognize that it is an honorable act to get out of the way and let others take charge when he or she cannot mobilize the motivation, the resources, and the actions to meet the demands of a challenging task. Leaders should make it possible for someone else who has the values, the competence, and the self-confidence to step forward. Such an "everyone is a leader" culture is certainly more potent than an "only managers are leaders" culture.

Strengthening Self-Belief

In addition to competence, then, self-confidence is critical to leadership credibility. Fortunately, there are at least four ways self-efficacy can be enhanced: mastery experiences, observation of role models, social support and encouragement, and reinterpretation of personal stress.[25] We'll examine each of these methods.

Mastery.   The first thing people can do to enhance self-efficacy is to learn to do the task well. This task, of course, is related to the competence criteria we discussed earlier. People must be given the training and experiences that enable them to master their performance. Mastery does not come in small doses. It cannot come from the usual two days of training and on to the next task. It requires ongoing training and practice. Carrigan's journey lasted five years, not counting her many previous years of work in education and human resources. She was also given the opportunities to learn the job of plant manager progressively. She had the chance to get feedback on how she was doing all along the way.

  Mastery does not come from learning to do the easy things superbly, however. It comes from learning to overcome the setbacks that occur in the process. Mastery comes from patience and persistence. It also comes from recognizing that *you* are the one who created the performance—it was not caused by luck, other people, a mentor, or the weather. To gain a sense of mastery, you need truly to believe that you can personally achieve high-performance results.

Modeling.   In previous research, we found that observing others was the second most important way people learned to lead.[26] The opportunity to watch others who have mastered a practice is extremely helpful to strengthening beliefs in self-effectiveness. To believe in their own abilities to master something, people need to see that it can be done well.

  But it is one thing to watch the CEO do something well and another to see someone in your own position excel at it. To increase your own self-efficacy, find opportunities to watch others like yourself performing tasks well. It could be anyone about whom you might say, "Hey, she's just like me. If she can do it, I can do it." Or "I know him. We used to work together. I didn't know he could do that. Well, if he can, I bet I can, too."

Support.   Hearing from those we respect that we are doing well is always uplifting. Social persuasion, as it is called, helps us learn to believe in ourselves. Everyone needs to hear words of encouragement if they are going to work harder to be successful. And the more task-specific the feedback, the better. If you are not getting enough realistic encouragement, then you should ask for it from someone you trust.

Support is also a matter of being in situations in which we are more likely to succeed than fail. Though people should always challenge themselves to learn and grow, prematurely placing yourself or being placed in a situation where there is a high probability of failure will not add to your sense of self. Try to structure the conditions for success by gradually raising the level of difficulty and by surrounding yourself with supportive individuals.

Reinterpreting Stress.   One day we watched a man bounce a soccer ball from foot to foot, foot to head, knee to knee. He even spun around several times and still kept the ball in the air. As we watched, he must have bounced it one hundred times before he missed and the ball hit the ground. Truly a master at work.

But when the ball dropped, he swore, kicked the ball hard, and stamped his foot. Learning to perform well can be frustrating, even for masters. It is hard, and often very stressful, work. When under stress, the body sends out signals. Based on these cues—aches, pains, and strains—we learn how we are doing. We read the signals from physical exertion and determine our limits. To continue the task at hand, we have to find ways to modify our beliefs about our capabilities when we feel those stress signals.

You can do this by enhancing your physical stamina through exercise, by using relaxation techniques, or by reminding yourself that this is hard work and it is natural for you to feel tired or irritable. However you respond, it is important that you not interpret the psychological or physical stress as a lack of ability. Do not allow your body to convince your mind that you cannot master leadership.

These same principles can be applied to assisting others in increasing their self-confidence. Having mastered a performance yourself, you might volunteer to help others learn it as well. You might offer them words of encouragement and help them to understand that stress is a natural part of the learning process.

Achieving Optimal Performance

In his research on optimal performance, University of Chicago professor Mihaly Csikszentmihalyi provides other clues to strengthening self-confidence. He has examined the attributes of work and leisure experiences that contribute most to optimal performance, or what he calls flow. Csikszentmihalyi offers four useful guides for building the confidence to be credible: setting goals, becoming immersed in the activity, paying attention to what is happening, and learning to enjoy the immediate experience.[27]

Setting Goals.   Goals are necessary to create flow because they focus attention on a few choices and challenges. Goals and challenges define a course of action, and they suggest the skills necessary to achieve the objectives. People need to pay attention to the results of their actions and compare those results to the goals. But most importantly of all, goals must be self-selected, not imposed from outside. One must own them.

Becoming Immersed in the Activity.   People who experience flow and optimal performance get totally engrossed in the activity. They are engaged in it, fascinated by it, preoccupied with it. Total immersion is characteristic of people who excel at what they do and who experience the joy of doing it. This deep level of involvement is greatly facilitated by the ability to concentrate.

Paying Attention to What Is Happening.   People who experience flow are not distracted. They attend to the activity constantly; they sustain involvement. This is obvious in professional athletes, but it is equally true of master painters or master listeners. In a similar way, to be masterful at leading, people must engage in it completely. Csikszentmihalyi reports that intense attention rids one of self-consciousness, which he sees as the most common source of distraction. Lack of self-consciousness is what makes deep involvement possible, and this in turn enables one to attend to the activity.

Learning to Enjoy the Immediate Experience.   By setting goals, getting involved, and paying attention, people learn to enjoy what they are doing even when the conditions are poor. One achieves a sense of personal control over the circumstances and is able to find joy in many little things.

Try asking yourself whether you are engaged in your work and leisure experiences in a way that produces optimal performance. Have you set goals? Are you immersed in the activity? Are you paying attention to what is happening? Are you enjoying the immediate experience? If your answers are not yes to each, you may not be developing the confidence to be credible.

CHARACTER: SUMMING IT ALL UP

Credo, competence, and confidence are the content of character. They are the substance of self, the subject matter that gives meaning to people.

Those who are clear about their values and beliefs have laid the cornerstones for a firm ethical structure. People who have developed the skills to enact their beliefs possess the moral capacity to achieve good ends with good means. People who have faith in their abilities to execute effectively and consistently even under duress and challenge display moral fortitude. Moral structure, moral capacity, and moral fortitude combine to make a distinguished moral force in the world.[28]

The quest for character is a noble one, though often baffling and frustrating. Just when we think we have grasped its nature, it evades us. Yet if we wish to be judged by the content of our character, we must decide what content we wish it to consist of.

Discovering your self is the first discipline of credibility, and now it is time to experiment with putting it into practice. In the closing section of this chapter, we provide specific exercises to help you in your quest. Following these suggestions, we move on in the next chapter to examine the second discipline, appreciating diversity. There we look at how leaders actively attend to and understand the varied and often conflicting needs, interests, aims, and aspirations of their constituents.

DISCOVERING YOUR SELF: FIRST STEPS/NEXT STEPS

We begin with exercises designed to enable you to explore further your leadership credo; then we move to competence and finally to confidence. There is no particular priority to these exercises, so choose those that most appeal to you.

▶   *Write and tell your stories.* When we interviewed Cam Starrett, we learned that she relies on reflection to bring her closer to self-knowledge. "I do it through a lot of reading, a lot of thinking, writing," says Starrett. "I've been a journal keeper all my life. I don't write every day; it's not a diary. . . . It's a journal of thoughts." Try keeping a journal yourself.

A journal is a record of your life story and one of the most powerful paths to finding meaning in your life. Your personal stories are also what make you unique. In many ways, all that others know about you are the stories that you tell.

But don't just write your stories. Try telling some to others. Tell your stories, talk about your memories and hopes. You may discover values and competencies that you hadn't considered.

▶ *Discover your life themes.* Our past is prologue. Although leaders look ahead to the future, they also look back to their past to discover forces that may propel them forward. When we explore our past, we may notice recurring themes. In discovering these, we can draw meaning from what might otherwise seem like a random stream of events. Our lives are frequently shaped by reaction to a significant event or personal hurt in early life. Elders and historical figures we've admired may have served as role models and may be the inspirations for the unifying forces that create meaning in our lives.

Books, too, may be critical. It is reported that Lincoln loved *Aesop's Fables.* His other favorites were the King James Bible, *Pilgrim's Progress,* and Shakespeare's plays.[29] What is the pattern here? All are rich in moral tales and in figurative language. Similarly, King was a student of the U.S. Constitution, a seminarian, and a student of the world's great philosophers.[30]

You might try discovering your life themes by exploring your own past. Begin by considering some of the following questions.

◆ What books made the biggest impression on you as a child? What values did these espouse?

◆ Who are your most admired historical leaders? What values did you learn from studying them?

◆ What older persons in your early life did you admire? What values did you learn from them?

◆ Can you recall suffering a hurt early in your life? How did you react? What purpose and challenge did you find in it? What values did it teach you?

▶ *Assess your values.* How can you know if you or others truly hold a value? Here are some questions to ask yourself about each of the values you have recorded on your leadership credo.[31]

♦ Did I freely choose this value? If it is an organizational one, do I freely choose to accept it?

♦ Have I considered other alternatives to this value and explored them fully?

♦ Have I considered the alternative consequences of this value?

♦ Do I truly cherish this value? Is it something I prize? Am I passionate about it?

♦ Am I willing to affirm publicly that I hold this value?

♦ Am I willing to act on this value?

♦ Am I willing to act on this value repeatedly, over time, in a consistent pattern?

If your answers to all these questions are yes, then your choices are firm. If you have said no to any of them, you might want to spend some time reexamining the values you have chosen.

▶ *Audit your ability to succeed.* If, as Pat Carrigan did, you want to be a plant manager, you have to know what knowledge and skills are required. If, as David Maister did, you want to continue to be of worth to your clients, you have to stay current with the problems that are of interest to them. Your credo provides you with a good starting place. But you must also identify the specific job-related competencies you need to master to lead your constituents.

How do your abilities compare to what the situation, role, and tasks call for? How well can you execute what you say you value? Where are there gaps? What specific knowledge and abilities do you have that will enable you to succeed in this environment? Which must you acquire? What experiences do you need to sharpen these competencies? Who is the very best in the world in your field, and how do you compare to that person? What can you do to become the best? Would your constituents respond to these questions in the same way?

Audits are only as effective as the questions you ask, so stretch yourself beyond the usual questions. Max De Pree, chairman of Herman Miller, is a master of inquiry. Annual reviews with his managers are no-holds-barred sessions that examine some revealing questions. He asks unusual and intriguing questions, such as, "What should grace enable us to be?" And he asks some highly challenging ones, such as, "Why does this organization need you?"[32] Try answering that one for yourself.

▶   *Make a personal development plan.* Carrigan and her managers worked out a five-year plan. Maister recommends a personal strategic plan for our professional careers. Whatever you call it, you need to take charge of your own work life. This is especially true now that the old covenant with organizations has been broken. You are responsible for your own development; you must not rely on someone in human resources or in management. You have to make a plan, give some focus to your development, and get on with it.

Be sure that your plan includes specific goals and activities in which you can immerse yourself. Pay attention to what is happening as you engage in the activities. Make sure that you learn to enjoy the immediate experience.

▶   *Evaluate experiences.* We suggest that you conduct a debriefing on every project, big or small. And we suggest that you review every single failure. Each work assignment is a chance to accomplish something—and an opportunity to learn. But to learn from it, you must take the time to do so.

We have found the following Experiential Learning Model from Pfeiffer & Company to be a very useful debriefing guide.[33]

Experience. First, focus on the project, task, or activity in which you have been engaged. Make sure that everyone has a common experience to use as the basis for discussion.

Publish. Next, ask "What happened to you during this experience? What were your feelings, your reactions, your observations?" Make sure that everyone has the opportunity to share their personal observations and record the raw data for later review.

Process. Together, look over the individual reactions and see if you can find any repeated patterns, common themes, and trends. Make note of these recurring dynamics.

Generalize. Make generalizations and inferences from the common themes. What fundamental principles might be at work here? Find ways to extend what you have learned beyond the specific project so that you can make use of the lessons in planning and executing future assignments.

Apply. Apply the new lessons you have learned to the next project and start the experiential learning cycle over again.

This process can be applied to personal projects; however, debriefings are most effective when done in a team setting with all the key participants in a project.

▶   *Observe master models.* Study individuals like yourself who have already mastered the skills you need. The skills might cover running a meeting, giving a speech, making a sale, negotiating an agreement, conducting an interview, or listening to feedback. Whatever the skill, watching those who do it well is extraordinarily useful. If you can't watch them in person, then view them on videotape.

Volunteer for an assignment to work with someone who excels in the skills you need. Become an apprentice. Apprenticeships are not common in most managerial roles, but they are in many trades and in some professions. In the legal profession, for instance, the role of law clerk is an honorable one. You may have to invent the role, but look for those assignments that provide opportunities to watch the masters in action.

▶   *Seek mastery experiences.* It is critical that you also afford yourself the opportunity to master distinctive competencies. Learn them. Since practice is one of the most significant contributors to self-confidence, practice the leadership basics—being challenging, inspiring, enabling, modeling, and encouraging—daily, just as a musician practices the scales.

Ask for coaching from a colleague who has mastered the art. One-on-one instruction is important in individualizing the skills. Break the task down (whether it is running a meeting or giving a speech or resolving a conflict) into discrete, learnable pieces based on achievable goals. Incremental progress is essential to acquiring skills. Measure and get feedback on your progress. Knowing how far you have gone in your quest to improve is very important to building self-confidence. Also remind yourself that you are the one responsible for your success. No one else is going to do the work to become the best you can be.

▶   *Ask for support.* Social support is one of the most powerful social psychological forces known. It is responsible for increases in health, moral reasoning, teamwork, and self-confidence. As you practice, ask others to give you constructive feedback on your performance. Practice in the company of people who want you to succeed as well as themselves.

Do not set up competitive situations where you know that others want mostly to defeat you. Do not engage in experiences where you know your performance will be clearly inferior to others. Of course, you must try to stretch yourself, but when trying to build your confidence, you will need the support of someone who will encourage you to improve.

▶   *Sum it up; write a statement of personal purpose.* As a final exercise in discovering yourself, bring it all together in a brief statement of your vision of greatness or purpose, what is often called personal mission.[34] To assist in that process, we have developed the five *P*'s of personal mission: proficiency, product, people, place, and purpose.

- Proficiency is the special skill, task, expertise, or talent that we possess or desire to possess at a level of personal mastery.
- Product is the activity we perform using our special proficiency.
- People are those individuals we most want to serve or with whom we most enjoy being.
- Place is the setting in which we most enjoy exercising our special skill or talent.
- Purpose is the benefit or result of exercising that skill or talent.

Underlying these five elements is a sixth *P*, the principles that guide your actions. These are the values you articulated earlier in the values-clarification exercise. As a summary exercise, write a brief (twenty-five to thirty words) personal mission statement, and list of your values on one page.

4

Appreciating Constituents and Their Diversity

For long-term success, we need to attract and retain the best people in the industry. To do that, we must create a company in which everyone can contribute his or her best, in which everyone is valued, regardless of differences.

Andrea Zintz
Ortho Biotech

In our programs on leadership, we make the point that leadership requires a pioneering spirit—that leaders are adventurers who actively seek out opportunities to change the way things are. They test their skills and abilities, experimenting with innovative approaches to getting extraordinary things done. In one of our leadership videotapes, we make this point graphically by showing a picture of a woman, neck deep in a swamp. She's involved in training exercises as part of Operation Raleigh, an international organization whose primary goal is leadership development.

With this image on the screen, we then state, "Leaders go places. The difference between managing and leading is the difference between what you can do with your hands and what you can do with your feet. . . . You can't lead from behind a desk. You can't lead from a seated position. The only way you can go anyplace is to get up from behind the desk and use your feet."[1]

That's what we used to say—until we received a letter from Richard O. Whitney, president of Disabled Programmers, a computer software services business. Whitney had used our videotape for a segment of a professional development program for his employees and was writing to highlight our comment that one cannot lead from a sitting position. He aptly remarked that our comments were flawed if taken literally. Whitney wrote, "More than 30 percent of our employees are people with disabilities. Several are in wheelchairs and I can testify that they lead very effectively from a sitting position."[2] In writing to us, Whitney helped us reconsider our statement and view it differently.

Our point that leaders are adventurers and pioneers remains valid, but the way we expressed it was thoughtless. What of those who are confined to wheelchairs, yet are as vital and energetic as leaders who are ambulatory? In our attempt to make the point more colorfully, we demonstrated that we did not truly appreciate a group of important constituents.

True leaders must understand deeply the hurts and bruises, joys and struggles, aims and aspirations of their constituents. Through carefully listening and being sensitive to the needs of others, we can recognize their needs and offer ways to fill them. However, people will follow our advice and recommendations only when they trust our competence and believe that we have their best interests at heart.

Understanding and appreciating constituents' needs and values—and thus establishing credibility—is made more difficult in today's complex work environment. Corporations are of necessity becoming more global, employing much more diverse work forces, responding to more demanding customers with wide-ranging needs, and facing more concerned shareholders. They are also developing closer relationships with fewer suppliers and are being asked to pay more attention to the needs of the communities in which they exist.

Leaders, whether in the board room or on the front line,

are at the center of a vast web of relationships that is today characterized more by variety than uniformity. They must become fully aware of the views and attitudes of their constituents, who may be very different than expected. Simply relying upon the "old boy network" or upon oneself as the source of understanding about values is insufficient, negligent, and even dangerous in today's business environment.[3] Furthermore, as organizational boundaries become blurred and we all work more within "networked" organizations, the significance of broadly defining and appreciating constituents is crucial. These days, constituents are not just "subordinates" but are just as often peers and other managers within the firm, suppliers, vendors, and partners outside it.

Leaders must reach out and attend to all their constituents if they wish to be credible. Credibility, like quality and service, is determined by the constituents, so leaders must be able to view themselves as their constituents do. It requires effort and new skills; one benefit is that a natural by-product of attending to other people is that they in turn come to trust us and we to trust them.

Harvard Business School professors John Kotter and James Heskett provide support for this perspective. They report that organizations with adaptive, performance-enhancing cultures have outperformed nonadaptive, unhealthy ones precisely because of their emphasis on attending to all of their constituencies (that is, customers, stockholders, and employees). By contrast, they found that in organizations with nonadaptive and unhealthy cultures "most managers care mainly about themselves, their immediate work group, or some product (or technology) associated with that work group."[4] Similarly, other studies show that having the interest of others in mind first, rather than personal objectives, is also critical to building customer loyalty.[5]

Leaders who are clearly interested in their own agendas, their own advancement, and their own well-being are not willingly followed. In fact, in a free and democratic society, they will be voted out. Just ask an elected member of government.

The credibility-strengthening process begins with the

clarification of a leader's personal values and beliefs, but only by being constituent-oriented can any leader ultimately become trustworthy. A firm credibility foundation can be established only when the leader truly understands and appreciates, even embraces, the aspirations of his or her constituents. Leaders must be clear about placing a value on others. Appreciating and paying attention are signals that leaders send about how important their constituents are to them and that constituents' input and ideas are important. It isn't enough for constituents to know what their leaders stand for and to recognize that they are competent. Constituents want to be appreciated.

A NEW ETHIC: SHIFTING THE FOCUS FROM SELF TO OTHER

With increasing clarity, executives are beginning to understand the need to balance high tech with high touch. They are seeing the necessity of more cooperation and a greater focus on others. Scholars and executives alike have recognized the impact of corporate culture and the ways that shared values (or alignment between personal and organizational values) make a difference.

For more than a decade, we have been involved in systematic studies, conducted in both the public and private sectors, about managers' values and the strategies for aligning personal and organizational values.[6] Our intention has been to take a broad look at managerial values because they are such a powerful force in organizational life. As we discussed in Chapter Three, values are at the core of our personality, influencing the choices we make, the people we trust, the appeals to which we respond, and the way we invest our time and energy. In turbulent times, they give a sense of direction amid conflicting views and demands. Knowing more about values enables us to appreciate differing points of view and areas of common agreement.

Our studies clearly show that there has been a shift in some critical managerial values over the past decade. We've noticed changes in the significance of certain values as follows:

- Quality and service are more important.

- Cooperative values are increasingly emphasized.

- Focus is shifting from self to others.

- Home/family interests are receiving greater attention.

Yet other managerial values remain as constants:

- Honesty and competence are key personal characteristics.

- Top management actions set the company's ethical tone.

- Customers are the organization's key stakeholders

Quality and customer service have become clear and deliberate corporate and managerial values; they are at the top of most corporate agendas. Neither of these concerns was even on most agendas just a decade ago. Yet today they are the rallying points, not just for corporate excellence, but for corporate survival.

What will it take to improve our future quality of life? As compared to ten years ago, we have found that significantly greater numbers of managers today feel that improvements will require a society with a cooperative value system rather than mechanisms and systems dominated by individualistic efforts. Few people envision a better future by simply letting the status quo continue. Greater appreciation is also reported for the importance of partnerships between the private and public sectors in meeting common objectives.

"Looking out for number one" is no longer the priority these days when people think about key stakeholders in their organizations. Greater attention is being focused on others in the organization, rather than being directed toward personal (self) needs. The higher importance ratings given to employees and subordinates signal growing recognition of the reciprocal relationship between those who are led and those who aspire to lead. Participatory management in the eighties has given way to empowered and self-directed work teams in the nineties and in the process has created new roles and responsibilities for management personnel. As facilitators and coaches, today's managers place greater emphasis on understanding the concerns of their work group members and supporting the efforts of others than did their counterparts just ten years ago.

Big shifts have been reported in the balance between work and home demands, with the nonwork side of our lives playing an increasingly important role. There are growing numbers of people willing to turn down a better job offer or promotion if it requires a significant change in life-style or a relocation. Supporting this trend, a *Time*/CNN poll finds that more than 66 percent of us would like to "slow down and live a more relaxed life," in contrast to only 19 percent who say they would like to "live a more exciting, faster-paced life."[7] Whereas executives had previously reported their careers as providing them the most satisfaction in life (54 percent versus 38 percent favoring home), in the 1990s they were reporting just the opposite—61 percent chose home and only 34 percent their careers. These trends create ongoing challenges for aligning personal and organizational values.

In short, the fast-track competitive value system that once was so typical of corporate America seems to be losing some of its luster. People want to find a more even balance between the demands of their personal and organizational lives. They don't want to have to dedicate (or sacrifice) themselves to one part of their lives at the expense of another. They see greater value in working together, especially as problems and issues increase in complexity, than in going it alone; this appreciation carries over from the living room to the plant and office.

Despite the massive changes of the past decade, our surveys make clear that in the area of values there are some dependable constants. The importance of leading by example has not diminished, and the personal qualities we admire most in others have not altered. For example, as we described in earlier chapters, people who are seen as honest and competent continue to be held in highest regard. These two personal values or characteristics stand out in relation to all other personal attributes in the people we would be willing to follow. Being inspiring and forward-looking continues to be essential for leadership as well. These findings remain constant across hierarchical levels, gender, age, and years of managerial experience. A twenty-one-year longitudinal study (1965–1986) investigating the values of an ideal manager, conducted within the Sperry Rand Corporation, reached similar conclusions.[8]

The relative ranking of organizational goals (for example, quality, service, effectiveness, morale, organizational leadership, productivity, efficiency, innovation, stability, profits, growth, service to the public) was also strikingly similar across the past decade. Generally, the order or prioritization of these various goals has remained the same. In addition, there continues to be considerable agreement on how important organizational goals are in the minds of managers at different levels in the hierarchy and in hundreds of different types of organizations. Customers remain on center stage as a firm's key constituents, and the interests of stockholders are viewed as best served when the organization meets its corporate objectives. Managers have a strong sense of agreement about the purpose of their enterprises.

Amid the changes and the consistencies, we see that people are no less committed to work but are determined to work differently. Included in this difference is a desire for more self-expression and organizational cooperation.[9] There are changes in what people are doing but not in what they are looking for from their work and leaders: a sense of meaning and shared purpose that justifies a personal commitment. Leaders recognize these needs and the importance of valuing them. They also recognize that their constituents now cover a wider spectrum than ever before and that to meet corporate objectives and constituent needs, leaders must broaden their perspectives.

ENRICHING PERFORMANCE THROUGH DIVERSITY

Whether on the floor or in the boardroom, Wall Street or Main Street, the fact is that we now live in a multipolar world. And it's increasingly a more democratic world. It's no longer possible to thrive in the business, government, or independent nonprofit sectors by being responsive only to the world as defined by a few, the elite. In order to be successful in a multipolar world, leaders in all roles, at all levels and in all walks of life, must learn to appreciate diversity.

The workplace of the twenty-first century demands appreciating (valuing) diversity, not simply tolerating it, managing it, or even being able to create a "melting pot." Surely the industrial revolution of the early 1900s, with its waves of immigrants and the movement of farm and country workers to the cities, brought tremendous diversity to the workplace. But the predominant strategy then was to forge a single type of work force in the same sense that Henry Ford promised his Model-T in every color the customer wanted—as long as it was black. Homogeneity was then achieved by conformity to the predominantly WASP-oriented values of the country's corporate and political leaders.

Such homogeneity is no longer feasible today. In fact, organizations themselves are also becoming more diverse. Increasingly, they are being radically designed around processes, not functions, with greater freedom of movement across "boundaries" within and outside the organization.

This diversity, individual and organizational, enriches us. Diversity is not a threat. In fact, it is an asset. Diversity is not simply good because it implies breadth of tolerance and empathy but because it will help us to be creative and innovative. By forcing ourselves to look at a wide range of possibilities, we will make better decisions and produce more accurate results. We are also made more adaptable and resilient. An organization valuing diversity has greater capacity to adapt and renew itself in a swiftly changing world. Indeed, given radically shifting business environments, it is imperative that organizations constantly challenge underlying assumptions in order to keep improving the process.

Diversity does, however, make the leaders' job more complex. With the greater resources, talents, and energy come new challenges and alternatives. More reaching out is required. More compassion and understanding are demanded, as is the ability to recognize that sometimes competing values and interests are legitimate and important. Today's multicultural world demands that differences be recognized and acknowledged. Overlooking real and relevant differences can hurt individual people and their productivity.

What makes for good working relationships between people with differences in gender, ethnic, and/or racial backgrounds? Research suggests four characteristics.[10]

1.   These relationships involve the whole person; that is, we do not separate business from pleasure but include and acknowledge our personal sides (such as family, interests, hopes, and dreams).

2.   A sense of shared history over time is developed in these relationships; we've been through good times and bad times with each other. We've laughed and cried together and learned from one another.

3.   These relationships are collaborative rather than competitive. Each person has certain strengths that can be counted on and well-known weaknesses that have to be taken into account.

4.   There is a strong sense that each person values and affirms the other. We are one another's supporters and admirers.

These characteristics are not restricted to relations between disparate groups; they contribute to successful interpersonal relationships. Period.

Being able to build relationships starts by learning how to understand and see things from another's perspective.[11] Asked why their marriage or friendship fell apart, two people might say, "We didn't understand each other any more" or "We didn't see things the same way." The same can be said about strategic alliances and mergers that fail to reap the synergistic benefits anticipated. And about executives. For example, studies from the Center for Creative Leadership have revealed that successful executives can become derailed because of their insensitivity and inability to understand the perspectives of other people. These managers undervalued the contributions of other people and made them feel inadequate. They listened poorly, acted dictatorially, played favorites, and failed to give (or sometimes even share) credit with others. The net result over time was that these traits and attitudes caught up with them. When these managers really needed the help of others around them, they were left to fend for themselves, ignored, isolated, and on occasion even sabotaged.[12]

We must therefore fully appreciate others to enable the relationship to work and to keep on track. The greater the extent to which we comprehend each other's perceptions, concerns, and values, the greater our ability to work together. But where and how do we begin?

SHOWING APPRECIATION BY LISTENING

As fundamental as it might seem, the best thing that leaders can do to show others they respect them and consider them worthwhile is to reach out, listen, and learn. Professors Suresh Srivastva and Frank Barrett of Case Western Reserve University underscore this point in their writings on executive integrity by noting that it is "not the content of the exchange that is central but the experience of being taken in and heard, which not only affirms the legitimacy of one's way of looking at the world but then allows one to begin letting go of some defensiveness because the experience of affirmation increases one's capacity to affirm others."[13] So, as leaders, we must not simply articulate our own philosophies. We must listen to others'. We must learn from them. Unfortunately, research by the Hay Group, covering one million employees in over two thousand organizations, reveals that only about one in three people respond favorably to questions about how well their company listens to them.[14]

Joe Campau is a machinist who has been with his company for more than eleven years. Writing in the company newsletter about his feelings for the company's total quality (TQ) efforts, he expresses well the common concern of people, regardless of organization or level, about whether or not management listens:

> Recently management has come to us (I emphasize those last three words—come to us) to seek our assistance and input in helping make this a better place to work. That has always been one of our goals, but, in the past, the management has seemed to turn a deaf ear toward our requests and recommendations. This has resulted in a vast polarization between management and the labor force.
>
> Management's aloofness to our plight down in the shop has resulted in the skepticism and guarded optimism toward the TQ philosophy. In a nutshell, a sad refrain emerges: "We've heard it all before." It would greatly enhance morale if we could rely on the management team to listen to our bitches, gripes and complaints about what needs to be done in the shop to make things run more smoothly. It would greatly enhance morale if management acted upon our concerns and helped resolve problems rather than remain stashed away in cushy offices, relying more or less on erroneous graphs and silly charts to determine the progress of the shopload—only coming out of their hole to speak with us long enough for the obligatory Christmas handshake.

If the management team desires to help us out of this quagmire, listen to us, develop a definite plan of action, resolve problems, get things done, obtain the supplies we need to do our jobs, then our efforts will be justified. If, on the other hand, we sense the runaround, the putoff, the condescending attitude that has prevailed all too often in the past, we will be worse off than we are now. Management will retain the reputation of not to be trusted, morale will surely plummet, and some of us will certainly feel foolish.

We expect—no, we demand honesty on management's part with no b.s. Management must listen to the things we have to say, regardless of how mundane or ludicrous that they may seem at the time. After all, they're important enough for us to mention them in the first place, and management should put forth a sincere effort to help us resolve the problems and conflicts that are sure to arise.[15]

In reading Campau's words, we feel his anguish. We come to appreciate that failure to listen increases cynicism and casts further doubt about leaders' intentions and trustworthiness.

In contrast, listening and being sensitive to the needs of others can provide substantial benefits. The Ford Motor Company asked car assemblers how to improve the manufacturing process. They wondered why so many different types and varieties of bolts, screws, and nuts were required in the assembly. Finding the right screw for the right coupling and the right-sized tools created more work. Apparently, the design and manufacturing engineers had not taken these requirements into consideration. But based on this feedback and working side-by-side with the assemblers, the engineers eliminated and substantially reduced the number of materials and tools. Millions of dollars were saved in direct costs and untold more saved in procurement costs and production time.[16]

Norm White, CEO at the State Energy Commission of Western Australia, points out another benefit of listening and responding to suggestions within the organization. On those occasions when he finds it necessary (generally because of policy changes mandated by the state government) to make nonparticipative decisions, he finds that because of his efforts to listen and hear their concerns, people in the organization are now more willing to trust his decision and go along with the change more cooperatively. Quite simply, White says, "I think they are starting to trust me."

As the lines increasingly become blurred about who's inside and who's outside the corporate boundaries, the simple requirement for increased trust is greater communication with those constituencies critical to our success. This means listening everywhere and to everyone. It means regularly walking the halls and plant floors, meeting often with small groups below the managerial level, and hitting the road for frequent visits with the troops, key suppliers, and customers. It may even mean learning another language if a large portion of your work force or customer base speak it. Building trust begins by building a personal relationship through listening.

Listening can't be achieved from a distance, by reading reports, or by hearing something secondhand. Our constituents want to know who we are, how we feel, and whether we really care; they want to see it from us in living color. Since proximity is the single best predictor of whether two people will talk to one another, we have to get close to people if we're going to communicate. And since most of our constituents cannot come to us, we have to go to them.

Beginning to Understand

To appreciate each person as unique, we need to acknowledge how little we may know and understand about that person. Ironically, the less we know, the more likely we are to underestimate how little we know. Unaware of our own ignorance, it is only with hindsight that we may learn of it. A stark example of this was General Motors's introduction of its Chevrolet Nova into Spanish-speaking markets without realizing that in Spanish *no va* means "it doesn't go."

A language difference is obvious. But misunderstandings

are rarely so simple as this. It is not unusual for any of us, when we have differences with another person, to believe that the other party needs to know more about our perspective. We find it much harder to recognize that we may not know enough about the other person. To start to understand someone else, ask, "What does he or she care about?" Once we understand more about other people's interests (concerns, wants, hopes, and fears) we are more able to meet their needs.

Trying to imagine the other person's situation and assuming his or her role can help us learn a different perspective. Ken Olsen, the founder of Digital Equipment Corporation, once took DEC executives to the loading dock from which the computers were shipped. He gave each executive a crowbar and asked each executive to uncrate a computer and set it up.[17] Replicating their customers' experience in receiving a DEC computer provided many lessons and helped widen the executives' perspectives. Appreciating customers' experience with a product is one step toward understanding that their experience may well be different than our own – and in critical ways.

Learning Anew

We also appreciate others when we adopt a learning attitude. Great leaders are great learners and keep their minds open about what people can contribute to an enterprise. This is to their advantage in working with people from diverse backgrounds. Those of us still becoming great leaders may need to acquire this skill by reexamining old assumptions. If we are to change our views, we may have to question some of our past decisions and actions (and fear that others, even our friends, will also question our past judgment and wisdom accordingly). This practice can make us uncomfortable and cause us to worry about losing face or looking stupid. Taking in new information, information that is contrary to previous positions and statements we've made, can make us psychologically insecure. Is it any wonder that appreciating other perspectives may seem difficult or awkward? How can we make this easier? How can we reduce the risk of being proven wrong?

The answers are really the other side of the coin about how we can increase the likelihood of being right. One way to make the process easier is by seeking out and remaining open to new information. Susan S. Elliott, president and founder of Systems Service Enterprises, a St. Louis computer consulting company, puts it this way: "I can't come up with a plan and then ask those who manage the accounts to give me their reactions. They're the ones who really know the accounts. They have information I don't have. Without their input, I'd be operating in an ivory tower."[18] A similar attitude is expressed by George Petley, general manager, Kewdale Structural Engineers (Welshpool, Western Australia). He acknowledges that the employees "know how to do this stuff better than I do. Some people like pretending that they are king of the hill, big boss, throwing their weight around and all that, but me, I know that what these people can do if you let them is terrific. We work together."

Another way leaders remain open and appreciative is by basing their self-respect not on what they already know, but on how well they are capable of learning. Stephen Dunne, account manager for Fujitsu Business Communication Systems, explains, "I learn most from working with others to resolve our team's current problems. I believe this attitude increases my credibility with our customers. They know that while I might not have all the answers, I am very responsive in making things work for them." Dunne relates how one of his former managers built credibility by admitting he needed to listen more to his work team. This manager "told us he had been reviewing some of our previous presentations. He discovered that earlier recommendations we had given him on an important project would be a better way to proceed. So he said, 'I think this team is trying to steer me in the right direction. I need to acknowledge that you were right. I should have listened more carefully at the time. Let's pull these files out again, backtrack a little, and understand this approach better.'" What Dunne remembers from this incident is not that his manager made a mistake, but that he should always listen carefully to others, especially when he did not agree with them initially.

One challenge in appreciating diversity is that people have a tendency to value their own contributions more than those of others. This has been demonstrated in a series of research studies by psychologist David Kipnis and his colleagues. They report how powerful people tend to attribute the success of their work unit to their own work more than to the efforts of the "less powerful" people they supervise. As a result of this inclination, the contributions of others can often be overlooked and our own overemphasized.[19] This can inhibit our willingness to search out diverse opinions unless we recognize how, as leaders, we are dependent upon others.

SOLICITING FEEDBACK

Leaders demonstrate that they appreciate diverse points of view by asking for feedback from their constituents. By being open to influence (necessary to fully appreciate diversity), leaders encourage people to provide more information.[20] Soliciting feedback is the reciprocal side of showing appreciation. We trust them, and they trust us. We listen to them, and they will be more likely to listen to us. For this to occur, however, informal and formal feedback opportunities need to be structured.

Three structures that have proven useful are 360-degree performance appraisals, skip-level meetings, and upward performance appraisals. Companies such as the Automobile Club of Southern California, Levi Strauss & Co., State Farm Insurance, TRW, Merck, Trygg Hansa, and Baltica augment traditional management performance appraisals with 360-degree performance appraisals. You can gain new insight into how your behavior affects others when feedback is solicited from everyone around you. Similarly, skip-level meetings, where your manager talks directly with the members of your team about your strengths and areas for improvement, also yield valuable information. At Esso Resources (Canada), employees complete our Leadership Practices Inventory and then meet as a group to summarize their feedback and prepare an upward performance appraisal regarding their manager's leadership effectiveness.[21]

Sometimes the feedback received in these sessions reveals actions and behaviors that are confusing, counterproductive, and even annoying to others. Many such actions can be rectified quite easily and quickly — once we know about them. Others require cooperative efforts and support from the team (in the same way that they would need support from you for any new behavior). And some of your actions won't be changed, but others can understand the rationale for them and you can be more sensitive to the impact such actions have on others.

Management scholar and author Peter Drucker has suggested that managing one's "boss" is relatively simple. The most important thing to do is to get together with your manager "at least once a year — and ask: 'What do I do and what do my people do that helps *you* do your job? And what do we do that hampers you and makes life more difficult for *you*?'"[22] This sounds like an obvious approach, but it is rarely done.

Drucker's advice works both ways. Given that leadership is a relationship, it is imperative that you go to your constituents often and ask, "What can I do to help you? What could I stop doing that would help even more?"

PROMOTING
CONSTRUCTIVE
CONTROVERSY

Appreciating diversity requires an investment of time and effort. But it pays off, and organizations are the beneficiary. Aware of the pitfalls of institutional unanimity, leaders resist the urge to hire only those people who look or sound or think just like themselves. They build dissent and controversy into the decision-making process so that people will be willing to speak openly and offer ideas contrary to their own. So look for good people from many molds, and then encourage them to speak out, even to disagree.

When team members actively promote varied ideas, the group becomes more resilient. Members are more likely to see their part within the whole, and their satisfaction becomes less contingent on whether they agree with the outcome. With diversity comes balance and protection against polarization, in which a conservative group shifts to an even more conservative position than any individual within the group might have taken or a liberal group adopts a more liberal stance.

When thoughtful dissent is encouraged, the result is much more than a heightened sense of collegiality: better decisions are reached. Psychology professors Janet Sniezek and Rebecca Henry have found that groups are generally more effective than individuals in making forecasts of sales and other financial data. And the greater the initial disagreement among group members, the more accurate the results. "With more disagreement, people are forced to look at a wider range of possibilities," Sniezek and Henry report.[23] In one of our own studies, we found that greater ethical reasoning was applied to difficult decisions by a group than by the group members deciding alone.[24] Open and sometimes heated discussion by the group members brought out ideas and perspectives that some had ignored or not even considered in their initial considerations. In articulating their views, members were encouraged to talk about their values and the principles involved in their decisions; the discussion was elevated to higher levels of reasoning as a result.

Effective leaders have been found to encourage dissent precisely because it does force clarification of assumptions and ideas. Leadership scholar Warren Bennis observes, "Whatever momentary discomfort they experience as a result of being told from time to time that they are wrong is more than offset by the fact that reflective backtalk increases a leader's ability to make good decisions. Former president Ronald Reagan suffered far more at the hands of so-called friends who refused to tell him unattractive truths than from his ostensible enemies."[25] Leaders promote a range of opinion by actively stirring up disagreement and by legitimizing the articulation of differences.

One surprising finding from research is that appreciating diversity encourages both open discussion and productive conflict management.[26] In a series of laboratory and field studies, management professor Dean Tjosvold and his colleagues have shown how diversity facilitates controversy—the open discussion of opposing positions and views—promoting the elaboration of different viewpoints, the search for new information and ideas, and the integration of apparently opposing positions. What Tjosvold refers to as constructive controversy copes with the biases of closed mindedness and inadequate evaluation of new information. It simplifies the problem and mitigates against unwarranted confidence in initial positions. This process in turn aids in understanding opposing points and the problem, fosters greater development of alternatives, and results in stronger commitment to high-quality solutions.[27]

What credible leaders intuitively do is demonstrate the constructive controversy process for their multiple constituencies. They explain their current position and ideas, presenting facts, information, and concepts that support their views, and provide a logical structure linking these premises to their conclusions. But they don't stop here, assuming theirs is the best or only possible decision. Credible leaders invite others to elaborate their own perspectives, which are often quite different and incompatible. These opposing ideas and positions challenge and provoke people's thinking. Appreciating diversity allows this controversy to stimulate innovative thinking and encourages actively searching for new information. Curiosity is aroused. Original positions are reclarified and reformulated. By paying attention to others' arguments, we find it easier to adopt their perspective and remember the facts, arguments, and reasoning they used to support their (alternative) position. This elaboration and search leaves us much more open minded and knowledgeable about the subject. We become less rigid, more capable of synthesizing and integrating different facts and ideas into new patterns and more responsive positions. Repeated exposure to diversity and controversy fosters more sophisticated, proactive responses, higher-level reasoning, and cognitive development.[28] And, as we'll see, how we handle controversy and difficult situations has much to do with the levels of trust we engender.

ENGENDERING TRUST

Trusting other people encourages them to trust us; distrusting others makes them lose confidence in us. We can help people trust us by the candor with which we talk about our behavior. Being open is especially important when discussing conduct that might look to others as inconsistent or incompatible with a prior promise. To enhance the reputation of being reliable, you need to deal honestly with problems before they happen. As long as the problem is not reoccurring, you build confidence about your trustworthiness by demonstrating your initiative and by reassuring the other party that you care about the situation and are doing something about it.

This approach is exactly what Steve Tritto took during a particularly difficult period for electronics manufacturer Emu Systems, where he was chief operating officer. The company had serious financial and cash-flow problems, and it couldn't really afford to stay current on the rent for its facilities if it was to rebound. Emu's chief financial officer (CFO) had already spoken with the landlord about foregoing lease payments, and the landlord had not been interested. Tritto decided to speak directly with the landlord again and explain the situation "although," recalls Tritto, "the CFO felt that basically I couldn't add anything."

Tritto and the CFO met with the landlord:

> I laid our cards out on the table with him, explaining that if the company were to survive, we weren't going to be able to spend $30,000 on rent. We needed this money to

buy parts and to pay people. But I told him what we were
doing to get back on track and why we felt this would
work and how he would get his money and so on. Essentially what I was asking of him was delayed rent payments
for nine months. He agreed. Our CFO—I didn't tell him
what I was going to do because I really wasn't sure myself—but when I asked for this concession, he almost fell
out of his chair; and when the guy said yes—well, he was
in a state of shock. Later on, during a casual discussion of
the meeting, the landlord said he agreed because he
believed what I told him. And we did make good on our
promises.

By being honest, Tritto enhanced his credibility. His
rationale for telling the truth was also relatively straightforward: "You can't be honest because you're afraid that they're
going to find out anyway; you have to be honest for the sake of
being honest, not because you think you're going to get caught
if you're not." Honesty is in fact primarily a moral choice.[29]

To be trusted, we have to extend ourselves by being
available, by volunteering information, by sharing our personal experiences, and by making connections with the experiences and aspirations of our constituents. As Tritto knew and
demonstrated, we must allow our constituents to know us.
Becoming trusted requires reciprocity, a willingness on the
part of both parties to enter into dialogue and conversations. It
also takes time because although trust may sometimes be
forged in moments of great drama, it is more likely to be
formed by many small, moment-to-moment, encounters. The
richness of the relationship between leaders and constituents,
like the intensity of a good sauce, is formed by letting the
various ingredients simmer together.

How then can you become trustworthy as a leader? How
can you behave in ways that facilitate trust? Research has
shown that certain key behaviors contribute to whether or not
others perceive one as trustworthy.[30] Examining your daily
actions with the following four questions in mind will go
a long way toward enhancing your reputation as someone
trustworthy.

1.   *Is my behavior predictable or erratic?* If your behavior is confusing, indecisive, or inconsistent, others cannot depend upon you to behave in certain ways in similar situations. They cannot make reasonable hypotheses about how you might react under new or different circumstances. Some degree of predictability or consistency is required in order for people to believe in you. Consistency means that the same personal values and organizational aims will influence what you say and do, that your preoccupation with quality or customer service (for example) will not give way to the shifting tides of fashion or politics.

2.   *Do I communicate clearly or carelessly?* Sometimes we make statements about our intentions, even if tentative in our own minds, without realizing that to others these are viewed as promises. If you frequently make statements that you don't intend as commitments but that others might reasonably interpret as such, they may well believe that you are unreliable. If you are clear about what you mean, there is less chance that others will find your statements misleading.

3.   *Do I treat promises seriously or lightly?* If we treat our own commitments seriously, others will too. If we take our promises lightly, others will also. Problems arise when people have different perceptions of the importance of both your word and the circumstances required to justify not keeping your promise. Further complications arise when people can't distinguish between wishes or vague promises on your part and those ideas to which you are seriously committed.

4.   *Am I forthright or dishonest?* If you knowingly mislead or lie—for example, making a promise you never intended to keep—then other people have good reason not to trust you. There is no such thing as a little bit of dishonesty. Discovering that someone has been deceitful casts doubt over everything he or she says or does. By the way, honesty doesn't require full disclosure. It does, however, require a clear indication of areas about which complete candor should not be expected and an

explanation of why it is not appropriate. Still, greater disclosure between people generally makes for better working relationships and easier resolution of problems should they arise.

Before people will be willing to follow a leader's vision or act on a leader's initiatives, they must trust their leader.[31] This trust cannot be demanded. Leaders must earn it before they can expect their diverse constituents to accept and act upon their messages.

TAKING RISKS
AND GAINING INNOVATION

Tremendous energy is unleashed within constituents when they have confidence in their leaders. They feel liberated, self-confident, and secure enough in their relationships to explore new territories and opportunities and take on fresh challenges. In this way, trust is the lubricant for individual and organizational change. The irony is that people cannot take risks unless they feel safe, unless they feel secure that they will not be unfairly treated, embarrassed, harassed, or harmed by taking some action. When we feel safe, our defensive mechanisms are not aroused because our self-esteem is not being threatened. We become more open (vulnerable) to outside influence and to learning.

We often see this take place in the context of leadership development programs involving outdoor initiatives (often referred to as "ropes courses"). In one of our recent experiences, the heftiest member of the group was fitted with belay equipment in front of the group, then lifted up and left dangling four or five feet off the ground. The facilitator then proceeded to tell us about the characteristics of the safety system—the harness, webbing, and rope. She then took a knife and systematically cut the fibers of the rope holding our compatriot until but one strand remained. After this demonstration, we were ready to put our trust in the system and face up to the challenges of descending steeply down (in this instance) into a darkened cave.

Questions of physical safety provide dramatic emphasis in this question of trust. Yet emotional safety is no less significant. At Total Autos, a moderate-sized car dealership outside of Perth, Western Australia, it's no longer difficult or threatening to convey ideas upward—thanks to increased accessibility. They've removed many of the physical demarcations between workers and management, and the management group is spending more of its time in the shop than in its offices. Indeed, both groups seem quite comfortable in one another's work areas. When the shop floor leader and several of the mechanics had an idea about changing the shop work flow, they took it directly to dealer-principal Manny De Canha. He listened; the plan was established.

De Canha makes it a point to be visible: "I want it to be easy for people to talk with me. Initially it's often chitchat. But as people become more familiar and comfortable with me, the talk becomes more personal, and I learn about the things they really care about. And one of the things we care about in common is making this business a success." What De Canha demonstrates is that when people know us they are more likely to trust us. And when constituents trust us, they feel safe with us. And when they feel safe with us, they are more likely to take risks with us.

Examples such as these and the research make clear that shared trust or lack thereof is a significant determinant of managerial problem-solving effectiveness.[32] Further, the more we trust those making decisions in an organization, the more satisfied we are with our level of participation in the process. This finding holds true even on those occasions when our actual level of participation is relatively low.[33] In organizations in which mutual trust does not exist, people are cautious, less open, less satisfied, less influential, more distant, and more inclined to leave at the first available opportunity.

There is still another compelling reason for encouraging trust: a climate of trust is good for your health. Several longitudinal studies have revealed that people with high scores on suspiciousness (the belief that others are not well-intentioned and good hearted) have a significantly greater chance of contracting a fatal disease. In one study in which 255 subjects were followed over a twenty-five-year span, those with higher scores on suspiciousness had more coronary heart disease and 6.4 times the mortality rate of low scorers (or trusting people).[34]

Clearly, it is in our best interests as individuals and as leaders to be trusted by all of our constituents. If people have faith in us, our behavior will generate fewer disputes. If we don't deceive others, they will have less reason to get angry or deceive us in return. If we are reliable and others know they can count on us, then our words and actions will have greater power to influence them. If we appreciate people and show that we take their interests to heart, they can trust us to lead. People will be less suspicious and better able to deal with legitimate differences. On all fronts, developing the trust of their diverse constituents is critical to leaders.

With these efforts, we can all become better able to appreciate and benefit from our differences, from our diversity. Weaving the richly varied threads of these together requires effort from everyone, effort that can be undertaken wholeheartedly only when trust is mutual. When it is, we can direct ourselves toward our shared values and common purpose, as discussed in the next chapter. The results that can then be achieved justify the personal and collective effort and commitment involved.

APPRECIATING CONSTITUENTS: FIRST STEPS/NEXT STEPS

Here we provide some practical steps you can undertake both to help increase your appreciation for constituents and their diversity and to build their trust in you as a leader.

▶ ***Be accessible—even at home.*** "I'm giving you my home phone number," Debra Scates, Santa Clara University's director of graduate education, tells new M.B.A. students at orientation, "because there may be a time, perhaps, when you are having a problem. The office is closed, maybe it's the weekend, and you need some help or someone to talk with. Give me a call at home, and we'll see what we can do." There is no other message sent that day more powerful than this one about how Scates trusts the students. And no other piece of information is written down by so many students. How many calls does she get at home? "Oh, maybe two or three in a year," she says, "but I am so happy that these people called because we can usually take care of their issue right away and put their minds at ease. Can you imagine how big this problem is on Monday morning after the student has stewed about it all weekend?"

Although there are many reasons why you may not want to give out your home number to everyone, ponder what really keeps you from doing it. Don't you trust people to respect your privacy? Balance this concern against the benefit of clearly communicating your trust and your accessibility to all of your constituents—and your focus on their needs.

▶ ***Listen everywhere and listen well.*** What we heard loud and clear from leaders and constituents alike, over and over again, is the importance of listening to what other people are saying. People know they are respected and valued when they are listened to. Being able to listen well is not easy. Dennis Longstreet, president of Ortho Biotech, a Johnson & Johnson company, says that the thing he had to adjust most in maintaining his credibility "was my listening skills because I think that most management, particularly white male management, has a tendency to listen for about ten seconds and then solve the problem. That's the way I was trained, that's the way I moved through the organization, and so I would attempt to fix problems quickly. That's not necessarily the style that works."

Do what it takes for you to become a better listener. No matter how good you think you are at listening, make an active plan to do something about being better.

You can listen better when you say to your constituents, "Tell me about that problem. I want to hear more about it. Can you give me any examples?" and conclude by asking, "What do you think?" Listening helps us to reduce our defensiveness and makes us more patient in hearing "bad" news. If you need another reason to improve your listening skills, consider this: no great idea ever entered the head through an open mouth.

▶ *Learn your constituents' stories.* What can you learn when you listen to someone tell a story? Think about what it tells you about the storyteller. Pay attention, and you can discover a great deal about values—what makes people laugh, what makes them mad, how they feel about other people, even how they feel about the company.

Furthermore, try asking people to tell you more about their stories, and what it means to them. Use this information as the basis for more conversations. What does the story mean to you? Exchange stories. And use them—giving credit as appropriate—to illustrate your appreciation of their insight and experiences. Relating another person's story can be a wonderful form of recognition.[35]

▶ *Step outside your cultural experience.* Let's use the analogy of art appreciation. How do you come to appreciate art? For some, it begins by reading books about art, artists, and the artistic process. Others start by going to museums and art galleries, looking at lots of paintings, and determining which ones they like or don't like and why. Some even start by trying to draw, sketch, or use watercolors themselves. The processes are similar for appreciating another culture. Read about that culture, its history, politics, and religion. Listen to the music and sounds of that people, group, or community. Watch films. Visit art galleries. Sample the food.

When possible, approach this task of becoming more appreciative by seeking the assistance of an "interpreter," someone who can show you around and help you make sense of the cultural data. Most people are really more than willing to help others learn about their culture—assuming that they are sincere in their interest and keep an open mind. Usually in this interchange, both parties will learn more about the other's culture, as well as gain insight into the subtleties and unexamined aspects of their own.

▶ *Keep in touch.* Meet and spend time with your constituents to get to know them. Once you've had the face-to-face communications that people prefer, supplement this with technological methods that enable you to stay in touch and be available.

At UNUM Corporation, all 5,500 employees (not just in their Portland, Maine, headquarters but in the one hundred-plus offices around the United States and England) are urged to sound off to CEO James F. Orr III through the insurance company's electronic mail system. He sits down each night to respond to that day's messages—sometimes answering with a personal phone call the next morning.[36] James Treybig, CEO and president at Tandem Computers, appears on a monthly television program broadcast over the company's in-house TV station. Employees around the world watch the show and call in their questions and comments. In a similar vein, within one week of Southern Pacific Lines' annual senior management conference, participants are provided with video highlights and copies of key handouts and slides so that they can hold "town hall meetings" with company employees about the railroad's strategic focus and concerns.

Keep in mind that no matter how effective the system,

such technological solutions as electronic mail, voice mail, videos, and video conferencing work best when the participants have first met in person.

▶   ***Become an employee for the day.*** Many companies invite their employees to step into the shoes of their managers for a day and learn about the demands and responsibilities of management. Why not turn that around and also have your management team take over the jobs of their nonmanagerial associates? That's what they do at the Florence, Kentucky, distribution center of Levi Strauss & Co. Pete Blackmore, general manager, says that he learns a great deal about how hard people work in getting pants out the door: "Spending time on the plant floor actually packing jeans and carting boxes around gives me a much greater appreciation for the talents required and pressures we place on people than anything I learn from reading reports generated by our human resources department. I also get to meet lots of people on an informal and first-name basis. Of course, they get to meet me on the same basis." Blackmore says that these actions by the management team foster its credibility throughout the organization.

Learn about what other people do in your organization. Honor your colleagues by periodically working along side them for a day.

▶   ***Hold a regular forum with key constituencies.*** As the marketing folks would put this idea, conduct a regular focus group with your key constituencies. Ask them to tell you about what they like and don't like about your product, services, programs, policies, jokes, or leadership practices. The important point is that you value their opinions and that you listen carefully to them.

You can also benefit from people bouncing ideas off one another in focus group or forum settings. You get a chance to test whether one person's or group's needs are idiosyncratic or common to everyone. In the process, everyone learns about what it takes to work together to achieve common objectives.

▶   *Ante up first.* There are no magical formulas for building trust. The process begins with one person's willingness to take a risk. A risk because ultimately that's what trust is all about. We take the risk that the other party won't harm us, physically or psychologically, with the information we share or the actions we agree to take on their behalf. In the beginning, there is no guarantee that the other party will also sufficiently ante up or play a win-win strategy in this trust game. What we do know is that people who have confidence in others are in turn seen by other people as trustworthy themselves. And vice versa: people who do not have faith in others are not perceived as meriting other people's trust.

If you're worried about putting your "money" up first, take heart in knowing that people who basically trust others are no less or more intelligent than those who are fundamentally suspicious or untrusting of others. Moreover, gullibility is unrelated to our propensity to trust or not to trust others. But unless you take the first step, trust cannot be created.

▶   *Know what "bugs" your constituents.* Knowing what managerial behaviors most commonly irk employees can help you avoid committing them. According to Mary Ann Allison and Eric Allison, coauthors of *Managing Up, Managing Down*, here's what upsets employees most about their managers: public reprimands, failure to get credit for ideas, unrealistic demands, unclear directions (followed by angry reproof when the job is not done properly), and angry, rude, condescending, or temperamental behavior.[37] Ask your constituents about whether there are things you do that bother them and then do something about these. (This may be the start of a small win, discussed next.)

▶ *Practice small wins.* Make it easier for people to trust you (and lower your risk in trusting others) by adopting a strategy of small wins. As an example, consider LuAnn Sullivan, branch office manager for Wells Fargo Bank.[38] Even though volume in the branch had not grown for several years, she believed that members of her staff could double the amount of their core deposits. How did they do this? She started small, by asking each person to write one more deposit or loan the next month than they had the previous month. And when staff members accomplished this objective, Sullivan congratulated them and again asked them to write one more than they had the previous month. Breaking down their overall goal into doable accomplishments (wins) placed the solution within each person's current capacity and reduced the amount of trust and energy required for each person to achieve his or her part of the solution.

So start small, with something manageable, and build upon your success. Or try relying on someone else just a little more than you do now, and see how it goes before making a long-term commitment. If there are difficulties, use this experience to problem solve for future encounters. When it works, venture out a little further the next time.

5

Affirming Shared Values

*Shared values are the glue
that hold this organization together.*
Shelley Brown
Aspect Telecommunications

Once there was a village in Nigeria, West Africa, where the people made their living by farming. The village lay in a large green valley that was lined with palm trees and bushes. Surrounding the village were fields dotted with crops of yams, cassava, corn, and other vegetables. Just beyond the fields was a deep river that the villagers called Baba, which means father. The river was a friend and a provider for the people: the men used it for fishing, the women washed clothes on its banks, and the children played in its waters. But in the rainy season, the river overflowed, and the people were fearful of its power. So, at a place where the river wound beyond the fields, they built a strong dam to hold back the water.

There was a man in the village named Modupe, which means "I am grateful." Modupe was a shy, quiet man whose wife had died and whose children were all married, so he had moved to the top of the mountain overlooking the valley and lived alone. There he had built a small hut and cleared a small piece of land to grow his vegetables. The people did not see Modupe often, but they loved and respected him because he had the gift of healing the sick and because he was one of them.

One year at harvest time, there were unusually heavy rains, but the crops had done well and there was much to do. No one paid it any mind. As Modupe stood by his house on the mountain, he noticed that the river had become swollen from the rains and was straining the dam. He knew that by the time he could run down to the village to warn the people of the flood, it would be too late and all would be lost. Even as Modupe watched, the wall of the dam began to break, and water started to seep through.

Modupe thought of his friends in the village. Their crops, their homes, and their very lives were in danger if he did not find a way to warn them. Then an idea came to him: he rushed to his small hut and set it afire. When the people of the valley saw Modupe's house burning, they said, "Our friend is in trouble. Let's sound the alarm and go up to help him." Then, according to custom, men, women, and children ran up the mountain to see what they could do. When they reached the top of the hill, they did not have time to ask what had happened—a loud crashing noise behind them made them turn around and look down into the valley. Their houses, their temple, and their crops were being destroyed by the river, which had broken the dam and was flooding the valley.

The people began to cry and moan at their loss, but Modupe comforted them. "Don't worry," he said. "My crops are still here. We can share them while we build a new village." Then all the people began to sing and give thanks because they remembered that in coming to help a friend, they had saved themselves.[1]

On another occasion, half a world away, people again worked together, this time after a 7.1 earthquake struck the San Francisco Bay Area on October 17, 1989. Sixty-three people lost their lives, thousands were injured, and over $6 billion in damages was reported. But behind these headlines were little-known stories of people, thousands of them, who opened their hearts and wallets to aid the victims of this terrible catastrophe. Friends, neighbors, and strangers offered comfort and shared resources. Earthquake or burst dam, hurricane or other disaster, we see that in times of need, people do come together; by helping others rebuild their physical community, they reaffirm their spiritual sense of community as well.

Leaders do not wait for a disaster or an external event to pull people together, however. Instead, they build community through shared values. They create consensus around shared values and rely upon those to resolve conflicts. Moreover, leaders build commitment to these values and get people to perceive themselves as part of a larger whole—and to become involved in collective actions and shared successes.

USING SHARED VALUES TO MAKE A DIFFERENCE

Shared values are the foundation for building productive and genuine working relationships. While credible leaders honor the diversity of their many constituencies, they also stress their common values. Leaders build upon agreement. Their efforts are not to get everyone to be in accord on everything—this goal is unrealistic, perhaps even impossible. Moreover, to achieve it would negate the advantages of diversity. But in order to take a first step, and then a second, and then a third, people must agree on something. There has to be some common core of understanding. If disagreements over fundamental values continue, the result is intense conflict, false expectations, and diminished capacity. There could be no agreement on the "specifications" of quality, customer service, or any guiding principle.

Recognizing that we hold shared values provides us with a common language with which we can collaborate. When individual, group, and organizational values are in synch, tremendous energy is generated. Commitment, enthusiasm, and drive are intensified: people have a reason for caring about their work. Individuals are more effective (and satisfied) because they are able to care about what they are doing. They experience less stress and tension. Shared values are the internal compasses that enable people to act independently and interdependently.

Organizations also benefit from shared values. Employees are more loyal when they believe that their values and those of the organization are aligned. They are more creative because they become immersed in what they are doing. The quality and accuracy of communication and the integrity of the decision-making process increase when people feel part of the same team.

For example, in one of our recent investigations, involving over one thousand managers in a range of different companies and industries, we found that those who shared their company's values and experienced congruency between their personal values and those of their company reported significantly more positive attachments to their work and organization than those who felt that little relationship existed (see Figure 5.1). These two groups, not surprisingly, also differed in the extent to which they found their management to be credible.[2] We found similar results when investigating the impact of shared values on managers in Hong Kong and Australia.[3]

A host of other researchers in a variety of disciplines have demonstrated empirically how shared values affect personal and organizational effectiveness.[4] For instance, an accurate understanding of job requirements and the organization's values has been shown to enhance people's adjustment to their jobs, as well as their subsequent level of satisfaction and organizational commitment. The fit between person-organization values has been shown to be a predictor of job satisfaction and organizational turnover a year later and of actual turnover after two years. Another study has shown how operating-unit performance and value congruency are linked.

In his book, *Managing with Power*, Stanford Business

Figure 5.1. Person-Organization Values Alignment.

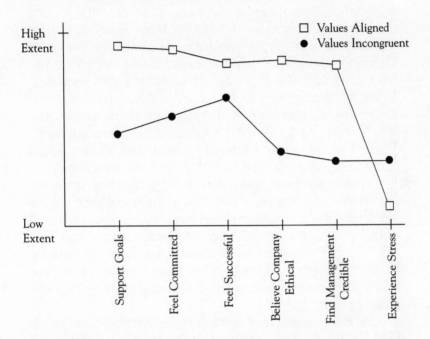

Note: All differences between the low and high groups were statistically significant at $p < .001$. Higher numbers represent more positive responses.

Source: B. Z. Posner and W. H. Schmidt, "Values Congruence and Difference Between the Interplay of Personal and Organizational Value Systems," *Journal of Business Ethics, 12* (1993): 171–177.

School professor Jeffrey Pfeffer gives yet another persuasive business argument for "speaking with one voice": power! Pfeffer's empirical investigations reveal that those organizational groups or departments with the greatest unity get more resources.[5] Pfeffer uses the word *unity* for agreement and consensus around paradigms—essentially what we have been referring to as shared values. Because of their unity, these groups also have more efficient internal and external communication. As a result, their coordination costs are reduced, and joint action is easier to achieve.

As an example, consider academic departments within a university. Once there is paradigm consensus, the faculty members are able to work together more easily, get more things accomplished, and receive more funds. Not being rife with internal conflicts, they can also form more effective coalitions in dealing with other departments for scarce resources. Since the average tenure of academic department heads is longer in units that are more paradigmatically developed, the chair's ability to speak for the department is strengthened.[6] These benefits are not limited to academia; similar points apply to departments within multifunctional organizations.

The truly great companies have known for years the importance of being clear about their vision and their values. And as more and more companies have become decentralized, pushing decisions out of corporate headquarters into divisions, from divisions into departments, and from one country to another around the globe, they have come to appreciate how values provide a framework for integrated and coordinated efforts.

And the same is true at the departmental, unit, and group level. In the business world, we ask how the organization's values fit into those of our department, unit, or group and vice versa. Where are there agreements? Are there conflicts? Can we find common ground?

FINDING COMMON GROUND

The leader's challenge is in learning how to achieve what John Gardner has called wholeness incorporating diversity. In his commencement address to the centennial graduation class at Stanford University, he said, "[Your goal is] not to achieve wholeness by suppressing diversity, nor to make wholeness impossible by enthroning diversity, but to preserve both. Each element in the diversity must be respected, but each must ask itself sincerely what it can contribute to the whole. I don't think it is venturing beyond the truth to say that 'wholeness incorporating diversity' defines the transcendent task for our generation."[7]

That phrase, wholeness incorporating diversity, comes to mind as we recall how communist control over the former Soviet Union disintegrated. The planet's security depends upon the ability of leaders from what is now called the Unified Commonwealth of Nations to create social, economic, and political systems (wholeness) that can incorporate long-suppressed differences. Similar challenges exist across the globe. At an individual level, the question is whether people whose individualities and self-interests have been long suppressed can appreciate sufficiently the need to engage in cooperative ventures.

One of the most common mistakes made in attempting to create shared values is announcing which are most important and should guide the department (or company). This approach may have worked in the old command-and-control hierarchies, in which managers told and sold values. It does not work in today's more diverse work environment. Instead, leaders must cast the net widely to capture the broadest possible understanding of constituents' values. Having listened, leaders and constituents must then learn to speak with one voice.

Determining the key shared values is not just a technical problem-solving exercise; it is a process in which the parties must participate and, together, design an agreement. The process itself is as important as the product, if not more so. Participation is vital, for people's perspectives change once they are involved. Having injected their own ideas into the final solution, they are able to make the agreement their own. They accept ideas they might have otherwise rejected. Developing shared values is thus more about asking people for their input than it is about telling them what is or is not important.

In developing shared values, there are several compelling questions. What values do we actually hold deeply? Do these make any difference in what we do around here? If the key question asked is "what principles should we have?" merely rhetorical statements will result, and people will respond with justifiable cynicism. As managers and organizations have discovered, it is just not enough to write the credo down. People must believe it for value-driven behavior to result.

Over the past decade, more and more companies, and functional units within them, have designed innovative processes for involving their constituencies in finding common purpose and building a community of shared values. One of the boldest experiments is taking place at Ortho Biotech, part of the Johnson & Johnson family of companies. Ortho Biotech is determined to create a new corporate culture that supports the contributions of all its diverse constituencies.

Initiated in 1992, Adventures in Cultural Enhancement (ACE) got its original impetus from the key players' involvement, years earlier, in a series of managing diversity programs. In June of 1990, when Ortho Biotech became a separate organization, Dennis Longstreet, the company's president, and Andrea Zintz, vice president for human resources, saw an opportunity to establish a distinctive culture for Ortho Biotech. Says Longstreet, "The spawning of it [ACE] was my experience in managing diversity and trying to change a culture. And then having an opportunity, a rare opportunity, to start a new company, we took diversity awareness to the next step, which is what do you do differently and how do you change norms and behaviors?"

At an early corporate strategy session, board members developed a statement of Ortho Biotech's business mission. Board members then joined with the existing managing diversity task force to form a new group—the Culture Development Committee (CDC). This was charged with creating a process to involve all employees in putting the new vision into action. In developing a vision statement, they went beyond the usual language about stockholders, customers, and employees. After heated debate, the board and CDC took the position that "we can only attain market leadership through maximizing the contributions of employees of all races, cultures, and genders."

According to Zintz, ACE was one of the ways that they intended to "involve all Ortho Biotech employees in building the kind of culture we most want for our company." Before ACE was a year old, two-thirds of the approximately 450 employees had participated in the program, in groups of seventy to ninety people. The invitation to the ACE program told employees that they could expect to be "actively involved in examining and challenging the vision statement" and that they would "participate in examining and defining the unwritten rules (norms) of the culture." Further, the invitation explained, "There will be an opportunity to learn and practice skills that will be useful in bringing about a work environment where everyone can take part in the success of our business."

The first day of the three-day experiential learning program was designed to enable people to feel safe with the process, the other participants, and management. It also focused on the skills of giving and receiving feedback and seeking and telling, skills the planners felt essential to collaboration and consensus building.

Day two began with a historical perspective. Longstreet, Zintz, Rich Gatens (chief financial officer and CDC chair), and other key leaders told their personal stories about the CDC adventure. They then described the new company vision and asked participants to think about such issues as:

- How does the Ortho Biotech vision fit with your personal vision, what you stand for?

- What do you like about the vision? What does it do for you? What concerns you?

- What's missing from the vision? And what would you like to change if you were to suggest a change?

After reflecting on these questions, participants formed small groups of about fifteen people to share responses and to produce a report from each group. Then the groups reassembled into a kind of fishbowl or open forum setting. A representative of each small group took a chair in the middle of the large group, along with all the members of the CDC. Two extra chairs remained open so that any participant who wanted to could come in and have a say. Group members could also take their representative's place in the center group.

Each group representative offered the CDC its feedback. These intense forums got to the heart of core issues of operating in a diverse environment — issues of race, gender, and level. And they were packed with emotion, especially for those who had invested personal energy in creating the original statements of vision, norms, and behaviors. Zintz says about her role as a CDC member, "I can't stress enough how hard it is for people who are leaders to hang in there. . . . You have to hang out a long time in the listening mode. . . . You earn your credibility with your constituents through really hearing them."

The unfinished business of day two was taken up at the start of day three. Affinity groups, small gatherings of people who had like issues and wanted to focus their attention on how the norms and behaviors did or did not address their key issues, were the forum for much of the day's work. These groups came up with changes and recommendations for improvements in the norms and behaviors statements. Representatives of each affinity group were selected to be part of another meeting of the CDC at which a final vision statement would be crafted.

Why go through this time-consuming and difficult process? Zintz explained to us, "Creating a company where everyone can contribute their best is important to our long-term success. It helps us attract and retain the best people in our industry, and when people feel good about where they work, they can perform their best. We often find ourselves working hard to meet short-term results. In contrast, the ACE program is an investment in our long-term success."

The program fulfills a number of important needs. In our research we have consistently found that constituents across a wide variety of industries and disciplines, from front-line employees to fairly senior-level managers, want from their leaders a clear response to two questions: Where are we going? Where do I fit in?[8] Clearly, people want to see the bigger picture, to understand that what they are doing makes a difference. Leaders recognize these needs and the importance of creating a sense of community.

CREATING A COOPERATIVE, PROUD COMMUNITY

Community is the new metaphor for organizations. In his book *Love and Profit,* seasoned Fortune 500 executive Jim Autry explains that the workplace is becoming today's neighborhood and discusses the role of community at work:

> By invoking the metaphor of community, we imply that we in business are bound by a fellowship of endeavor in which we commit to mutual goals, in which we contribute to the best of our abilities, in which each contribution is recognized and credited, in which there is a forum for all voices to be heard, in which our success contributes to the success of the common enterprise and to the success of others, in which we can disagree and hold differing viewpoints without withdrawing from the community, in which we are free to express how we feel as well as what we think, in which our value to society is directly related to the quality of our commitment and effort, and in which we take care of each other.[9]

Creating a community requires promoting shared values and developing an appreciation for the value of working cooperatively and caring about one another. In an organizational sense, unless we know what we have in common, there can be no compelling purpose that justifies people's commitment to the community of the organization. Indeed, for a strong community and for strong and vibrant organizations, we must be willing to make other people's problems our own and to solve them together. Leaders recognize that the metaphor of community goes a lot further in unifying people than does the standard hierarchy. They energize people to take actions that support higher organizational purposes rather than self-interests. Leaders show how everyone's interests will best be served by coming to consensus on a collective set of shared values and common purpose. They structure cooperative goals and point out how collaboration will allow the team to make the most of its resources. They indicate that individuals will be rewarded to the extent that the team succeeds and the group as a whole will be held responsible for failure. Leaders establish strong expectations that employees will develop work relationships in which they trust one another and deal openly with problems and conflicts.

Recent studies document the central role played by community in the relationship between leaders and their constituents.[10] For example, leaders who establish cooperative relationships inspire commitment and are considered competent. Their credibility is enhanced by building community through common purpose and by championing shared values. In contrast, competitive and independent leaders are seen as both obstructive and ineffective.

Advocating Cooperation

Relationships characterized by cooperation (community) have higher levels of productivity and resource exchange (sharing) than competitive relationships. In a variety of situations, cooperative goals have been shown to create higher expectations of assistance, more actual assistance and greater support, more persuasion and less coercion, and more trusting and friendly attitudes in power relationships than competitive goals. Cooperative objectives are seen to result in better progress on the job and more efficient use of resources than competitive or independent goals. Beyond that, they also strengthen confidence in future interactions. When there is community, leaders and employees assist each other by sharing resources and expertise, integrate different points of view and ideas to solve problems, discuss issues to reach mutually satisfying agreements, show initiative, consult with others, and follow proper procedures.[11]

The cost of competitive or independent relationships is

steep. Researchers find that the work situation is characterized by both parties being unwilling to help and giving low priority to the task, viewing the problem only from their own perspective, refusing to discuss problems, strictly following job descriptions, ignoring advice, working in isolation, and failing to follow procedures.

Despite more than a decade's worth of evidence supporting cooperation—evidence from classrooms, offices, and factories—the benefits from competition continue to be overemphasized, primarily at the expense of cooperation. Changing this emphasis is a difficult and critical task. Why is it critical? First, success often depends on sharing resources efficiently; this task becomes nearly impossible when people have to work against one another. Second, competition generally does not promote excellence: trying to do well and trying to beat others are simply two different things.[12] As management professor Dean Tjosvold explains in *The Team Organization*, forging unity requires people on the team to perceive themselves as part of a community, where their goals are cooperative and they are united in their purpose. Leaders cannot make team members believe their goals are cooperative; team members must decide for themselves. They must be involved in developing this unity.[13]

How then do we convince people that they are members of a cooperative team, part of a community, and in the process support shared values and common purpose? To start, people must affirm that the team has these values and purpose—and that success depends upon them all reaching these goals.

Building Consensus

Organizations must enable employees to explore and understand their common agendas. Projects requiring the team as a whole to make a set of recommendations, develop and produce a new product, or solve a problem all enhance the alignment of individual and corporate actions. Further, the task itself promotes cooperative behavior and a sense of community when team members realize that the work requires them to coordinate their efforts. Leaders structure the work flow so that the process of getting the job done demands that one person's efforts have a direct impact on the activities of another and vice versa.

Organizing the work so that individuals must cooperate and making certain that people recognize how their roles are interconnected are crucial. Leaders ensure that people discuss how their responsibilities supplement each other and how no one can be effective unless everyone fulfills their responsibilities. Through this dialogue, people learn enough about each other and their respective functions to know how to help each other. But are people generally helpful? A review of several hundred studies has found that most people are genuinely interested in assisting others.[14] The secret is making certain that people feel comfortable enough with themselves to ask for help and to be gracious with their help. When the fear of "losing" to a teammate diminishes, the need to gain personal power also decreases. Power sharing replaces power struggles. Empowering people confirms their basic worth and encourages them to seek continuous improvement, a process that creates a supportive and helpful environment.

When faced with rapidly mounting losses ("a bankruptcy in progress") at semiconductor maker Monolithic Memories, Irwin Federman (then CEO and president) made use of these ideas. He knew he needed to build consensus and empower people—and fast. So he called everyone together:

> I told them what a bunch of losers and misfits we were and that I was surprised they weren't ashamed to go home to their families every night. And I said I was surprised because individually everybody looked pretty good, but collectively we amounted to less than a slag heap. I couldn't understand why, if we really thought we were worth a damn, we didn't act that way. Well, we kind of chatted and yelled and agreed and laughed nervously like that and even in those first few days you could sense that something was happening. I had struck a responsive chord. It's called pride.

What Federman did was to create agreement about key values (like personal responsibility) and put them into the context of community—acting responsibly on behalf of the common good. Monolithic developed a theme: if you find a problem, you own it. Finger pointing quickly became obsolete because fixing the blame was no longer meritorious. Fixing the problem was.

Costs were a problem, but it wasn't clear how spending could be reduced. Federman explained:

> I certainly didn't know how to do it. But I got the managers together and said: Look, if the top line ain't bigger than the middle, the bottom line will be red, and we have no margin for red any more. None—not a little, zero, nada! So either we fix it, or say what the hell and go out looking for new jobs full-time right now. So they closeted themselves for two days, traded dollars, negotiated priorities, and came up with a break-even plan for the next four months. And, of course, I said that was great, and I trusted them to do it so much that I didn't want to get in the way, or have their progress encumbered by delays in approvals. So I increased everybody's purchasing authority by 10 times and said now you don't need my approval.
>
> They were stunned, but purchase orders did not get written, and expenses nose-dived, and in four weeks we did a $660,000 profit turnaround, which included shipping about 40 percent more product, a level from which we never retreated. Giving folks that kind of authority had a significant ancillary benefit in the self-esteem department.[15]

And they trusted one another and believed that by adhering to a shared set of principles they could achieve their purpose. A community was created in which people saw themselves as part of a whole, understood that working together was better than doing their own thing and that others could trust them and that they, in turn, could count on others.

The point of departure for building consensus at Levi Strauss & Company (LS&CO.) was different than at Monolithic Memories in that there was no immediate crisis. In fact, it took more than two years of intense discussions among the Executive Management Committee members (eight top-ranked executives) to hammer out the LS&CO.'s Aspirations Statement, a major initiative to redefine and give meaning to the values that would guide all Levi employees. But they discovered that it wasn't enough to just come up with these and expect people to understand why they were important, why or how they would be implemented, or just how seriously they were to be taken.

So LS&CO. developed and implemented an intensive five-day experience to immerse managers and professionals in LS&CO. aspirations.

This experience, called Leadership Week, is the center-piece of the company's strategy to enable employees to understand what these aspirations mean and in so doing build consensus about their importance for both individual and corporate vitality. Another purpose of Leadership Week is enabling people to learn how to put aspirations into practice. More than twenty sessions a year are conducted for small groups of about twenty-five people at a time. And in order to send a clear signal of the importance of this process to the company, at least one member of the Executive Committee or some other senior manager participated in every weeklong session when the program was launched.

"Since you can't train anybody to do anything he or she doesn't fundamentally believe in, Leadership Week is designed to give people an opportunity," explains Chairman and CEO Robert Haas, "to reflect on their own values and to allow them to say what they want to get from their work. In most cases, people learn that their personal values are aligned with those of the company." Participants also come to realize that others have similar values and problems. Suddenly, they don't feel so alone and can see how the company's values unite them in common purposes. Support networks are created, with people's own self-confidence increasing as a consequence of feeling these bonds.

In addition to the knowledge and awareness that are

promoted during Leadership Week, participants are provided opportunities to develop the skills needed to talk about their values and their own aspirations, to minimize the gaps between what they say and what they do, and to link key actions and decisions (some of which may be quite different from what they've done or felt expected to do in the past) to being "aspirational."

During Leadership Week, people achieve greater clarity about their own personal values and discover how being "aspirational" gives them the opportunity to live out these personal values within their corporate existence. Discussion of aspirations provides a way for people to talk about the often-difficult trade-offs inside a company. For example, is it aspirational to close a plant when the company is having a good year? Aspirations force people to be explicit about all the factors involved in making decisions and fosters consensus around key issues and consistency in decision making. Dialogue continues long after participants return to their work.

Yet an Aspirations Statement and Leadership Week are not enough. Leaders recognize that commitment to shared values must be reinforced through collective actions, most typically in everyday organizational policies, systems, and programs.

USING ORGANIZATIONAL SYSTEMS TO REINFORCE SHARED VALUES

In the process of affirming shared values, leaders get people to identify themselves as a group and set the expectation that they will share in some long-term benefits. Recognizing this interdependency — realizing that no one works all alone — creates a strong sense of obligation to assist and support one another. Nurturing this sense of connection and belonging between people creates a natural incentive to engage in cooperative behavior.

Frequent interactions and cooperation are a way of life at Hewlett-Packard because founder William Hewlett encouraged HP engineers to "develop products useful to the person at the next desk," then sell them to all "the 'next desks' in the world." In searching for ways to remain internationally competitive, former CEO and president John Young built on this "next desk" orientation and added shared work activities. He emphasized that each employee was both a customer and a supplier, and he asked all employees to work together to set mutual expectations, standards, and measurements to improve product quality at every stage.

Employees were empowered to live by Young's motto "Don't make or accept junk," and the results were dramatic: HP increased quality levels nine times in a few years. In so doing, the company saved $542 million in manufacturing inventory costs and $150 million in money owed by customers, as just two examples.[16]

Continuous quality improvement is a clear benefit, but are there others? Another important outcome of people helping each other is that mutual respect increases. For example, after observing U.S. Air Force trainees interact in three-person teams during a management simulation, researchers noted an encouraging link between cooperative behavior and race relations. They concluded that "helpful teammates, both black and white, attract greater respect and liking than do teammates who have not helped. This is particularly true when the helping occurs voluntarily."[17]

In high-performing, strong-culture organizations, this cooperative teamwork begins even before the first day on the job. It starts with the recruitment process and carries through into promotions.

Recruiting and Hiring

An organization's recruitment and hiring programs are critical for reinforcing and sustaining common values. Organizations must attract employees who already share at least some of its key values and whose needs are likely to be met by working there. In the course of updating his book, *The 100 Best Companies to Work For in America*, Robert Levering noted that people were increasingly looking not just for jobs, but for workplaces whose cultures were in harmony with their personal values. Further, he determined that the best firms were finding people who fit the company rather than a specific job.[18]

Paul Cook, chairman of Raychem Corporation and its CEO for more than thirty years, asserts that one of his most important jobs was always that of finding the right people: that means "learning how their minds work, what they think about, what excites them, how they approach problems." The top management at Raychem spends a huge amount of effort (Cook estimates that he spends 20 percent of his own time) on recruiting, training, and interviewing.[19]

For the work teams that are responsible for hiring their own colleagues, the question of shared values and fit with the group's norms is paramount. Motorola shows potential employees a video in which the company's values are explained. This includes everything from the key principles — uncompromising integrity and a constant respect for others — to daily expectations, such as a drug-free workplace. Understanding these values and expectations helps people screen themselves before they sign up.

Orientation

Orientation programs also play an important part in transmitting shared values. How do Disneyland and Disney World rely on teenagers to manage crowds of sixty thousand people per day and to keep the place clean, the rides exciting, and the experience fun? It's tradition. Specifically, it's the traditions passed on in "Traditions 101," a two-day orientation program. Here every new employee (even the ninety-day summer hires) meets Walt Disney (through videotapes) and learns about his vision and the underlying values in which every customer is a "guest" and every employee a "performing artist." They are quizzed about traditions and come to understand the reason why every rule, policy, and procedure is important. The result? Shared values.

Training and Development

Shared values are also strengthened and reinforced in training and development programs. For example, white-collar employees at Matsushita spend a good part of their first six months in what is called cultural and spiritual training to help build common vision and values. They study the company credo and learn how to translate it into daily behavior and even into operational decisions. Japanese companies aren't the only ones to engage in cultural and spiritual training, however. The equivalent experience at Philips is called organization coherence training. Santa Clara University offers "understanding the Jesuit tradition" to its lay faculty. At El Camino Hospital, the phrase is "learning the El Camino Way." At Unilever, it's called indoctrination.

In fact, Unilever spends as much on training as on research and development, not only because of the direct effect of upgrading skills and knowledge (the importance of which we discuss in the next chapter), but also because training plays a central role in inculcating values and a common vision. For example, Unilever has a policy of placing 100 to 150 of its most promising overseas managers on short- and long-term job assignments at corporate headquarters each year. This approach helps corporate decision making by injecting perspectives that are fresh and close to the market. It also gives the visiting managers an immediate sense of Unilever's strategic vision and organizational values. As one of the expatriates in the corporate offices has said, "The experience initiates you into the Unilever Club and the clear norms, values, and behaviors that distinguish our people—so much so that we really believe that we can spot another Unilever manager anywhere in the world."[20]

Promotions

The question of who gets promoted in the organization is another key determinant of whether or not people believe that shared values make a difference. Promotion decisions made solely on the basis of technical competence run the risk of undermining commitment to shared values. Promotions should reflect the strength of employees' commitment to the company's values, as well as technical competence (much as training should clarify a company's values and provide technical skills). At LS&CO. and at many other strong values companies, the top executives are rated annually in terms of how they have supported the company's values. For example, to make certain that employees recognize the seriousness of Levi's corporate values, one-third of managers' bonuses depends on their ability to manage "aspirationally"—the "how" of management rather than the "what." Says CEO Robert Haas, "In some areas of the company, it's weighted even more heavily. The point is, it's big enough to get people's attention. It's real. Giving people tough feedback and a low rating on aspirational management means improvement is necessary no matter how many pants they got out the door."

The message is that leaders must be vigilant about ensuring that organizational systems communicate a consistent message about shared values. But first, there must be agreement on those values.

RECONCILING
VALUES DILEMMAS

Differences and obstacles are often found along the road toward wholeness and alignment of personal and organizational values. The first step in reconciling differences is to explore our own inner territory, so that we are clear about what is important to us and what we are seeking in a relationship. The second step is understanding the other party's perspective. If unable to reconcile value differences, people all too often blame a stalemate on the personality or basic nature of others. This practice is generally ineffective and unfair. Behind any impasse usually lie some very good reasons — from the other person's vantage point.

Leaders appreciate these differences and take them into consideration when building what Harvard Professor William Ury, in *Getting Past No*, calls a golden bridge. This bridge makes it easier for people to surmount the four common obstacles to agreement: it's not my idea; this doesn't meet my needs; this may embarrass me; and you're asking too much, too fast (so it's easier to say no). Instead of starting from where we are, pushing our ideas or values (which is everyone's natural instinct), Ury urges beginning where the other party is "in order to guide them toward an eventual agreement."[21] This process means actively involving other people in devising the solution so that it becomes their idea, not just ours. It also requires discovering and then satisfying their unmet needs. It means helping them to save face. (Each of us almost always has a constituency or audience whose opinion we care about outside of the immediate situation.) It also means making the process of reconciliation and agreement as easy as possible.

Take the example of how conflicting values were brought into alignment at The Tom Peters Group (TPG). In 1992, TPG decided to try an 80–9 schedule, in which employees work eighty hours in nine days and then get the tenth day, a Friday, off. The schedule had a lot of potentially desirable benefits: a boost to associates' morale, a little more time for personal and family matters, two fewer days of commuting each month, fewer cars on the road, and a learning experience in some innovative work practices.

Yet there were some problems to iron out. The 80–9 schedule had to enable associates to continue serving customers responsibly and responsively, to meet the shared value of "genuine client delight." Since another shared value is being a "collaborative community," associates met to work out a system to implement the proposed new schedule in a way that would best delight both clients and associates.

The associates seemed enthusiastic about the opportunity to have twenty-six three-day weekends each year, and everyone wanted to make the process work. Since TPG is a small business of about twenty-five people, coverage was the biggest problem. Associates therefore divided themselves equally into two teams, such that each business unit and each function would be represented every Friday and every customer request could be fulfilled. Then came the problem.

TPG had one receptionist, and there was not a second employee to cover when it came her turn to have a Friday off. Among the options (hiring a temporary receptionist every other Friday, hiring a second receptionist, sharing the job equally, and keeping the receptionist on a forty-hour schedule), the alternative with the most support seemed to be job sharing. Each associate would perform the receptionist function about once a quarter.

But job sharing was not the unanimous choice. One associate remarked, "This is not a commune. This is a business." Others supported this view and pointed out that in a business not all tasks should necessarily be divided up equally. Being a collaborative community did not mean every person had to do every job. Not only were some people more talented at certain jobs than others, but some work did not lend itself to interruptions every other Friday. Shouldn't sales and training folks be out in the field with customers? And what would happen if a sales or customer service representative was at the reception desk handling the phones when one of the representative's accounts called? How could saying "I have phone duty and can't help you now" be consistent with the value of genuine client delight?

The issues posed quite a dilemma. Regardless of which obstacles to agreement were at work, it appeared that being a collaborative community and genuinely delighting customers made competing and contrasting claims in this instance.

At first, the resolution seemed to be a choice, an either-or situation. But the associate's reference to "commune" pointed to the basic nature of the problem and led to its eventual reconciliation. The word *commune* shares its origin with the words *community* and *communication*, all of which arise from the word *common*. There did not have to be a choice between delighting customers and collaborating. It could be an opportunity to find new choice combinations meeting both of these values. The question of who should cover the phone was at its core a problem of what associates should and should not share. Above all else, what associates had in common was the need to *collaborate to create value for the customers.*

Viewed from this integrative perspective, associates decided to share the receptionist role every other Friday. The experiment enabled associates to learn that values conflicts can be reconciled into new combinations rather than forced into either-or choices. It was also a particularly valuable lesson in resolving a dilemma arising from principles (values), not positions; problems, not people.

How might leaders help in situations similar to this one? When values collide, a leader must act to resolve these issues. As Charles Hampden-Turner, a senior research fellow at the London School of Business, warns, reconciling value dilemmas is not without risk: "Confronting dilemmas is both dangerous and potentially rewarding. Opposing values 'crucify' the psyche and threaten to disintegrate both leader and organization. Yet to resolve these same tensions enables the organization to create wealth and outperform competitors. If you duck the dilemma you also miss the resolution. There is no cheap grace."[22]

The process of resolving problems is aptly framed by the word *reconcile* because it literally means to "unite again." Scholars at the Harvard Negotiation Project have proposed the need to be "unconditionally constructive" in the process of getting people together.[23] This requires thinking about adopting a strategy in which both parties improve their ability to work together and advance their substantive interests, regardless of whether the other party responds as they would like. It means that the guidelines are good for both parties: they are, in fact, as good for the other person as they are for ourselves. The six parts to this strategy are summarized in Table 5.1.

When principles conflict, it may be possible for leaders to

Table 5.1. Unconditionally Constructive Strategies and Results.

Strategy	Benefit to the relationship	Personal benefit
1. Balance emotion with reason.	An irrational battle is less likely.	I make fewer mistakes.
2. Try to understand.	The better I understand you, the more empathetic I am, the fewer the collisions we will have. We are more likely to come up with solutions that address real needs.	The less I shoot in the dark, the better the solutions I can invent and the better able I am to influence you.
3. Inquire, consult, and listen.	Through two-way communication, we both participate in making decisions. Better communication demonstrates a genuine interest in the other person's needs and ideas and improves our decisions.	I reduce the risk of making a mistake without giving up the ability to decide.
4. Be reliable.	It tends to build trust and confidence.	My words will have more impact.
5. Be open to persuasion; try to persuade.	If people are persuaded rather than coerced, both the outcome and compliance are better.	By being open, I keep learning; it is easier to resist coercion and the urge to fight if one is open to persuasion.
6. Accept the other as worthy: worth dealing with and learning from.	To deal well with differences, I have to deal with people and have an open mind. This openness makes the generation of mutually satisfying possibilities more likely.	By dealing with people and reality, I remove obstacles to learning the facts and to persuading them on the merits.

Source: Adapted from R. Fisher and S. Brown, *Getting Together* (Boston: Houghton Mifflin, 1988), 40.

resolve them by looking for a new combination: a higher-order value, a new interdependency. The total-quality movement is a higher-order resolution of a values dilemma. Organizations used to speak of lower or higher reliability, as if it were a trade-off. By talking about total quality, involving the entire system and its processes, organizations found that they could increase speed, improve collaboration, reduce waste and cost, and improve margins. The principle of total quality helped move the dispute from an "us" versus "them" mentality to one of "we are in this together."

But we must not assume that all dilemmas will be resolved to favor previously prescribed shared values. Not all of these will be appropriate for all time. Sometimes new ones emerge as our world changes. Witness the issues of diversity in the workplace and the environmental movement. Wise and credible leaders build in processes that enable communities to renew themselves.

Renewing community and commitment to common purpose can make a strategic contribution to a company's success and adaptation over time. They are essential processes if we are to keep from being blinded by rigid adherence to a set of principles that no longer make sense and that might otherwise become more rigid than the rule book they replaced.

That's exactly why, at companies such as Levi Strauss, Johnson & Johnson, and Ortho Biotech, employees are surveyed as to how well their company's vision and values are being executed in their operating units and to identify areas where improvement is needed. As one example, Dennis Longstreet, Ortho Biotech's president, did have some questions about the Johnson & Johnson credo. But, as he says, "I had the chance to change it" as part of the credo challenge process; when the session was over, he didn't change anything. Having had the opportunity to discuss, affirm, or alter it if necessary, he states, "The result was I buy into it fully and can defend it to anyone."

This experience made a very strong impression on Longstreet and served as one of the catalysts for Ortho Biotech's own credo challenge. Says Longstreet, "If I give people the chance to challenge where we are headed, get their input on the basic principles of the company, and we adjust them and we all agree on them, then I don't have to worry about letting people know where we're headed and convince them. They're all on board, and we all are headed in the same direction." For leaders, renewing community is akin to the sailor's practice of taking a nightly sighting of the stars to make certain that the ship is still going toward its intended destination.

It makes sense to develop our shared values, our own credos, and then assess them. In the process, we affirm that everyone is still supportive. In addition, leaders must stave off decay and keep their communities vibrant by continually cultivating and renewing the capabilities of the people in the neighborhoods. By developing our constituents, essentially turning them into leaders themselves, we ensure that new, different, and often challenging perspectives are brought to bear on shared assumptions and unexamined paradigms.

Leaders also realize that shared values do not necessarily mean shared skills; some of these must be developed. Before a group can live up to its principles, it must have the competence and confidence to act on them. If we, as members of an organization, do not have the skills, resources, or supportive climate in which to achieve our common purposes, we will not have credibility. Nor will we feel self-efficacious or proud of ourselves. In the following chapter, we explore the leader's role in developing capacity within the community and among our constituents so that we can take the next step: do what we say we will do.

AFFIRMING SHARED VALUES: FIRST STEPS/NEXT STEPS

Here we provide some practical steps and exercises to help you in determining, maintaining, and renewing shared values and in starting the process over again.

▶ *Get together to start drafting your group's credo.* Soliciting people's ideas and listening to their concerns are critical. At the early stages, look for feedback; it is not the time for yes or no decisions. Ask such questions as "What interests of yours are not well represented?" "In what respect is it not fair?" "How would you improve upon it?" If people resist giving you their ideas or giving you feedback on yours, try to involve them by offering them a choice or list of alternatives. Once they select an alternative, it becomes their idea. A Chinese proverb is useful in this regard: "Tell me, I may listen. Teach me, I may remember. Involve me, I will do it."

Circulate draft versions of the credo in which you've incorporated everyone's ideas. Revise the draft, and if necessary ask for more criticism. Gradually you will build consensus as people begin to think of the draft as their own. And it will be!

▶ *Make sure there is agreement around values.* Focus on understanding shared values. Ask constituents to write down what they believe are the key values of the team (department, unit, or company). How much agreement is there? Clarify what is vital, and determine what is secondary. Try including some of your relevant customers, suppliers, vendors, and even shareholders in this discussion. Present hypothetical situations involving potential value dilemmas, and ask people to consider what actions they would take. Have them link their proposed actions to key principles. Take a recent organizational or team decision, and analyze it for agreement with shared values.

▶ *Conduct a values survey.* The best way to know what people think is to ask them. But what if you have lots of people? Send out a survey and find out what they think. For example, we prepared an aspirations survey for Levi Strauss. Distributed to over twenty-five hundred managers throughout the company, the survey focused specifically on LS&CO.'s aspirations and how well people understood them, supported and believed in them, and perceived that "living them" made a difference — whether they were reflected in key actions and decisions. The results helped illuminate which aspirations were clearly understood and where confusion existed, discrepancies between personal and work group alignment with the aspirations, and the intensity with which aspirations were held and being implemented. Analyses helped pinpoint particular problems and opportunities. Readministrations of the survey showed an ongoing commitment to aspirations and their continuing importance (proving that they weren't just a fad) and allowed people to see areas of consistency, change, and improvement.

The process works. Assemble your constituents. Have them determine the key values and design the shared values survey. Have them analyze their own data and decide what it means.

▶   *Connect values with reasons.* In Chapter Three, we talked about studies in which it was found that the only teacher behavior that was effective in raising the moral reasoning of school children was the Socratic question "why?"[24] A similar case can be made for leaders and their constituents. The importance of certain values may seem self-evident. But we have seen that commitment is facilitated when people know that the values are not just their own, individually, but are shared by others, endorsed, and put into practice by their organization. Moreover, providing a rationale for the value helps people to remember it. It also helps them to apply the "logic" of that value to new and different situations and circumstances, and promotes a consistency in the interpretation and enactment of important principles.

In General Electric's values statement, for example, key values are identified and their meaning and importance described. Consider the business value of being *lean*. What it means is to "reduce tasks and the people required to do them." Why is leanness a value? It is "critical to developing work cost leadership." Or the individual value of *dignity*. What it means is to "respect and leverage the talent and contribution of every individual in both good and bad times." Why? Because "teamwork depends on trust, mutual understanding, and the shared belief that the individual will be treated fairly in any environment."

▶   *Structure cooperative goals.* We've seen how essential it is that community members perceive that they are interconnected and have cooperative goals. There are several strategies useful for structuring these.[25] For instance, discuss the team's vision and have members explore how the vision can be best achieved by everyone working together. Or have the team analyze the factors critical to achieving its vision. Have the team identify what needs to be done, determine priorities, resolve differences, and assign people to various roles and responsibilities. Or keep track of the team's productivity by having everyone average his or her individual output to form a group average for some specified period (perhaps weekly). People then see that they are responsible for keeping their own output up and for helping others to improve theirs. Another strategy is to promote group learning. Have each person teach another team member about his or her job or task responsibilities. Encourage cross-functional and interdisciplinary learning.

You might also try a technique that Tom Melohn, former CEO at North American Tool & Die Corporation, used to reinforce collaborative values. At monthly all-employee meetings, Melohn would occasionally give employees the envelopes containing the paychecks of other employees. He would say, "Frank, do you realize that Larry earned part of your paycheck?" "Eleanor, do you realize that Bill earned part of your paycheck?" Then he asked each employee to find the person whose name was on the envelope and to give him or her the paycheck. This ceremony reinforced the idea that people were interdependent and working for the same shared goals.

▸   ***Make sure everyone knows the business.*** How do you know if your constituents understand the common purpose? Do they know the business you are in and why? Get a cross section of people together, and see if they can answer some of the following questions, as they relate to your company or business unit. How do we make money (profit)? Who are our toughest competitors? What have our annual profits and revenues been over the past five years? What do our customers see as our differential advantages in the marketplace? Who are the five senior officers in our organization? What new products or services will we initiate in the next six months?

Many more questions could be asked. But the point is this: if your constituents can't answer such relevant business questions as these, how can they work together to transform shared values and common purposes into reality?

▸   ***Be an enthusiastic spokesperson for shared values.*** Speak enthusiastically about shared values. Talk about your common purpose and the importance of community. Let people know that everyone is in this together, that what they are doing is important, and that their contributions make a difference. Constituents are filled with energy and enthusiasm when their leader speaks with passion about shared beliefs. Your task is to keep people focused by constantly and publicly affirming shared values.

Researchers have documented the importance of speaking out on behalf of shared values and how it contributes to creating community. At an East Coast university where there was a publicized incident of an African-American student receiving hate mail, researchers randomly stopped students walking across campus and asked them what they thought of the incident. Before the subject could respond, however, a confederate of the researchers would come up and answer first. One response was something like, "Well, he must have done something to deserve it." The confederate's alternate response was something like, "There's no place for that kind of behavior on our campus in the 1990s." As you might expect, the subject's response was more often than not just like the confederate's.[26] This study illustrates clearly the importance of "affirming" and why as leaders we must speak out strongly on behalf of our values and get others on the line to do the same.

▶ *Accumulate yeses.* The key word in agreements is *yes.* It is a magical word and a powerful tool for bringing people closer. When people say yes to one another, their relationship changes; a potential argument is transformed into the beginning of a reasoned dialogue. To build agreement, be on the lookout for opportunities to say yes as often as possible: "Yes, you have a point there." "Yes, I can understand that." Say yes as often as possible and try to get as many others as possible to do the same.

Don't say, "But . . ." or "yes, but . . ."; say, "Yes, and . . ." When people hear but, they think you disagree with them and that you are about to try to prove them wrong. Unfortunately, an all-too-common reaction is for them to stop listening. People will be more receptive if you first acknowledge their views with a yes and then preface your own with an and. In this way, your views can be seen as an addition, not a contradiction, to their point of view.[27]

▶ *Go slow to go fast.* Keep the importance of making it easy for people to say yes firmly in mind. If agreeing on a program of shared values seems daunting, divide up the task. Each small agreement can then open up more opportunities. Start where people are, with the easiest issue for them to agree with. Move progressively from the easiest to the more difficult issues. In this way, you can get people in the habit of saying yes and showing them that agreement is possible.

But if this step-by-step, small-win process won't work because people are reluctant to make even a small agreement, don't press for an immediate concession. Set people at ease by reassuring them that they need not make a final commitment until the end. This approach is what Varian, an international, high-tech company, did in negotiations with a Chinese customer for purchase of a $2.5 million inspection system.

The customer sent a delegation of ten people to the United States to resolve a host of issues and finalize the purchase. The Varian team reviewed the issues and started with the easiest ones first. As Bill Cologgi, manager, continuing engineering, explains, "We spent two days dealing with each of the lesser issues, working on and achieving collaborative solutions and establishing increasingly positive rapport with the customer team. Finally, the 'big' issue was the only one left. All involved knew that a win-win solution had to be found. And all of us, both Varian and the customer team, strongly wanted it to happen." Because of the positive relationship already established, neither side was willing to drive for a zero-sum solution. They spent the better part of a day exploring dimensions of the problem, looking for a breakthrough idea. When the idea—a rather simple solution— came, it was met with exuberance by all sides. "We could never have conceived of the solution, or consummated an agreement," says Cologgi, "if we had not had an overwhelming desire on both sides to reach agreement. This desire had been built up by months of going slow with no commitment required, followed by three days of negotiations with incremental agreement that built up a powerful positive relationship between the parties."

▶ *Establish a sunset statute for your credo.* Tom Peters, noted commentator on organizational excellence, has remarked that "all good ideas are eventually oversold. Corporate vision and values are no exception." He's openly skeptical of people's ability to review and update their vision and values regularly and suggests "there ought to be a 'values sunset statute'—throw out a third of your values every five years, or burn the lot and start over every 10 years."[28] Perhaps there is some merit in his suggestion. Rather than waiting for chance or circumstance, it may be a good idea to rethink your team's credo periodically. After all, many people will probably have left your group since the original inception of your shared values statement, and some of the new people will not feel included in this part of your organizational history. Although certain values will endure (as we discovered about managerial values in the last chapter) and others will change (some slightly and some considerably), the process of reviewing and prioritizing can only reinforce the team's unity of purpose and commitment to its shared values.

CHAPTER

6

Developing Capacity

How can your company grow if your people don't?
Johan Beeckmans
ITT World Directories

Tim Firnstahl owns a chain of four restaurants in and around Seattle. At each restaurant, considerable efforts are taken to ensure world-class customer service and to make the customer happy. The company motto, We Always Guarantee Satisfaction (WAGS), is a shared rallying cry, focusing the more than six hundred employees on the same company game plan. Each employee signs a contract pledging WAGS follow-through. The WAGS logo is everywhere—on report forms, training manuals, wall signs, shirts, name tags, even underwear!

After a while, however, Firnstahl noticed that the guarantee and all the hoopla surrounding it weren't enough. Employees had responsibility but had not been taught to make use of their new authority. As a result, says Firnstahl, "They tried to bury mistakes or blame others. I saw it every time we tried to track down a complaint. The food servers blamed the kitchen

153

for late meals, and the kitchen blamed the food servers for placing orders incorrectly."

Firnstahl realized that he needed to give the workers the authority to make the guarantee stick. He had to eliminate hassles for both customers and employees. No forms, no formal approval would be needed. Instead, if an error or a delay happened, any employee could provide wine or dessert on the house. Employees could pick up an entire tab if necessary. They were given guidelines and urged not to get bogged down in them. In new training programs, employees learned that every customer is different and that they should do whatever it takes to make sure all patrons enjoy themselves.

Employees were wary at first. As Firnstahl related, they needed to be convinced that "they wouldn't be penalized for giving away free food and drinks. But once they got used to the idea, employees liked knowing the company believed so strongly in its products and services and it wholeheartedly stood behind its work—and theirs. . . . Their power as company representatives increased their pride in the business and that in turn increased motivation."

Employees quickly became creative in carrying out the guarantee. For example, when a customer ordered a margarita—as it was made at another restaurant—the "bartender called the bartender at the other restaurant and, bartender to bartender, learned the special recipe." When an elderly woman who had not been in the restaurant for years ordered breakfast, which was no longer served, the waiter and chef "sent someone to the market for bacon and eggs and prepared the breakfast she wanted."

The bottom line is larger profits, and people often ask where Firnstahl finds "such wonderful employees." Firnstahl's response is that their employees are "better than most because they have the power and the obligation to solve customer problems on their own and on the spot. Giving them complete discretion about how they do it has also given them pride. . . . The people who work for us know we take our guarantee seriously and expect them to do the same."[1]

The essential task of leaders, as Firnstahl discovered, is to develop continuously the capacity of their constituents to put shared values into practice. Constituents cannot do what they do not know how to do. Credible leaders strengthen constituents' competence and confidence. This enhances the team, department, or organization's ability to perform and meet their promises and builds the credibility of the leader. Because the unit is more competent and people are more productive, the leader's reputation grows. Leaders realize that only by investing in their constituency can their asset base expand.

If we are to clarify values, build understanding and commitment to shared values, and create communities where people perceive cooperative goals and mutual respect, then we must concurrently establish the capacity of people and work teams to take on their new leadership responsibilities. Constituent participation and development has moved from the stage of curious experimentation to a competitive necessity. Alvin Toffler, in his book *Powershift*, explains, "The old smokestack division of a firm into 'heads' and 'hands' no longer works . . . the knowledge load and, more important, the decision load, are being redistributed. In a continual cycle of learning, unlearning, and relearning, workers need to master new techniques, adapt to new organizational forms, and come up with new ideas."[2]

Therefore, leaders must develop the capacity of people in the organization to act on the shared values in ways that increase the organization's credibility with its constituents. To develop capacity, leaders must expand or realize the potentialities of the people and organizations they lead; they must bring them to a fuller or better state. Leaders must assure that educational opportunities exist for individuals to build their knowledge and skill. Leaders must provide the resources and other organizational supports that enable constituents to put their abilities to constructive use. In our more complex "informated" organizational world, this obligation means going beyond the traditional definitions of jobs and classifications. It means increasing the scope of work for everyone, especially those on the front lines. Leaders earn their credibility by fulfilling their promise that everyone is a leader.

LIBERATING THE
LEADER IN EVERYONE

The cover of a recent *Fortune* magazine shows a group of seven employees huddled around a gigantic carton of cereal. This is a work group at the General Mills cereal plant in Lodi, California, whose productivity increased nearly 40 percent since these employees became responsible for managing themselves without a "boss." The headline asks "Who Needs a Boss?"[3] Who, indeed.

Myth has it that leadership is a function of position. Nonsense. Leadership is a set of skills and practices that can be learned regardless of whether or not one is in a formal management position. Leadership is found in those in the boiler room and those in the board room. It is not conferred by title or degree. In fact, often those responsible for the smooth and successful operation of organizations, from the youth soccer league to the church fellowship, have neither.

We have learned from our research that within effective teams the behaviors of individual contributors are practically identical to those of leaders. Scores from individual contributors on the Team Leadership Practices Inventory reveal that there is more leadership exhibited among the individual members within high-performing work groups than within equivalent low-performing work groups. United in a common cause, every member of the team becomes responsible for providing leadership. Self-led teams outperform teams that are tightly managed, either by a controlling supervisor or the team members themselves. Self-led groups are more effective than self-managed groups.[4]

Developing capacity requires us to ask ourselves about the assumptions we make regarding the abilities of the people we lead. Just how far are we willing to go to develop the skills people need to contribute to making our shared values a way of life?

Credible leaders turn their constituents into leaders. This is the essence of how leaders get extraordinary things done in their organizations: they enable people to act. It is not a case of the *leader* doing something or even telling others what to do but of *everyone* wanting to work together for a common purpose, one that is aligned with shared values. "My personal best as a leader," explains Alan Daddow, regional manager with Elders Pastoral in Australia, "simply involved being able to maximize my staff's potential." Organizational effectiveness depends upon the sharing or distributing, not the hoarding, of leadership.

Empowerment is an important concept but one often misunderstood; perhaps it's even an obsolete term. The problem with empowerment is that it suggests that this is something leaders magically give or do for others. But people already have tremendous power. It is not a matter of giving it to them, but of freeing them to use the power and skills they already have. It is a matter of expanding their opportunities to use themselves in service of a common and meaningful purpose. What is often called empowerment is really just taking off the chains and letting people loose. Credible leaders in this sense are liberators.

You can sense the liberation by recalling our earlier discussion (in Chapter Two) about how working with credible leaders makes people feel: alive, valued, turned on, enthusiastic, significant, capable, and proud. Credible leaders make us believe we can make a difference; they liberate the leader within.[5] In so doing, they make a significant difference in our lives and in the organization. Interviews with female leaders over the past thirty years document how developing capacity, "enabling others to do their best," was central to their effectiveness as leaders for social reform as well as to the achievement of institutional excellence.[6]

Credibility is enhanced when leadership is distributed across the organization. This practice requires that everyone in the organization behaves as if he or she were a leader. But liberating the leader within doesn't just happen. It evolves as a result of many contextual decisions and must be viewed as an ongoing and continuous process.

Competence, confidence, choice, climate, and communication. These are the five essentials to developing capacity so that everyone can act in a free and responsible way. We must have the knowledge and skill to DWWSWWD. Fostering and sustaining liberated people and teams is vital to an organization's ability to maintain its credibility. Indeed, the only sustainable competitive advantage any business has is its reputation and the ability to deliver what it has promised. We must have the latitude to make the choices based on what we think should be done. We must believe we can do it. We must work in a climate that encourages taking some risks and experimenting, knowing that we will make some mistakes but learning from our experiences. And we must be constantly informed about what is going on in order to keep up to date. This framework is the constituent equivalent to the process discussed in Chapter Three for discovering your self. In a sense, the leader acts as an educator, helping others to learn and develop their skills and providing the institutional supports required for on-going, experiential learning and maturation.

BUILDING COMPETENCE: EDUCATE, EDUCATE, EDUCATE

Credible leaders invest in developing people's skills and competencies. In Toronto, MICA Management Resources Corporation's survey of senior executives revealed that organizations that invested more than the average amount of money on training enjoyed higher levels of employee involvement and commitment, better levels of customer service, and greater understanding of and alignment with company visions and values. This finding was consistent with a recent Conference Board of Canada study showing that spending money on training and development was a profitable investment.[7] These results should not come as any surprise, but apparently many companies and their managers have failed to realize that learning on the job is critical. In fact, over the past sixty years, it has contributed more to productivity increases than technology or capital.[8]

In measuring the gap between U.S. and Japanese auto makers, researchers at Massachusetts Institute of Technology examined the amount of time given to training and working in teams. U.S. auto plants devoted about 46 hours of training per worker compared to 370 hours per worker in Japanese auto plants in North America. The percentage of time employees worked in teams was less than 20 percent in U.S. plants and over 70 percent in Japanese ones. Training and teamwork were seen as the most important reasons that it takes 16 percent less time to produce a new car in an auto plant in North America run by the Japanese than by Americans — and with 21 percent fewer defects.[9]

Training is at the top of winning companies' agenda these days. And not just any training. These companies emphasize training that is linked to their strategic initiatives, whether about quality, service, partnership, community, diversity, or other values. Training was the backbone of the Ford Motor Company's efforts in the 1980s to restore its competitive position after years of continuous erosion of its market share. Many things happened, but most significantly Ford got smart about people and started developing their capacity.

Ford's Education, Development and Training Program (EDTP) offers courses that are strictly devoted to personal development and are entirely separate from technical training. Every plant has an EDTP committee, which surveys workers, finds out what courses they want, and schedules them at convenient times. Life/education advisers help workers figure out what they would like to learn and how to go about learning it.

How does all this work? At Ford's Van Dyke, Michigan, transmission and chassis plant, the training and educational initiatives have come together. The technical training committee is staffed by fourteen hourly workers and two trainers. In large part, the skilled tradesmen on the committee decide what kind of training should be offered. Each of them keeps in close touch with co-workers so they know what the training needs are. The tradesmen are also largely responsible for deciding when training is not appropriate, when the problem might be one of motivation, for instance. They research the content, sources, and delivery methods of training; in some cases, they even help design it. They work directly with the vendors who provide the agreed-upon training.

This committee is also taking a larger part in deciding what kind of equipment to buy for the plant. For example, the committee has suggested that all equipment be fitted with identical control mechanisms to cut down training time on new machinery.

What good does all this training, especially classes unrelated to technical requirements, do for the company? Ford believes that "you can't quantify the benefit." More importantly, it doesn't even want to try because that's missing the point. Company and union officials believe that the more education and knowledge workers have, the better workers they will be. From the workers' viewpoint, if "quality is to be job number one," then the company cannot in good conscience *not* invest in developing the capabilities of its people. Training is what makes Ford's employee involvement process credible and is a part of Ford's rise. Of the changes, Jim Bradley, a longtime pipe fitter, member of United Auto Workers Union Local 2280, and one of those serving on the Van Dyke plant's technical training committee, says, "Now I love to come to work. Things have turned around here 180 degrees."[10]

OFFERING CHOICES, ENCOURAGING OWNERSHIP

Choice builds commitment. Choice necessitates ownership. Jack Stack, CEO, explains what ownership means for his constituents at Springfield Remanufacturing Corporation: "We have a company filled with people who not only *are* owners, but who *think* and *act* like owners rather than employees. That's an important distinction. Getting people to think and act like owners goes far beyond giving them equity. . . . Owners, *real owners*, don't have to be told what to do — they can figure it out for themselves. They have all the knowledge, understanding, and information they need to make a decision, and they have the motivation and the will to act fast. Ownership is not a set of legal rights. It's a state of mind."[11] Leaders create real owners by making certain people have choices to make about what they do, especially in how shared values are implemented.

Harvard Business School professor Leonard Schlesinger and his colleagues have written extensively about how choice is required for organizations and their employees to provide exceptional customer service. They have observed that responsive service and extra employee efforts emerge when employees have (1) latitude, or the necessary leeway to meet customer needs, and (2) discretion, or sufficient authority to serve customer wants.[12] Remember the extraordinary accomplishments of the employees at Firnstahl's restaurants when they were authorized to guarantee satisfaction.

But lest we think these ideas apply only to front-line service personnel, consider this study of the Fortune 200. Companies that allowed higher spending authority substantially outperformed those that didn't. Over the past two decades, thirteen of the top two hundred companies outperformed the other 187 organizations. Only a few factors separated the top thirteen from the rest of the pack. One was a much higher spending authority at the divisional level. For example, divisional managers in the most successful firms could spend up to $20 million on their own signature. At the other organizations, managers were authorized for only one-tenth that amount.[13] People who do not exercise any choice cannot feel responsible, nor can they make a difference within their organization.

BSD, a software inventory control company with thirty-six offices worldwide, provides proof of the increased effectiveness that comes with choice. The company organized itself into customer-focused teams responsible for selling, designing, installing, and supporting a given customer in a specific area. To grow, each team had to seek out smaller customers within its geographic area (a requirement that meant changing the product) or move into new geographic areas once it had sold out its initial market. Sensing an opportunity for people to assume increased responsibility, learn, and grow, BSD's president asked the group, "What can you do to assure that each customer gets the best service, from the best trained person (with all the skills necessary to provide that best service), at the same time assuring that you continue to learn and grow and don't stagnate?"[14] The president turned the decision (the choice) over to those people who had to make the decision work.

As James Belasco, management professor and consultant, reports, given this choice, the people "decided to hire a whole new team to sell to smaller customers in their original geographic area, and hire new people from new geographical areas to sell there. They set up a rotation system within the teams to assure that individuals learned all the skills and set up an internal monitoring system to assure that the skills were current."[15] Their system worked, and the teams are extraordinarily successful. The more than seven hundred people in the company are now organized into sixty-two semiautonomous teams, each responsible for hiring, training, and maintaining superior levels of service to their customers throughout the world.

Providing people with choice—discretion and latitude—liberates the leader within and contributes to greater productivity. As mayor of Madison, Wisconsin, Joseph Sensenbrenner was convinced that developing his constituents' capacity was essential and that the concept of continuous improvement could be applied to the public sector.[16] He decided to begin with the city garage. Complaints were rampant, especially about how long repairs took. The problem was painfully apparent: the garage didn't have the right parts in stock.

The parts manager explained that the problem with stocking parts was that the city purchased many different makes and models of equipment virtually every year. The fleet included 440 different types, makes, models, and years of equipment. Why? City policy was to buy "whatever vehicle had the lowest sticker price on the day of purchase."

One mechanic explained to Sensenbrenner, "It doesn't make any sense. When you look at all the equipment downtime, the warranty work that weak suppliers don't cover, the unreliability of cheaper machines, and the lower resale value, buying what's cheapest doesn't save us anything." The parts purchaser agreed: "It would certainly make my job easier to have fewer parts to stock from a few reliable suppliers. But central purchasing won't let me do it." On to central purchasing: "I understand what you're saying because I hear it from all over the organization. But there's no way we can change the policy. The comptroller wouldn't let us do it." What did the controller have to say? "You make a very strong case. But I can't let you do it because the city attorney won't let me approve such a thing." Onward to the city attorney, who cheerfully replied, "Why, of course you can do that. All you need to do is write the specifications so they include the warranty, the ease of maintenance, the availability of parts, and the resale value over time. Make sure that's clear in advance, and there's no problem. In fact, I assumed you were doing this all along." For Sensenbrenner, this was a stunning disclosure. The problem was thus not incompetent workers but a flawed system that failed to allow people sufficient individual discretion. Involving front-line employees in problem solving, rather than blaming them or ignoring them, brought about huge improvements in productivity and morale. The 24-step purchasing policy, with multiple levels of control, was cut to just three steps. This simplification gave people latitude and discretion, key elements that enabled them to become more involved and to provide good service.

Without latitude and discretion, without choice, people cannot lead, cannot make a difference. This conclusion applies to making quality products and multimillion-dollar organizational decisions. If people have no freedom of choice and can act only in ways prescribed by the organization, then how can they respond when the customer or another employee behaves in ways that are not in the script? Even if they think they know what needs to be done and feel they could do it, they will have to ask the "boss" what to do. And if their boss doesn't know, the question will go to the next higher boss. And up the ladder it goes. Choice is central to feeling ownership and expanding people's capacity to act on the values that they espouse.

INSPIRING CONFIDENCE

At its core, liberating the leader within is not so much a management practice or technique as it is a psychological process that affects individuals' intrinsic needs for self-determination.[17] Each of us has an internal need to influence other people and life's events in order to experience some sense of order and stability in our lives. Feeling that we can adequately cope with the events, situations, and people we confront puts us in a position to exercise leadership. People feel powerless when they perceive themselves as lacking control over their immediate situation or lacking the capability, resources, or authority needed to accomplish a task.

Working with credible leaders bolsters people's self-efficacy and fosters greater self-confidence. Leaders take actions and create conditions that strengthen their constituents' self-esteem and internal sense of effectiveness. From this process comes the repeated sentiment "my leader believes in me and so I can also believe in myself."

In an innovative series of experiments, Stanford University professor Albert Bandura and University of Western Australia professor Robert Wood have documented that self-confidence affects people's performance. In one study, managers were told that decision making was a skill developed through practice: the more one worked at it, the more capable one became. Other managers were told that decision making reflected their basic intellectual aptitude: the higher their underlying cognitive capacities, the better their decision-making ability. Working with a simulated organization, both groups of managers dealt with a series of production orders that required various staffing decisions and establishing different performance targets. Managers who believed that decision making was a skill that could be acquired set challenging goals for themselves, even in the face of difficult performance standards; used good problem-solving strategies; and encouraged organizational productivity. Their counterparts, who didn't believe they had the necessary decision-making ability, lost confidence in themselves as they encountered difficulties. They lowered their aspirations for the organization, their problem solving deteriorated, and organizational productivity declined.[18] Comparisons of the results between these two groups of managers are shown graphically in Figure 6.1.

Another interesting finding was that the managers who lost confidence in their own judgments tended to find fault with their people. Indeed, they were quite uncharitable about their employees, regarding them as incapable of being motivated and unworthy of supervisory effort: given the option, the managers would have fired many of their employees. In a real-world parallel, as General Motors officials visited the NUMMI (New United Motors Manufacturing, Inc.) plant in Fremont, California (a joint venture between GM and Toyota), they were overheard to wonder where NUMMI "found such great workers." The GM officials failed to realize that these were the exact same people who had previously been responsible for such shoddy workmanship and tumultuous union-management relations that forced the closing of the old GM plant.[19]

In another study, one group of managers was told that organizations and people are easily changeable or predictable. Another group was told, "Work habits of employees are not that easily changeable, even by good guidance. Small changes do not necessarily improve overall outcomes." Those managers with the confidence that they could influence organizational outcomes by their actions maintained a higher level of performance than those who felt they could do little to change things. Those in the latter group lost faith in their capabilities.

Figure 6.1. How Conceptions of Ability Affect Confidence, Goals, Strategies, and Performance.

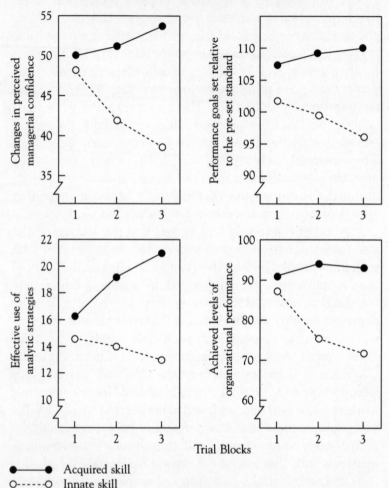

●——● Acquired skill
○-----○ Innate skill

Source: R. E. Wood and A. Bandura, "Impact of Conceptions of Ability on Self-Regulatory Mechanisms and Complex Decision Making." *Journal of Personality and Social Psychology 56,* 1989.

As their aspirations declined, so did organizational pérformance levels.[20] These results are shown in Figure 6.2.

As these studies illustrate, having confidence and believing in our ability to handle the job, no matter how difficult, are

Figure 6.2. How Beliefs in Controllability Affect Confidence, Goals, and Performance.

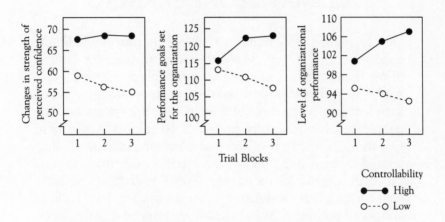

Source: A. Bandura and R. E. Wood, "Effect of Perceived Controllability and Performance Standards on Self-Regulation of Complex Decision Making." *Journal of Personality and Social Psychology 56,* 1989.

essential in promoting and sustaining consistent efforts. Fostering self-confidence is not a warmed-over version of the power of positive thinking. By communicating the belief that constituents can be successful, leaders help people extend themselves and persevere.

Although the effort may begin with words of encouragement, support, and praise, the most effective means of raising people's self-confidence is achieved through actual experience; that is, providing them with an opportunity to perform successfully. An initial experience with success, followed by a series of small successes over a period of time, initially forms the basis for enhancing people's sense of personal effectiveness. The leader's challenge is to create situations for small wins, structuring tasks in such a way that they can be broken down into manageable pieces, with each success building up the person's sense of competence. Creating a climate where learning is stressed and people feel comfortable making mistakes is also critical.

CREATING A CLIMATE FOR LEARNING

Developing capacity requires that leaders provide a climate conducive to learning. As we discussed in Chapter Four, a prime requirement for people to be capable of learning—able to change and develop new skills—is an environment in which they feel safe. They must be able to trust the system and the people involved. Results from our Readiness Assessment Questionnaire have revealed that a learning climate, characterized by trust and openness, is a critical precursor for any successful organizational change effort.[21] With trust and openness comes greater willingness to communicate about feelings and about problems. As individuals are listened to, more information becomes available, and people discover greater common ground and reasons to engage in cooperative behavior. They have less motivation to defend either themselves or the status quo and are ready to take on the leadership challenges associated with, for example, customer service and continuous quality improvement. "After all," says Daven Moldrich, corporate manager, Westpac Banking Corporation, "when we're here to learn, then it is us against the problem. We are not trying to figure out who is wrong but to learn what isn't working so we can correct it."

Learning is also about making mistakes. In any new endeavor, there is a learning curve: performance generally goes down before it goes up. Think about the last time you installed new software on your personal computer. What happened to your productivity at the start? As leaders, we need to make it easy to learn from mistakes. We must place the emphasis on maximizing learning; too often for managers the concern is with minimizing errors.

Leaders are great learners, and they regard mistakes as learning opportunities, not the end of the world.[22] And this attitude is true not just for themselves, but also for their constituents. In fact, because they appreciate that mistakes are an essential part of the learning process, leaders develop their constituents' capabilities by helping them break out of old patterns of thinking. Mired down in a numbing daily routine, people often behave automatically, stop thinking for themselves, and form unquestioning attitudes, or mindsets, based upon the first information they hear.[23] Leaders encourage their constituents to question routines, challenge assumptions, and, with respect to appreciating diversity, continually look at what is going on from changing perspectives.

How we get into mindsets is well illustrated in a classic psychological experiment. One group of people was shown a collection of familiar objects and told specifically what they were. For example, "This is a hair dryer," and "This is a dog's chew toy." Another group was shown the same objects but told conditionally, "This *could be* a hair dryer," and "This *could be* a dog's chew toy." Some time later, the experimenters intentionally created a need for an eraser. Only the second group, those who had been conditionally introduced to the objects, thought the dog's chew toy could be used in this new way.[24] The intuitive understanding that a single thing is or could be many things, depending upon how you look at it, is central to the learning climate created by leaders. Adopting a "could be" attitude, envisioning many possibilities and alternative scenarios, promotes creativity. Further, it fosters confidence in people's capabilities and their adaptability.

Breaking mindsets is an important component of what the best companies do to practice *kaizen* (which means "continuous improvement") and become what Ikujiro Nonaka, management professor at the Institute for Business Research of Hitotsubashi University (Tokyo, Japan), has described as the "knowledge-creating company." He reports that the "centerpiece of the Japanese approach is the recognition that creating new knowledge is not simply a matter of 'processing' objective information. Rather, it depends on tapping the tacit and often highly subjective insights, intuitions, and hunches of individual employees and making those insights available for testing and use by the company as a whole."[25]

For example, Nonaka describes the Osaka-based Matsushita Electric Company's efforts to develop a new home bread-making machine. The product developers were having difficulty with the kneading process. Employees had analyzed the problem in detail, even comparing X rays of dough kneaded by the machine and that kneaded by professional bakers, but to no avail.

> Finally, software developer Ikuko Tanaka proposed a creative solution. The Osaka International Hotel had a reputation for making the best bread in Osaka. Why not use it as a model? Tanaka trained with the hotel's head baker to study his kneading technique. She observed that the baker had a distinctive way of stretching the dough. After a year of trial and error, working closely with the project's engineers, Tanaka came up with product specifications — including the addition of special ribs inside the machine — that successfully reproduced the baker's stretching technique and the quality of the bread she had learned to make at the hotel.[26]

Matsushita's unique "twist dough" method is attributable to Tanaka's research and efforts and fresh way of looking at the problems. The result has been enormously successful: the new bread-making machine set a record for sales of a new kitchen appliance in its first year. But this might not have been, had the company not supported Tanaka's creative approach.

At United Electric Control Company, people have worked hard at creating a climate for learning. Recognizing that the more ideas, the greater the probability of a good one, vice president of operations Bruce Hamilton explains, "A person may come up with nine ideas that save a dollar apiece, then the tenth saves $50,000. People hate rejection. If you reject the first few, you don't get that last one." United Electric Control learned this lesson the hard way.

Over the previous twenty years, employees had contributed what averaged out to just over one idea a year to the company's suggestion box. The procedure was difficult and (because management was thought to implement ideas without giving employees credit), potentially not worth the effort. Since installation of the new system, which rewards the process of thinking of ideas, about 90 percent of (the approximately 350) employees contribute ideas. About two-thirds of all ideas are implemented.

One big reason for this turnaround is that employees think about things that they can do (or invent) to help them work faster or more accurately or more comfortably, rather than pointing out what other people are doing wrong (and need to get right). The result is an aquarium test to ensure that parts are watertight and a spool rack to relieve the pain of lifting spools of wire. Just day-to-day improvements, inspired by involved and liberated people. The benefits to the company? Since 1987, inventories have been cut by 60 percent, work in progress has been reduced 90 percent, on-time deliveries have increased from 65 percent to 95 percent, and sales have expanded over 30 percent.[27]

PROMOTING COMMUNICATION AND FEEDBACK

Sharing information is a critical determinant in developing people's capacity. Cheryl Breetwor, president of ShareData, shares information in her open-strategy sessions at the company. Instead of closeting a small group of key executives to develop a strategy based upon her own agenda, she holds a series of meetings over several days and allows a larger group to develop and help choose alternatives. As a result of having all the information, everyone knows what to do and why. Plus, having been involved in developing the plan, people are committed to it; their ownership is increased.

Communication and feedback are at the heart of "the great game of business," which is how those at Springfield Remanufacturing Corporation (SRC) passionately refer to their management/leadership system. The idea is that the best way to run a company is to make certain that everyone knows the rules of the game; that is, how the company makes money and generates cash. As CEO Jack Stack points out, at most companies, "No one explains how one person's actions affect another's, how each department depends on the others, what impact they all have on the company as a whole. Most important, no one tells people how to make money and generate cash. Nine times out of ten, employees don't even know the difference between the two."[28] So people at SRC are taught the rules (including how to read an income statement, what retained earnings and equity are, and so on) and shown how to keep score and follow the action. Then they are given the information necessary to do both.

For example, all the supervisors get together weekly in the "great huddle" to present their numbers so that they can all be added, subtracted, and totaled. Within thirty-six hours, virtually everyone in the company has the latest information on where the company stands and what every person and department will need to do to improve the score. To back this up, a complete detailed financial statement is published every month and available throughout the company.

Leaders understand that unless they communicate and share information with their constituents, few will take much interest in what is going on. Unless people see and experience the effects of what they do, they won't care. When leaders share information rather than guard it, people feel included and respected. A greater two-way flow of information is created. Sharing information also lets everyone know the reasons behind decisions and the ways they are linked to shared values and common purpose. When people have the same information and understand that they are part of a community, with common values and shared interests, the results flow. Finally, everyone can sing in unison, from the same page of the same song sheet.

Studies show that people's motivation to improve their productivity on a task increases only when they have a challenging goal and receive feedback on their progress.[29] As Figure 6.3 shows, goals without feedback and feedback without goals have little effect on motivation.

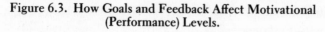

Figure 6.3. How Goals and Feedback Affect Motivational
(Performance) Levels.

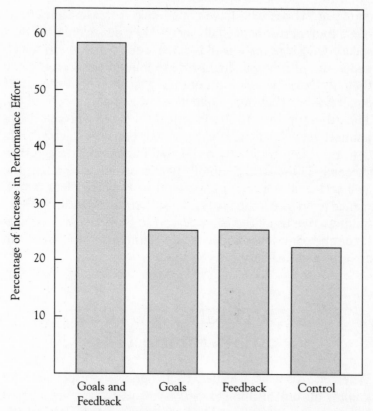

Source: A. Bandura and D. Cervone, "Self-Evaluation and Self-Efficacy Mechanisms Governing the Motivational Effects of Goal Systems." *Journal of Personality and Social Psychology* 45, 1983.

With detailed feedback that includes such factors as quality, quantity, timeliness, and customer service, people can become self-corrective and can more easily understand their interconnectedness with the big picture. With feedback, they can also determine what help they need from others and who might be able to benefit from their assistance.

But what happens when feedback shows that performance has fallen short of aspirations? Won't this information be discouraging? It depends upon people's beliefs in their capacities. Those who doubt their abilities are easily discouraged. Those who have confidence increase their efforts when their performance falls short. They persevere until they succeed. This point was illustrated well in a study in which people rated how satisfied or disappointed they were when their performance fell short of their goal and about their level of confidence that they could attain the goal in a second try. They then performed the task again. People who felt disappointed with a deficient performance but were highly confident that they could attain the goal increased their effort to succeed. Those who doubted their capabilities to attain the goal and were not too disappointed by their deficient performance abandoned the goal and lost their motivation.[30] These findings give us all the more reason to build people's competence and confidence and to create a climate in which they can assume responsibility.

FOSTERING MUTUAL RESPONSIBILITY

When everyone is a leader, each person is responsible for guiding the organization toward its future. Everyone has a part in keeping people aligned with the values. It is not just the manager's job. Indeed, the whole point of liberation is that people take initiative to do something. When we have freed the leaders within our constituents, people will go right to fixing the problem instead of just fixing the blame. When something needs to be done, everyone will feel compelled to do it—and will not wait to be told or asked.

But with the freedom to take initiative comes accountability for our own actions. If each person is a leader, then each accepts the responsibilities of leadership. In this sense, everyone is a citizen, someone who directly participates in enriching and renewing the community. It's as simple as picking up a piece of paper on the streets of your local town or from the hallway or plant floor next to where you work. You could step over it, saying to yourself, "I pay taxes; public works should clean up" or "It's not my job to pick up paper. The maintenance group picks up the trash." But leaders don't wait for others to do something. They take responsibility for making it happen, even if it means picking up the paper themselves and then enlisting others in doing the same.

These examples illustrate that liberating the leader within demands building and ensuring the credibility of our constituents, whether in restaurants, the military, high technology, basic manufacturing, or information services. Capacity building is necessary because we have to be able to do what we say we will do. If we can't, then we lose our credibility. That's as true for the CEO as the front-line worker and as true for any individual as it is for the team. Developing capacity involves building the skills, knowledge, and attitudes of the entire work force at all levels to DWWSWWD. We must not make a promise we can't keep to one another or to our customers, families, and communities. Developing capacity is a fundamental part of keeping our promises as leaders.

The fact that individuals or organizations have the capacity to be consistent with their values does not, however, mean they are. Shared values and capacity do not guarantee results. In the final analysis, credibility is earned through credible actions that are supported and consistently reinforced. If a group is to live up to its values, its members must use their skills on a daily basis. For example, we may as an organization espouse diversity, but if we do not daily show our respect for others who are different; if we do not recruit, select, and hire people with varied backgrounds; if we do not appraise performance on diversity; and if we do not link performance and rewards, then diversity is just a convenient political slogan.

Leaders play a central role in translating promises and preparations into performances. They go first; they tell the stories, they recognize consistent actions. In the next chapter, we'll take a look at the leaders' role in serving the purpose of the organization and the individuals in it.

DEVELOPING CAPACITY: FIRST STEPS/NEXT STEPS

In the following exercises, we provide some practical tips to use in taking steps to develop your capacity as a leader and that of each of your constituents.

▶   *Stop making decisions.* Rather than making decisions yourself, see to it that those responsible for implementing decisions make them. Even more importantly, make sure that they want to make the decisions, want to bear the consequences of them, have the necessary information to make good ones, and have the training to recognize good and bad decision criteria. This new role requires that you learn to ask questions more than give answers and be willing to give up responsibility and authority.

Some people worry about what others will think about them and their performance if they don't make decisions and give answers. Typical concerns are "Will I lose their respect?" and "Will they think I'm not earning my salary?" These issues are usually not even on the minds of liberated people: they are too busy enjoying their jobs. They don't have any problem redefining a manager's job to serve them so that they can do their own work better.

▶   *Stop talking at staff meetings.* The problem with most staff meetings is that the "boss" is the only one who talks — classic one-way communications. Even if the "boss" explains that he or she wants to listen, we all know that this doesn't always happen. At best, it is one person talking to the "boss" while the rest of us listen.

At your own staff meetings, do you talk more than 25 percent of the time? When you dominate in this way, you are communicating that you don't value other people's contributions, that they have little to offer. If that's really the case, stop having the meetings. Staff meetings should be an opportunity for people to see the big picture, learn about what others are doing, and appreciate how they can help one another. For leaders, these meetings should be important opportunities to develop capacity.

► **Set up coaching opportunities.** Provide people with meaningful learning opportunities, preferably ones in which you can participate as a coach. That's just what Gary Miocevich, managing director of VEEM Engineering in Western Australia, did. No one else in the hundred-person, customized, high-quality engineering firm thought it was such a great idea when Miocevich said that the chair responsibilities for their weekly staff meetings would be rotated so that everyone could improve his or her skills in leading meetings. In fact, after the first several months, it was a disaster. Some people were good at chairing the meeting, others used the position to dominate, many lost control, and a few had no interest.

Miocevich took another try at it. He knew that one of the problems was that he hadn't trained the other managers in how to head an effective meeting. In rotating this responsibility, he hadn't provided any learning opportunities—that is, no one got any informational feedback about what they did well or areas they could improve. Moreover, by the time one person's turn to be chair came around again, whatever vicarious learning might have taken place was forgotten and lost.

This time, Miocevich had each person lead the meetings for a month. One person was formally assigned to give feedback to the individual chairing the meeting, and this responsibility rotated at each session. Special attention was focused on identifying improvements from one week to the next. In the process, each person at the meeting began picking up ideas about what worked and didn't. Miocevich noticed that after a while most people began recognizing the behaviors in themselves that made the chair's job so demanding and often unrewarding and began shaping up on their own. As a further benefit, these managers also improved the way they ran their sessions with their own staffs; several have begun rotating the chair's position in these meetings as well.

▶   *Invite people to assume responsibility.* Be on the lookout for situations to induce people to assume responsibility. As a first step, consider adopting the approach taken by Frieda Caplan, founder and CEO of Frieda's Finest, a California-based marketer and distributor of unusual fruits and vegetables: "When I face a tough decision, I always ask my employees, 'What would you do if you were me?' This approach generates good ideas and introduces my employees to the complexity of management decisions."[31] Go one step further by inviting employees to take the actions necessary to implement their decisions. And back them up.

▶   *Give everyone a customer.* There is another *c* to add to our developing capacity list (competence, confidence, choice, climate, communications), and that is customers. Make certain everyone in your organization has a customer. Call this customer focus whatever you want (retail bankers call it relationship banking), but introduce this practice today.

Make certain that whatever people are doing, they have another individual or group in their mind that they are serving. Otherwise, they will feel alienated from their efforts and unable to be as responsive as they could be. Having a customer also enlarges most people's understanding of not only what they do but also what the company overall does. It typically puts each person in direct contact with other parts of the business.

At Springfield Remanufacturing Corporation, hourly employees are sent out to talk with customers whenever possible. One of the results, according to CEO Jack Stack, is that "everyone realizes that there were real people at the end of their remanufacturing process, that businesses out there depended on the quality that they produced. Everyone realized that they had responsibilities not only to themselves and their company, but to the customer as well."[32]

Having customers makes people feel important and significant. "I really like it," says Larry Williams, auto mechanic for Total Nissan, "when customers come back and ask for me personally. They say they really liked the way I fixed their car, and they want me to work on it again. That makes me feel great. Proud. I really want to make sure they keep asking for me."

▸ **Have an open house.** Want to make certain that your constituents feel proud about your department or company? Hold an Open House. Let people bring their spouses, children, aunts and uncles, grandparents, next-door neighbors, and friends into their business. This is a great way to build pride and self-esteem and let people feel important: "See where I work? See what I do. Let me tell you what I do, what *we* do, and why it is important." Invite your customers, suppliers, and vendors to join you.

▸ **Share the big picture.** Imagine that you have a five-thousand-piece jigsaw puzzle. You dutifully hand out each and every piece to your constituents and exhort, "Now you have all the resources you need to complete this project. Go to it!" What do you think they will say to you? How often have you been handed an assignment, given a budget, staff, and other materials, without ever really understanding what it was that you were being asked to produce? People need to know what the picture on the puzzle box looks like.

A few years ago, a group of executives from a Fortune 500 firm traveled to Midlothian, Texas, to Chaparral Steel, one of the world's most productive steel companies. They wanted to learn how the company managed its teams so successfully.

One executive asked, "How do you schedule coffee breaks in the plant?" A Chaparral manager replied, "The workers decide when they want a cup of coffee." "Yes," said the executive, "but who tells them it's okay to leave the machines?" As the Chaparral manager commented later, "The guy left and still didn't get it."

Chaparral workers know when to take a coffee break because they're trained to understand how the whole business operates. They know the "big picture." Once trained in the "Chaparral process," a worker understands how his or her job relates to the welfare of the entire organization. Financial statements are posted monthly in the mill, including a chart tracking operating profits before taxes—the key measure for profit sharing.[33]

▶   ***Enrich people's jobs.*** The content of the jobs at such companies as Chaparral Steel and Springfield Remanufacturing Corporation is not particularly glamorous. Yet these companies and others like them have been able to augment people's work so that they feel important and connected to the big picture. You can best liberate the leader within your constituents by understanding how the contextual factors of their jobs may contribute to lower feelings of personal effectiveness and reduced motivation. The most common reasons are excessive bureaucracy, authoritarian supervisory styles, nonmerit based reward systems, and job design.[34] The latter area may be one you can have significant influence over.

Make certain that peoples' jobs are designed so that they know what is expected of them, and provide sufficient training and technical support so people can complete their assignments successfully. Enrich their responsibilities so that they experience variety in their task assignments and opportunities to make meaningful decisions about how their work gets accomplished. Create occasions for them to form networks with others in the organization (including both peers and senior managers). Involve them in programs, meetings, and decisions that have a direct impact on their job performance. Take a careful look at what your constituents are doing in their jobs and determine — with their input — where you could be enriching their positions and consequently fostering greater self-confidence.

▶   *Let constituents be the teachers.* Peter Drucker points out, "knowledge workers and service workers learn most when they teach."[35] He finds that the best way to improve productivity is to have people instruct others. Have a star salesperson present "the secret of his or her success" at the company's sales conference, or have the top surgeon give a talk at the country medical society. School teachers have realized a similar principle: the learning of older children can be enhanced by having them tutor younger students. In this process the learning of both parties is strengthened.

Most of the work force at Syntex consists of highly competent scientific and professional employees, but many had very little formal understanding of how businesses operate. A cross-functional group of employees was charged with determining what people needed to know in order to work effectively in a faster-paced and more self-directed work team environment. The first course they designed was about product flow. They made a video to explain how products move from one department to the next in the development, production, and distribution process. Drew Garland, a research scientist on the committee, says, "The next course we are designing, with the help of our cost accounting department, will teach basic cost accounting to all employees. We are also designing a course in production control for all employees and a technical course for nontechnical employees." The courses are designed by the people who have questions about how things work and are staffed by teachers (experienced personnel in that subject or department) as well as learners. "Teaching others about business basics," states Garland, "makes me and others in my area more capable of integrating business thinking into our technical proposals. Ultimately, we are all more successful."

The teaching can also be informal. A study by Xerox's Palo Alto Research Center revealed that service personnel learn more of what they need to know about fixing copiers by swapping stories than they do from reading the company's manuals.[36] Instead of breaking up the gang by the water cooler, make opportunities for storytelling at informal get-togethers and loosely organized off-site meetings.

▶   *Use modeling to develop competencies.* Modeling is being used in a wide variety of settings to develop intellectual, social, and behavioral competencies. The method that produces the best results, according to Bandura, includes three major elements: "First, the appropriate skills are modeled to convey the basic competencies. Second, the people receive guided practice under simulated conditions so they can perfect the skills. Third, they are helped to apply their newly learned skills in work conditions in ways that will bring them success."[37]

Determine the competencies you want to develop, and then break complex skills down into subskills. Demonstrate, generally via videotape, an illustration of the desired skill (or behavior), incorporating many brief examples. Use "models" that are similar to your audience (since having respected peers as teachers is particularly effective). As people perfect their skills, especially new ones, provide informational feedback on how they are doing. Focus on the corrective changes that need to be made, instead of emphasizing what was wrong or flawed.

Keep in mind that feedback should be given to build confidence. This result is achieved by calling attention to successes and improvements, while correcting deficiencies. Finally, give people the opportunity to practice new skills, especially in situations where they are likely to produce good results. Sufficient success using what they have learned is necessary so that they believe in themselves and in the value of the new ways.

7

Serving
a Purpose

*You can't be motivated by self-interests and expect to be a
leader. The instant you feel exempt from the standards of
the organization, you cease to be a leader. A leader
galvanizes people by living their shared vision.*
Cheryl Breetwor
ShareData

When we called Harvester Restaurants in London to ask if we
could interview executive director Keith Henesey and personnel and training director Sue Newton, we weren't prepared for
their response. They felt a telephone interview would not be
sufficient to tell the story and instead volunteered to fly from
England to California to talk with us face to face. Not one
other person we have interviewed has ever made such an offer.
And nothing better illustrates the dedication of these two
leaders to serving their company, its people, and its mission.

When we sat down for the interview, we knew we were in
for a unique experience. Before they would let us ask them any
questions about their company, they insisted we listen to a
three-hour orientation on the Harvester brand, its mission and
values, and their way of making things happen. They pulled
out a forty-six-page presentation called "Making a Difference"
and proceeded to tell us dozens of stories about what indi-

vidual team members had done to take ownership for Harvester's mission. Our tape recorder registered the energy level: there are more bangs on the table to make a point than in any other interview we conducted.

This may have been unique for us, but not for the team members or suppliers of Harvester. Mission training — known as "getting on the Harvester Bus" in Harvester jargon — is required of all full-time and part-time employees and of suppliers. It is the training program on the values, commitments, and beliefs at Harvester.

Harvester is obviously doing something right. Sales from 1991 to 1992 were up 4 percent from the previous year; operating profit was up 8 percent; and trading profit increased 5 percent. These accomplishments occurred in a restaurant market that declined by 10 to 12 percent. Effectively, then, Harvester is beating the market by about 15 to 20 percent.

From our discussions with Henesey and Newton, it became clear that Harvester's success can be attributed to a great extent to the methodical way the company has built credibility with team members and guests (their terms). They have clearly articulated a Harvester philosophy of doing business and have unified team members and suppliers around it. They have created the necessary systems and structures and learned the individual behaviors required to practice intensely what is preached.

Henesey offers an illustrative example: "We were going around a restaurant into a pub and saw a seat with all the stuffing hanging out of it." When the manager tried to block it from view, Henesey sat down in the worn chair. He then "got the manager, got the regional manager, and said, 'Okay, where does this fit in the mission? This is absolutely horrific. There's a hole, and there's stuffing coming out of it. Where does that fit in?' Shuffling their feet, they said, 'Well, you know, money is tight.' I said, 'Whoa! It does not say our business is hospitality, but only when money's available.'" In this instance and in his interview with us, Henesey was quite clear that the leader's job is to serve a purpose, so that these people can in turn do their jobs of serving the company's constituents — the guests.

Leaders serve a purpose and the people who have made it possible for them to lead. They put the guiding principles of the organization ahead of all else and then strive to live by them. They are the first to do what has been agreed upon. In serving a purpose, leaders strengthen credibility by demonstrating that they are not in it for themselves; instead, they have the interests of the institution, department, or team and its constituents at heart. Being a servant may not be what many leaders had in mind when they choose to take responsibility for the vision and direction of their organization or team, but serving others is the most glorious and rewarding of all leadership tasks.

As we've said, the best guidelines about how to lead come from the ideas of customer service, not management books. Like any service, leadership is only as good as its execution at the time of the actual delivery. If an airline promises "friendly skies" but treats passengers rudely, it is not credible, despite on-time departure performance. If an accountancy promises accuracy but performs sloppy audits, it is not credible.

Similarly, when leaders affirm the shared values of an organization, they are promising that these values will be kept consistently. The leaders are also saying implicitly that they will be the first to live up to these promises. The ultimate test of leaders' credibility is whether they do what they say. In the doing is where leaders prove to others that they are truly serious about quality or respect or innovation or diversity or whatever the stated value.

The concept of servant leadership is not new. Nearly twenty years ago, Robert Greenleaf pointed out that "the great leader is seen as servant first, and that simple fact is the key to [the leader's] greatness."[1] Greenleaf, who had spent thirty years as a Fortune 50 senior executive, spent the last years of his career reflecting upon and organizing what he had learned about successful business and professional people. He observed that those people who believed foremost in the concept of service, who were servant leaders, were also successful leaders. It was their belief in serving others that enabled these executives to provide leadership and that made others willingly follow. Leaders are those people who are serving a purpose and are willing to act on what they believe.

Leaders believe in what they are doing. They have faith and do not need proof and evidence that something is right. Rather, it makes sense to them at a deep, personal level. Since there is no freeway to the future, they call upon an inner magnetic north to guide their actions and adventures forward.

"Our business was doing okay, better than our competitors," says Bob Branchi, managing director for Automotive Holdings, whose car dealerships accounted for nearly one in every four new cars sold in Western Australia. "But I had this feeling that what had caused us to be successful in the past was not going to be sufficient for the future. I don't know exactly when I began to feel this way or what caused it, and I can't give you any concrete data that says we needed to change. I just knew that we did." And on that basis — whether we call it faith, intuition, divine inspiration, or a personal agenda — Branchi is spearheading a culture change for the organization, along with many personal changes in shifting from managing to leading.

Because of their faith, leaders are always searching, exploring, and discovering what lies just beyond the horizon. Their strength is first of all an inner strength, as we have described in earlier chapters; it comes from knowing who they are, what they stand for, and where they are trying to go. But though servant leaders have a strong inner sustaining spirit to guide and support their adventures, they are also willing to "know experimentally."[2] Even given the data they have (which is always incomplete and messy), they are willing to act. Based upon their actions, they learn about what has worked, what has made sense or didn't, and subsequently use this insight to navigate and teach others these lessons. At the core of their inner strength is a fundamental belief that somehow "things" could be better than they are now. Like the sculptor, their task is to liberate the work of art trapped within the stone.

The leader's clarity of purpose and ability to articulate both the vision and shared values give certainty and purpose to others who may be unsure, who are afraid, or who would otherwise have difficulty achieving greatness on their own. As noted political scientist and historian James MacGregor Burns has pointed out, leaders elevate the human spirit: "Their purposes, which might have started out as separate but related . . . become fused [raising] the level of human conduct and ethical aspiration of both the leader and led, and thus it has a transformating effect on both."[3]

This connection between leaders and their constituents brings us back to Greenleaf's nearly two-decade old prophecy: "A new moral principle is emerging which holds that the only authority deserving one's allegiance is that which is freely and knowingly granted by the led to the leader in response to, and in proportion to, the clearly evident servant stature of the leader. Those who choose to follow this principle will not casually accept the authority of existing institutions. Rather, they will freely respond only to individuals who are chosen as leaders because they are proven and trusted as servants."[4]

Leaders must make certain that other people's highest priority needs are being taken care of first. They must ask whether those being served are growing—becoming healthier, wiser, freer, more autonomous, more capable—and are more likely themselves to become servant leaders. The service of leaders is the basis of their credibility.

Credible leaders set the example for others; they are willing to hold themselves to the same set of standards as others. Credible leaders go first. They truly walk the talk.

GOING FIRST

Leaders take the first step because doing so demonstrates their faith in the idea, program, or service. Going first provides tangible evidence of the leader's commitment. It demonstrates the leader's willingness to experiment and learn from the inevitable mistakes of trying out new concepts. Moreover, by going first, leaders serve their constituents' desire to know more about the unknown; constituents can learn from their leaders' experiences and feel more comfortable knowing that they are not alone.

When the Agriculture Division of Ciba-Geigy conducted its "Being the Best" leadership development program, its president, Leo Bontempo, attended every one of the sessions, lending his personal support and presence to the ideas taught in the program. Bontempo started each program by sharing his feedback from the Leadership Practices Inventory. He talked about what he had learned from this feedback and what he was doing to be a better leader. This action made it easier for others to talk about their own feedback with colleagues and constituents, even about areas in which they had been disappointed or surprised.

What the leader does is the single most important factor in demonstrating to others what is acceptable — and unacceptable — behavior in our organizations. Effectively, the leader's behavior is the model we use to determine or calibrate our own behaviors and choices. Beyond this, the leader's behaviors and actions generate intensity around shared values. In order for the shared values to make a difference in how the organization runs, the leader must adhere to them in ways that are evident to his or her constituents.

It is not just the big decisions (for example, should we open or close a plant?) that set the example. Hundreds of little opportunities each day are even more telling examples of what our leaders do or don't stand for. Where do they park? What questions do they ask? What events do they attend? Constituents see how and whom leaders serve by what they say and do. And if the music and dance don't go together, we can hardly expect to achieve great performances.

One way to ensure that the music and dance do go together is to keep time. To keep track of how we spend it, that is. How we spend our time is the truest tangible indicator of our priorities, of what we think is important. Constituents can measure how serious their leaders are about key values by observing how much time is spent on them. Who in the organization would take seriously exhortations about innovation when few can remember seeing these managers do anything new or different? Leaders consciously allocate their time and energy in service to shared values.

Each year, James R. Houghton, chairman and CEO of Corning, visits forty to fifty Corning locations around the world. Houghton has a commitment to "beating the drums of quality." He therefore meets with as many people as possible, and the emphasis of these meetings is almost exclusively on progress toward world-class quality goals. He understands that how he spends his time communicates the real importance of issues. It is thus to his credit that an analysis of his calendar reveals that he spent nearly one-quarter of his time devoted to quality-related activities.[5] His example sends a powerful message to constituents that Corning's CEO is serious about quality—and they should be, too.

Recently appointed as county manager of Fulton County, Georgia, John Stanford faces enormous challenges, not the least of which is restoring people's faith that the government's purpose is to work for them. As Stanford says, "My constant theme, both inside and outside, is what good are governments if they don't give back to and serve the people?" He is enthusiastic and diligent about encouraging "every member of the work force to practice that and getting the citizens to understand that's the way we are attempting to behave...to make the government give back to the people and make a difference in the lives of the people."

Stanford wants to make certain that his constituents understand this commitment. Three or four nights a week, he talks with some community-based organization. He holds meetings with employees every other week in three different locations in the county. In addition, he holds quarterly meetings at eight different locations in large auditoriums. Stanford includes a newsletter with employees' paychecks every two weeks. He also handles nearly fifty electronic mail messages daily and a weekly TV show. There is little question about Stanford's priorities: he is investing his time to make sure that others know that he is serious about having a responsive county administration.

By going first, being visible, and demonstrating priorities

by their investment of time and energy, leaders become role models. The significance of role modeling is underscored by a study involving the cadet wing at the Air Force Academy. Each cadet squadron (110 to 115 undergraduates) is supervised by an active duty officer, called the air officer commanding (AOC). Cadets were asked to select what they believed the AOCs' primary role to be. Their most frequent choice, chosen five times as often as the next possible alternative, was "officer model," defined as a "person who exemplifies what you want to be, acts the way you would like to act, and balances a task and people orientation." Subsequent analyses revealed that the performance (military, academic, and athletic) of cadets was significantly associated with the extent to which they perceived their own AOC as a role model; that is, evaluations as a role model were directly correlated with actual performance measures of individuals under their command.[6]

The significance of servant leadership is aptly illustrated in this cadet's description of his AOC: "She helps us out instead of trying to hurt us. She isn't insecure and power hungry like the other four AOCs I've had. She's concerned about teaching us to be capable officers instead of about teaching us to be capable cadet regulation followers." Another AOC is described this way: "His greatest strength is that he allows us to run our own squadron—he trusts us enough to do it. In essence, he treats us like junior officers." These are succinct descriptions of admirable and credible leaders.

STAYING IN TOUCH

To sustain credibility, leaders must stay in touch with constituents. If they don't, if they remain invisible, they contribute to the credibility gap described in Chapter Two. Leaders must be in touch: they must know the issues, the customers, and their constituents.

Clarke Otten, president of Professional Swedish Car Repair in Atlanta, does an admirable job of staying in touch and serving the customer. He sets aside an hour or two each day to call the previous week's customers. Being called by the president of the $1-million company makes a big impression. The calls also let employees know that Otten is in touch with customers and that they really matter. If customers have any problems, Otten learns about them right away and can "address the problem right on the spot."[7]

To get in touch, leaders must become more visible with their constituents. Getting—and staying—in touch is not just for the good times but also for moments of crisis and upheaval. It means being willing to take the "hot seat" on occasion. For example, in the mid 1980s, Ken Bertaccini, an AT&T vice president, was given the task of terminating eight thousand employees, the largest single cut in the entire history of the company. How did he do it?

Bertaccini gathered large employee groups and reported the reasons for the layoffs in person. He outlined the profile of those most likely to be cut, the treatment those laid off would receive, and the possibilities for those who would remain. When he finished one of these grueling deliveries, a man approached him onstage. This twenty-year veteran of the company knew his job was in peril. Tears were streaming down his cheeks, but as he got to Bertaccini, he said, "Thank you for treating me like an adult."[8] It was a difficult situation, to be sure, but Bertaccini's credibility and willingness to be visible to constituents made a difference.

Credibility is earned through human contact—in the hallways, on the factory floors, in the retail shops, in the classrooms, and on the streets. Credible leaders take the time to listen and learn.

Impressive listening skills have been identified as one common characteristic of credible leaders.[9] A willingness to listen carefully to constituents and, if necessary, to hear the bad news keeps leaders from becoming isolated from critical feedback. When they can get information from a variety of sources, across functions and levels, they are able to know what is going on. To serve others well, leaders must be in touch with them, listen to them, and respect them. Ever try getting good service at a restaurant when your waiter or waitress is never around, is too busy, or seems to think that something you have asked for was too much bother?

Leaders demonstrate that they value others when they listen to them, trust them, and are receptive to having others point out their own mistakes or other problems. Shelley Brown, vice president of human resources at Aspect Telecommunications, summed it up this way: "It's important to have some people around you who will tell you that there are problems and who will help you sort through them and won't try to mask the problems. I really value this in working relationships, personal ones as well."

Being able to listen to the news, good and bad, is a basic ingredient for staying in touch. When things are going well, it's not all that difficult to hear the good news. It's how we react to news about mistakes and difficulties that may be the better indicator of whether or not constituents feel like keeping us in touch. From the constituent's perspective, the question is always, "Do they still shoot the messenger with bad news?"

Walter Kiechel III, assistant managing editor of *Fortune* magazine, spoke with numerous executives and learned what they did to really hear what others had to say.[10] They told him that you have to be very careful about how you receive "bad" news. Even if the news makes your blood boil or bursts your illusions, you need to ask even-tempered questions and to be able to thank the person sincerely for bringing this unpopular (but never unwanted) information to your attention. When serving a purpose (rather than a personal agenda), assume that the "facts are friendly"; appreciate that without valid and reliable information, the ability to be an effective problem solver is diminished. You must be careful to enable people to discuss anything without having to mince words. The focus should be not on whether or how someone made a mistake but on doing the right thing.

Establish an atmosphere in which people feel comfortable about speaking up long before anyone worries about whether the news is good or bad. When people have the same values, sharing information becomes all that more easy; they can say, "I know that my leader will be interested in knowing about this, because of her interest in. . . ."

Staying in touch, then, means that leaders must remain approachable. According to what Kiechel learned, executives run the risk of becoming unapproachable, and therefore out of touch, because of their "imperial trappings — the cavernous office, the executive dining room, the dark-windowed limo" — and because of their appearance of being always busy. He suggests establishing "regular times when people know they can come to see you. Better yet, go to their offices to talk to them. Take colleagues out for the occasional lunch or dinner, no agenda, just a little friendly 'What's on your mind?'" He also cautions leaders to be careful about booking their daily or weekly calendar so full that people who want or need to talk with them can't get on the schedule. Leaders who wish to stay in touch with their constituents always have time to get out of their offices (or off the telephone) to step down the hall, over to the lab, or visit the plant to find out what is going on.[11]

Finally, when we recognize the importance of staying in touch, we appreciate the importance of responding to people, issues, or problems by listening first so we can obtain sufficient information to understand their concern. The prayer of St. Francis, "Lord, grant that I may not seek so much to be understood as to understand," captures this shift in emphasis required by servant leaders.

Steve Tritto is currently in the business of helping companies and their leaders deal with difficult situations, whether business turnarounds, restructuring, layoffs, or downsizing. His credibility is key. He recognizes just how important it is that he be approachable and accessible. Tritto told us about his fireside chats during his tenure as president of one company. He would meet every other week with twenty-five or so people selected alphabetically, crossing over department and rank. There were no set agendas, and people could raise any issue they wanted. Much as these chats were major opportunities to exchange information, Tritto explained that they were more significant than just that:

I used to think that the main benefit of a fireside chat, or at least the intent of them, was twofold—one was to be able to get information from people about the issues that were of concern to them without any filtering, without it going through several layers of management before it got to me; and secondly, that people would be able to hear my point of view on different issues without the filtering by the time it gets to them. And to some extent, those chats served that purpose. But using hindsight, what I have learned is that the greatest benefit of those fireside chats was that I could stay in touch with everybody in the company having access to me as the president of the company.

Having access, Tritto explained, made a difference: "It was much easier for me to get support and maintain a level of trust as a result of those meetings." It wasn't the content of the meetings that was as important as the concept. They proved that Tritto would sit with employees and discuss issues. People found they could give their opinions, and he would listen and respond. And, as Tritto said, the way he responded "either made me real or dishonest, or maybe it allowed me to convert them to my way of thinking, or maybe they'd just say, 'Hey, I really have to go back and think about this again,' but the fact that we could discuss our points of view candidly and honestly led them to say, 'I can trust this guy, he's not a bad guy. Let's give this a go.'" By staying in touch, Tritto was able to become real to his constituents and underscore the meaning of some basic values.

MAKING MEANING, DAILY

In the course of our everyday comings and goings, we have many opportunities to stand up on behalf of shared values and demonstrate our commitment to a common purpose. Many of these occasions arise from small incidents, such as the way we greet someone on the telephone, handle an interruption, bring up an idea, or introduce an associate to another colleague.

Probably no single one of these behaviors makes a difference by itself, but over the course of time they add up and present an easily recognized pattern or way of being that either promotes or discourages trust. We learn whether or not we can count on our leaders by watching them operate in a wide variety of settings. Consistency reveals to us both a depth of conviction and an internal integration of words and actions.

During our seminars, we often ask participants whether or not they think that the people back in their organizations are talking about them while they are away. Amid some laughs and worried brows, the answer is almost uniformly yes. But the issue is not whether people talk about us, but what they say.

In thinking about what people say about us when we are away, it is important to recognize that leaders are present in the minds and hearts of their constituents. People ask themselves, "What would our leader do about this? What criteria would she use to make that determination? How would he respond to that customer concern? What has she done when faced with this dilemma?"

Jim Shunk, personnel manager of Hewlett-Packard, finds that he still looks to how an admired leader handled difficult situations, many years ago: "I remember how he could let people vent their feelings and anger — yell and scream as if he had personally caused their problem — and still listen calmly and with empathy. And when we'd done something that was right (proper) but it still wasn't the right (fair) thing, he'd move mountains to rectify the situation for one and all. Whenever I'm in doubt, I think about what he would say and do."

Leaders make an impression. They leave their footprints in the sand, and these become guides for those who come behind. To the extent that people have positive and consistent images of their leaders in their heads, they will want to be like them and act in ways that are consistent with shared values. In contrast, if their leaders are inconsistent and inconsiderate, they will not want to emulate them or put into practice the values their leaders espouse.

Consequently, it is important to think carefully about the meaning we are creating with our actions. Consider this recent cartoon. The first drawing shows a sign in the woods that states, "Do not feed the bears." In the second, a large bear stands next to that sign. The bear is holding a sign that reads, "I am a giant gopher." Leaders, like this well-evolved bear, are able to frame or reframe reality and by so doing make meaning.

Making meaning is one of the first tasks for leaders in serving a purpose. Leaders get their constituents to care. Whatever the purpose, leaders endeavor to create a meaning with sufficient emotional impact to make their constituents confident and excited about the endeavor. There was a time when we believed that managers should be unflappable. This sense was well captured by a *New Yorker* magazine cartoon that showed a male executive, complete with suit, trenchcoat, wing tips, hat, and briefcase with a bland expression on his face. The caption read "the agony of defeat." The next caption read "the thrill of victory"—and the image of the executive was identical.

It would seem that it didn't matter whether these were the best of times or the worse of times. Managers and executives were not supposed to let others know how they were feeling. The net result was constituents who were equally cool, analytical, aloof, and uncaring. Workplaces were uninspiring. People saw their jobs like that of Sisyphus: they moved the rock up the hill each day, day after day, only to see it roll down again at night.

Think about your business for a minute. What would make you weep? That's a question often asked among the management team members at Herman Miller. Thinking about this question and others like it helps them get in touch with and focus on the elements of their business and contact with customers, suppliers, vendors, associates, and the like which they feel most deeply about. Ultimately, what leaders do is to enable their constituents to care—to care about what they are doing and why they are doing it, to know it makes a difference. But none of this can happen without knowing what it is that our leaders are concerned about. What would make them weep?

How can we learn enough about our leaders to be able to answer that question? As we've seen, leaders must be approachable to allow others opportunities to get to know them. Leaders must also volunteer information, both to make meaning and to show how it is meaningful to them.

BECOMING A STORYTELLER

When serving a purpose, leaders educate their constituents about the values and actions that are important and make a difference. In this educational process, leaders give meaning to actions, activities, and events that might otherwise divert people from the chosen path. Leaders have a responsibility to teach others the values, the way things are done around here, to teach the discipline. Some of the teaching is formal, classroom-like teaching. But most is informal, day-to-day teaching. Experience is the best teacher, and when learning the aims of an organization, it typically takes the form of critical incidents. These are the stuff of stories and legends.

The ancient art of storytelling is perhaps the major way that leaders teach. Many of the stories come from the critical moments that leaders confront or their own experiences of going first. We'll talk more about the sources of stories in the next section. For now, let's look into why credible leaders must master the art of storytelling.

Leaders' messages about purpose and values are important in educating people. The way those are framed is crucial, and the process by which they are communicated is just as significant. Several people can present the same basic message and yet receive entirely different responses from their audience. How we educate and how our messages are communicated are major distinguishing factors in whether what we have to say will be remembered, endorsed, and followed.

As management professor Jay Conger says, a leader's words "often assume their greatest impact as symbols rather than as literal meanings."[12] This impact is especially felt when words are used to tell a story. Stories serve as kind of a mental map that helps people know, first, what is important (that is, purpose and values) and, second, how things are done in a particular group or organization. Stories are powerful educational (leadership) tools.

Researchers in speech communications explain that stories "excite the imagination of the listener and create consecutive states of tension (puzzlement-recoil) and tension release (insight and resolution). The listener is not a passive receiver of information but is triggered into a state of active thinking."[13] The listener must consider the meaning of the story and try to make sense of it. By this process, the listener is engaged; attention and interest are fostered.

Social psychology helps explain why rhetorical devices (such as stories, analogies, and metaphors) are persuasive and effective ways to communicate ideas.[14] Statistical summaries, facts, and policy statements, because they are generally abstract and bland, lack impact and are treated as uninformative. In contrast, stories, analogies, and metaphors have a substantial impact on decision making; information is more quickly and accurately remembered when it is first presented in the form of an example or story, particularly one that is intrinsically appealing.[15]

Organizational sociologists Joanne Martin and Melanie Powers have demonstrated the power of stories in fostering beliefs. They compared the persuasiveness of four different methods to convince M.B.A. students that a particular company really practiced a policy of avoiding layoffs. In the first method, they used only a story. In the second, they presented statistical data that showed that the company had significantly less involuntary turnover than its competitors. In the third, they used the statistics and the story; and in the fourth, they employed a straightforward policy statement made by a senior company executive. Those presented with the story alone believed the company's claim about the layoff policy more than any of the other three groups.[16]

What we communicate in stories and examples is remembered by others in proportion to its vividness. The Center for Creative Leadership's Innovation and Creativity Research Group explains vividness in two ways. First, the story is about a real person and is clearly grounded in time and place. Second, it is told in colorful and animated language.[17]

Here's a particular story that illustrates these characteristics. Often repeated around one company, it reinforces the need to cope with the unexpected. At the end of a day of interviews, a candidate being recruited had met with everyone except the company's president. There seemed to be clear consensus that the young man should be hired. At 5:30 P.M., he met with the president, who promptly asked if he would join him and another manager for drinks. At a nearby bar, the president called his wife and the spouse of the manager to join them for dinner. The candidate went off to dinner having yet to begin his interview with the president. Dinner ended at midnight, and still nothing like an interview had occurred. Then the president asked the candidate to his home for the actual interview. Surprised, the young man balked, saying that it had been a long and exhausting day and he would prefer to see him in the morning.

Needless to say, there was no interview the next day and no job offer. The president and others often repeated this story to illustrate that the company needed those who were willing to "roll with the punches" and "to go the extra mile." The story vividly and powerfully illustrated what the president saw as important—and communicated much more effectively than statements ever could that employees should be willing to demonstrate flexibility and commitment.[18]

A warning: since stories may become part of the folklore of the organization, be sure that they fully reflect shared values. The story just related, for instance, would need to be reframed or retired if the company also wished to emphasize diversity. As told, recruits with family responsibilities and without full-time, live-in help would obviously be placed at a disadvantage. As values change, new stories need to replace the old in order to show the new way being forged.

TEACHING WITH
MOMENTS OF LEARNING

We often learn how to put shared values into practice when critical incidents demand it.[19] These are times that require leaders to step in and make decisions based on matters of principle. Often the most dramatic occur when a key principle is at stake or when someone's behavior is inconsistent with the stated values. We call these moments of learning. When leaders stand up for our beliefs, they let others know that they are willing to put their personal careers or personal safety on the line in service of shared values.

Moments of learning are great teaching opportunities. They are moments, both large and small, when we (both as leaders and constituents) put our credibility on the line: do I do what I say I will do? The following two stories illustrate how leaders responded to critical incidents and in so doing taught their constituents about serving a shared purpose.

Standing Up for Beliefs

As vice president of the Westinghouse Steam Turbine Division, Gene Cattabiani was faced with an extremely hostile labor-relations environment and the fact that the Steam Turbine Division was not especially profitable.[20] Costs had to be cut and productivity improved. It was clear that much of the opportunity for improvement was on the shop floor. Yet the animosities between labor and management made productive negotiation seem unlikely.

Cattabiani decided that he needed to break this impasse and begin to change attitudes on both sides by treating union leaders and the work force with honesty, respect, and openness. Instead of having information passed on from the labor-relations vice president to the union leadership, Cattabiani decided to give a presentation on the state of the business to all employees. This had never been done in the long history of the division.

Other senior managers wondered if this was necessary. Wouldn't it be easier, and maybe more effective, to have someone else make the presentation? Cattabiani was firm. His format was a slide presentation, simple but complete and clear, followed by questions from the floor. To reach the entire work force, he had to repeat the presentation several times to groups of hundreds of workers.

The initial presentation was disastrous. Cattabiani wanted people to see that the business was in real trouble and that their jobs depended on forming a new relationship with management. But the workers assumed that management was trying to trick them again. They heckled Cattabiani mercilessly all through the slide show and shouted abuse and threats during the question-and-answer period.

Cattabiani persisted and made the full series of presentations. Even though it wasn't clear that people understood his message or believed it, some important changes were noticeable. For instance, when Cattabiani went out on the factory floor (which his predecessors had done only when giving customers a tour), people began to nod in recognition—a big improvement from spitting on the floor as he walked by.

Whenever Cattabiani spotted a heckler, he would walk over and say something like, "You really gave me a hard time last week," to which the response was usually something like, "Well, you deserved it!" Such exchanges invariably led to brief but very open dialogues: clearly people were listening.

Suddenly, Cattabiani had become "a creature of flesh and blood, someone whose opinions had some value"; he was credible and not "an ordinary useless manager." Leaders, like Cattabiani, who serve the purpose and principles of the organization often make sacrifices, face ridicule, and suffer verbal abuse because they believe strongly in what they stand for. In fact, it is this faith that sees them through difficult times.

Handling Inconsistencies

In confronting inconsistencies, we are required to address the gap created by doing something less than what we promised. Steve Tritto recalled for us how he handled an inconsistency between a company's promise of reliability and what it delivered:

> Early on in my tenure... we shipped a new product line that was supposed to turn our financial difficulty around and get the company growing again. The product was shipped prematurely. It was behind schedule, and it was

unknowingly shipped with a lot of bugs in it. We took a lot of chances. We cut corners on the testing, and it backfired. There was a bunch of very expensive dead-on-arrival instruments. We had a 50 percent return rate in the first ninety days, and our dealers were absolutely furious with us.

A couple of months after that occurred, we had a scheduled dealer meeting. I told the marketing people that I wanted to meet with the dealers. The director of sales and director of marketing practically begged me not to give a presentation on the subject of this product. They would say, "Steve, these are not computer guys, these are music retailers. These are tough guys. . . . They're out to kill you. Let us do it. We know them. We've been through this before. We know we can scream back and forth at one another and then go and have a beer. But don't you get up there; it's suicide."

But Tritto insisted. He explains:

I walked into the meeting room with our dealers present, and you could feel the tension. I mean, you could cut it with a knife. There were guys who were really very ticked at our company. I gave a presentation that described what happened. I owned up to the fact that we cut corners; we didn't test it as we should have; we took risks that we shouldn't have. I offered to take all shipments back. I described how the problems would be fixed and how long it would take. I said that we absolutely screwed up, and I'm sorry, and the only thing I can tell you is that we're never going to let this happen again. We're probably going to make other mistakes of a new kind, but we're never going to ship a poor product again. I took fifteen minutes to just communicate what happened, why it happened, what we're doing about it, and to say I was sorry. All the tension was immediately diffused. I didn't leave them anything to complain about. I didn't realize that they had never experienced this before from a corporate executive in this business. And a mix of these things gave me a certain degree of credibility with them that I was able to call upon later.

These same dealers, who had been so angry, would actually end up making loans to the company several months later. The national sales director got $2 million in advance orders, all on a handshake—no paper, no contracts, no written agreements. But, according to the sales director, he wouldn't have received the advance orders if these dealers hadn't believed in Tritto. He cited the way Tritto handled the meeting as an essential factor in the dealers' backing. By directly confronting an inconsistency between what the company said and what it did, Tritto put principle before politics and personal image. He believed that the credibility of the organization was at stake and that it was only right to address these issues personally and directly. This entire incident was a moment of learning for Tritto and his constituents.

LOSING AND REGAINING CREDIBILITY

Despite our best intentions, despite our pursuit of flawless leadership, despite our efforts to be open and humble, we sometimes fail. Sometimes circumstances change, and we can no longer do what we said we would do. Sometimes we don't have the competence or resources to do what we said. Sometimes we make errors in judgment or choose the wrong strategies. Sometimes we just mess up. No human being is exempt from failure. The trouble is that leadership failures and human frailties can sometimes seriously damage our credibility. It is therefore important to understand, as Tritto did, what we can do to regain credibility if ever we lose it.

We have maintained that leadership is a service relationship. So in searching for guidelines on how to recover from failures of leadership, we have learned the most from observing how customer confidence can be regained after a service failure. Customer service researchers Leonard L. Berry and A. Parasuraman have found that "satisfactory problem resolution sharply increases customers' willingness to recommend the company and significantly improves their perception of the company's service quality."[21] Our research suggests a similar pattern with regard to leadership. It *is* possible to regain credibility. When leaders satisfactorily respond to their failures of leadership, constituents are willing to continue to follow.

To understand the steps necessary to recover from a mistake that damages a leader's credibility, put yourself in the role of a restaurant customer for a moment. Imagine that you are having a lunch with an important client or friend, and the server spills coffee all over your new suit. What do you expect the server to do?

In this situation, people's first response is usually that they expect an apology. They also expect some immediate action to rectify the problem — quickly providing a cloth to blot the spill on the suit and cleaning up the mess on the table or floor. Depending on the severity of the stain, some people also expect the restaurant to offer to pay for the cleaning or even for a new suit. These reactions represent three of the most common expectations of service recovery.

Recovering from mistakes that damage leadership credibility is similar to service recovery. It requires the three responses just discussed and more: accept, admit, apologize, act, amend, and attend. We call these the six A's of leadership accountability.[22]

When we asked people what a leader should do if he or she makes a mistake, the universal response was "admit it." To admit means that we first have to accept personal responsibility for our actions and (in the case of leaders) those of our organization. Then we have to publicly acknowledge that we have made a mistake. But because of legal concerns or a fear that admitting a mistake may hurt credibility, many times leaders either deny or attempt to cover up any wrongdoing, thus assuring damage to their reputations.

But does admitting mistakes really damage credibility? If clients and colleagues know we have failed, will they be more likely to think we are incompetent? Our evidence suggests that attempting to hide mistakes will be much more damaging and will actually erode credibility. When we asked people what behaviors best defined an honest person, the response "admits mistakes" was mentioned second only to "tells the truth." There is no better way to demonstrate our honesty to our constituents than owning up to our mistakes. By admitting we are wrong and then doing something about it, we can strengthen our credibility rather than destroy it.

Offering an apology is another important step in rebuilding credibility. It lets constituents know that we are concerned about the impact or problem our actions may have created.

Quick action to deal with the immediate consequences of a mistake needs to follow an apology. A quick response lets others know that you are going to do something about the problem *now*. If possible, get others involved at this stage. Sharing the problem and asking for suggestions tells others that you trust their judgment in tough times; this appreciation for the talents of others contributes to leadership credibility.

Making amends for mistakes is a necessary but often overlooked part of the rebuilding process. In service recovery, this is often referred to as atonement. A leader's error can cause undue hardship to others. A poor choice of strategy or failure to respond to competitive threats may cost jobs or require cuts in expenses. The advice we get is that if others have to suffer, the leader should also. People don't expect us to resign for an honest error or lapse in judgment, but they do expect some form of reparation or personal participation in the hardship. The amends should fit the problem.

And finally, to make sure that they are attuned to the influence their actions are having on restoring lost credibility, leaders should pay close attention to the reactions of their constituents. They need to ask for feedback and to be non-defensive in listening to constructive criticism. Attentiveness helps to determine if the recovery actions are working and what else needs to be done to regain credibility.

Constituents tend to be forgiving, up to a point. To use a typically American metaphor, a rule of "three strikes and you're out" seems to govern how many mistakes leaders can make before losing their credibility. The first time a leader makes a mistake, people can place the fault on the process.

The second time, people can say the leader didn't have the necessary skills. But after the third miss, people tend to conclude that the leader is beyond help and is not deserving of continued allegiance. The problem begins to be seen as part of a recurring pattern of personal shortcomings.

We echo a warning, however, from Berry and Parasuraman about recovery efforts: "When the company's reputation for service reliability is already poor, a weak recovery effort shatters whatever level of confidence might still exist."[23] A poor recovery process can actually do harm. When it is necessary to embark upon rebuilding, leaders should do it right, or they might as well not do it at all.

Of course, even excellent recovery is no substitute for leadership. A reputation for being a strong and credible leader depends upon continuous attention to the disciplines of discovering, appreciating, affirming, developing, serving, and sustaining. But when those inevitable mistakes do occur, a thorough recovery effort can renew a leader's reputation.

In serving a purpose, leaders earn their credibility by going first, whether it's admitting a mistake or teaching others what to do. Servant leadership is about spending time and investing energy in setting a positive example. It involves sharing stories of exemplary performance, standing up for beliefs, and confronting critical incidents. This is how leaders give meaning to shared values. But if leader and constituent actions are to be consistent over time and if changes are to be long lasting, they must be supported by systems and structures that reinforce the appropriate norms and behaviors.

ESTABLISHING SYSTEMS AND STRUCTURES

Credible leaders go beyond personal actions to build institutional systems and structures that support the purpose being served. These may be at the unit, department, or functional level. Or they may be companywide. In any event, constituents take us most seriously when all of the supporting organizational mechanisms reinforce our individual commitments to common values and purpose.

For example, Harvester has developed systems to support each of its six value sets: guests, people, sales and profit, quality, suppliers, and style. As Henesey notes, "If you have the right culture, the right structure, and quality people, you must have the right systems to deliver the values."

Guest Values

Every quarter, Harvester is visited by a paid, unannounced mystery guest who evaluates the establishment on external standards, "moments of truth" achievement (Harvester's phrase for each guest-team member interaction), hospitality in the pub and restaurant, and standard delivery in the pub and restaurant. Each business receives a full report directly and is expected to develop an action plan to respond to needed areas of improvement.

People Values

Harvester's recruitment and selection systems support the fit of people and values. One of the most distinctive features of the people system is the job spectrum, written by high-performing people in each role. The job spectrum breaks the accountabilities down to enable people to perform their jobs more effectively and to be able to keep score on how they are doing. For example, the team manager spectrum identifies eighteen specific accountabilities. Also delineated are eight stages, each with clear descriptions of what must be attained to move from one stage to the next.

Harvester makes extensive use of recognition systems to celebrate successes. There are formal awards such as Team Members of the Year, Coaches of the Year, and sales, quality, profit, and people awards. Then there are the more spontaneous, informal recognitions, such as YIPEE! ("You've Inspired Pride and Enthusiasm in Everyone!") awards, given to those who have done something that is uplifting, and Pink Memos.

Pink Memos must be handwritten and presented face to face. They can be given by any team member for actions that support the Harvester mission or inhibit it. Ninety-nine percent of the Pink Memos are for facilitative actions. Newton tells with great pride of a team member who began a presentation in front of the entire head office by presenting a pink memo to the commercial manager "because she worked four weekends, she stayed four nights, just to help me get this computer program right." At Harvester, people have taken ownership of the recognition process.

Sales and Profit

Reward systems go beyond awards and recognition. At Harvester, everyone is rewarded based on their job and salary scale; everyone receives a bonus when there is overachievement of budgeted profit; and managers also receive a bonus for achieving people and quality targets. Harvester has adopted a unique horizontal promotion system to enable people to be recognized by their organizations, to enhance benefits, and to offer more visibility, better perquisites, and a higher salary.

Quality Values

Among the systems to support quality is the "meal critique." All Harvester people, including suppliers, who eat in a Harvester critique the experience for the team manager. Harvester also has an in-depth quality assurance system covering kitchen, restaurant, pub, cellar, and administration.

Supplier Values

Systems exist to make suppliers full-fledged partners in the business. They attend Mission Day; Values, Commitments, and Beliefs Day; and conferences and divisional meetings. Harvester recognizes high achieving suppliers with awards for Supplier of the Year and Partner of the Year.

Style Values

And finally, systems are in place for the "style" values. There are mandatory communication systems, including annual conferences for manager/coaches, half-year divisional meetings for manager/coaches and key team members, quarterly consultative meetings, quarterly head office meetings, monthly business reviews, monthly business presentations, and weekly and monthly unit meetings. Written communications keep members on track: there are weekly bulletins, monthly winners, and a quarterly *Harvester Times*. Team members are constantly reminded of Harvester's values, commitments, and beliefs.

With values and common purpose as a foundation and the leaders' actions as stepping stones, organizational systems and structures provide the reinforcement mechanisms for ensuring that constituents can lead themselves. Leaders are not satisfied until everyone "gets it" in the same way that they do and until everyone in the organization serves that purpose. The result? As one of Harvester's team members, Andrew Jones, puts it, "Once you're so bought into the values, you get up in the morning and you clean your teeth in the values, and then you know that you can do anything because you just believe in the values and you know you're not going to screw up because if it fits with the values, it's going to be right."

But not all constituents think and feel as Andrew Jones does. Leaders also have to deal directly with the cynicism, frustration, and despair that constituents may feel. Leaders have the responsibility to keep hope alive. In the next chapter, we turn our attention to how leaders can sustain hope.

SERVING A PURPOSE: FIRST STEPS/NEXT STEPS

Many of the ideas we've presented in this chapter require a shift in perspective. Here are some exercises to help in the process of making that shift to being the servant leader.

▶   *Manage by storytelling.* We have already discussed how
    stories are teaching tools, powerful strategies for getting
    your point across, and more likely to be remembered by
    your constituents than policy pronouncements, lists, or
    statistics. In his book, *Managing by Storying Around*,
    David Armstrong, vice president at Armstrong Interna-
    tional, offers some additional reasons why storytelling is
    an effective leadership practice. It's simple: anyone can
    tell a story. It's timeless: stories are fadproof. It's univer-
    sally appealing: everybody, regardless of age, gender,
    race, listens to stories. It's fun: stories are enjoyable. It's
    also a useful form of training, a good method for empow-
    ering people, an effective recognition device, a strong
    recruiting and hiring tool, a useful sales technique, and
    an excellent way to pass along corporate traditions.[24] An
    added benefit is that telling stories forces you to pay more
    attention to what your constituents are doing. To find a
    good story, be on the lookout for someone who is doing
    something to contribute to your group's expectations.

What makes a good storyteller? Personal stories. Tell a
story that you know something about or that you and your
audience can personally relate to. Talk from a first-person
perspective. If you are feeling truly excited about a particular
activity or goal, show it. If you are deeply concerned about
competitive threats, show it. Allowing your emotions to surface brings excitement to your voice and increases your natural tendency to use gestures and to smile (generally lightening
up your face). Start your story by relating an heroic deed.
Think of a clever title for the story to capture people's attention and help them to remember (catalogue) it. Give your story
a theme, and be willing to repeat it. Keep the story short. Use
people's names. Verify all facts. Be sure to end your message or
story with its moral: a conclusion that demonstrates concretely
the intended message or lesson to be learned.

▶   ***Create heroes.*** Like it or not, people already tell stories about you. So be sure that when you handle critical incidents, you explicitly link your actions and decisions to shared values. In this way, you can provide the basis for positive stories about yourself.

The stories *you* tell should be about others, about what constituents are doing to put shared values into practice, and should demonstrate their commitment as "disciples." Telling stories about others gives you the chance to reinforce that everyone is a leader. Hearing a story about people similar to themselves (those with whom they can identify) also stimulates them to learn how to take such actions themselves. Talking about heroes encourages everyone to do the right thing. Besides, people seldom tire of hearing stories about themselves and others they know. Such stories tend to get repeated, and the moral of the story gets spread far and wide in the organization.

▶   ***Speak with confidence.*** We look to our leaders for guidance. We need to feel that they know what they are talking about. Begin by doing your homework, for being prepared bolsters your natural self-confidence. When speakers are nervous and lack self-assurance, they speak at a lower volume and make many errors such as incomplete sentences, long pauses between words, and omitted portions of words or sentences. Speak with confidence, and you will avoid these mistakes and build the trust of your constituents.

Research points to differences between styles of presentation perceived as confident or powerful versus those seen as powerless. The powerless style includes speech hesitations ("ah," "you know," "uh"), polite phrases ("please," "thank you"), questioning voice tones at the end of declarative statements, and hedging phrases ("I think," "I guess," "kinda"). The powerful style lacks these qualities and instead portrays the speaker as more goal directed and straightforward. In a study of these two styles, it was found that study participants rated speakers using the powerful style as more potent, attractive, and credible.[25]

▶ **Reduce fear.** As a leader, the better your interactions with constituents, the easier it is for you to serve them now and in the future. You must therefore appreciate the behaviors that create fear so that you can be careful to avoid or extinguish them in your service encounters with constituents.

Certain abrasive and abusive conduct — such as glaring eye contact, silence, brevity or abruptness, snubbing or ignoring people, insults and put-downs, blaming, discrediting or discounting, aggressive mannerisms, job threats, yelling and shouting, angry outbursts, and physical threat — erect very thick walls of antagonism and resentment.[26] The effect is the same whether or not these behaviors are intentional. Others (for example, decision making behind closed doors or failure to acknowledge or respond to people's input and suggestions) create tension for people primarily because of their ambiguity. Enigmatic actions include reasoning inconsistently, acting cool and aloof or impolite, playing favorites, claiming credit for others' ideas, communicating indirectly or through others, and being secretive.

You want to reduce these fear-producing behaviors and actions because the feelings they create work against the service relationship — in fact, they destroy it. All of them show a lack of caring, interest and respect for the other person (your constituent). They assume that the "subordinate" is to serve the manager rather than the reverse. Eliminating these actions, some of which may be quite subtle, from your repertoire is essential to shifting from boss to servant leader. Open gestures, friendly looks, an inviting tone of voice, and candor all encourage others to trust you and want to make commitments about shared values.

▶   ***Ask questions.*** As a leader, the questions that you ask are
a potential teaching opportunity, a moment of learning.
They focus people's attention. The key is to think about
the "quest" in your question. Where do you want to take
this person with your question? What do you want this
person to think about? Asking questions forces you to
understand what you are trying to teach and achieve.
Consider carefully which two or three you want to ask
about critical values and actions. As Donna Goya, vice
president for human resources at Levi Strauss & Co.,
says, "We never make a personnel decision without asking, 'is this consistent with our aspirations?'"

Questions asked in the Socratic tradition also develop
people. They help others escape the trap of their own paradigms by broadening their perspectives and taking responsibility for their own viewpoints. Asking good questions, rather
than giving answers, also forces you to listen attentively to
your constituents and what they are saying. This action demonstrates your respect for their ideas and opinions. According
to Dennis Ham, university statistician for Curtin University
(Western Australia), asking questions is also the best way to
locate and then solve problems. He typically begins providing
service by asking his constituents several questions. What
information do you require? What would you like to know
more about that you don't know now?

If you are genuinely interested in what other people have
to say, ask their opinion, especially before giving your own.
Asking what others think facilitates participation in whatever
decision will ultimately be determined, increases support for
the decision, and reduces the risk that it might be undermined
by either inadequate consideration or unexpected opposition.

Another benefit is that asking other people for their ideas
and listening to their suggestions enhances their self-worth.
People feel more important when they know that they can
come to you with their ideas and be given a fair hearing and
that you consult with them and value their counsel before
making decisions affecting them.

▶   *Hold yourself accountable.* Use the same standards and criteria for yourself that you apply to others. If customer service is important, find time to spend with customers. All three Nordstrom brothers report that their most productive times are spent on the floor, talking to the frontline Nordstrom employees about meeting customer needs.

If your message is that "we're all in this together," then make certain your own actions reinforce this message. As two examples, eliminate special parking privileges, and make certain that all company desks are of the same size. If you have new programs directed toward the company's quality initiative or training programs that address critical issues, make sure you attend every session. Listen to what people have to report about what the firm is doing right and what it needs to do differently. Simply put, the point is this: don't ask anyone else to do something you are not willing to do yourself.

▶   *Keep score.* Another way to hold yourself accountable is to "keep score" by collecting data from your constituents regarding your leadership practices and your commitments to shared values. In a broader way, this is also another strategy for keeping in touch. Consider using some of the questions that Clark Smith, manager of technical publications at Fujitsu-ICL, asks his constituents: "Is my style suitable for the work we do? Do you think I am capable of leading us toward greater excellence and opportunity? Have I helped you to achieve your personal goals? Do you trust me with your training plan? Am I consistent with the values I communicate and the decisions I make?"

Maintaining credibility requires you to seek 360-degree feedback: that is, feedback from your manager, customers, vendors, peers, colleagues, associates (employees), and shareholders. Do more than just collect the data. To ensure that all parties know the feedback will be taken seriously, make it public.

Marcus Stafford, manager of human resource training for the Bank of Western Australia, regularly collects data from his constituents and finds it invaluable. On one occasion, after assuming a new managerial position, he found from the feedback that he was doing well on challenging and stretching people. But it also said that people were not always able to complete each assignment with attention to detail. "This made me realize," says Stafford, "that I was inadvertently stressing activities or quantity over quality, and so we all got together and talked about the data and what it meant." Stafford explains, "You might not like the feedback. But it is the only way you can develop yourself as a leader. And this really validates that I care about and pay attention to what others think!"

Tony Harding, human resource manager for the Australia Post (the postal service), returned from one of our leadership workshops and shared his Leadership Practices Inventory data with his team. He told us, "We had one of the best conversations ever about leadership, where the team is heading, what each and every one of us needs to be doing better, and so on. We are definitely going to do this on a regular basis."

▶   *Conduct a personal audit.* Audit your daily routines. Determine whether or not you are spending sufficient time on matters consistent with your shared values. Use these as the basis for planning your weekly schedule. Let values be your guide, not old habits or the in-basket. Assess your daily calendar. How much time are you spending modeling shared values? How do your appointments contribute to communicating and reinforcing shared values? Look at the agenda for your meetings. What topics are discussed? Are the ones related to your shared values at the top? Bob Galvin, chairman of the Executive Committee of Motorola, restructured his policy committee meetings so that quality was the first item on the agenda; he would walk out after quality issues had been discussed and before financial matters were introduced.

Audit your questions. Which ones do you usually ask in meetings, one-on-one conversations, telephone calls, and interviews? How do these help to clarify and gain commitment to shared values? Make a list of searching questions that correspond to each of the shared values. At every opportunity, ask others these questions, getting them to be more conscious about what they are doing to put values into practice.

Look at how you deal with critical incidents. How did you respond to the most recent one? To what extent did your actions teach lessons about the most important shared values? In your next interview, use your shared values as the basis for the interview questions. Whenever you start a new relationship with a supplier, begin by providing a copy of the company credo. Talk about the kind of organization you are, and explain that the supplier should know these facts if it is going to be in business with you.

Audit your internal memos. How are you using them to foster commitment to shared values? Look at your in-basket. What percentage of your in-coming mail relates to shared values? What might explain this? Audit rewards and recognitions. Who's being recognized? Do these people exemplify best the values you want reinforced? When someone gets recognized, do you clearly indicate the value (or standard) on which the reward is based?

Have your evaluation done by someone other than yourself. Make the results public. Explain what's right and what's working. Set in motion changes that will realign your actions and behaviors to serve your purpose more consistently.

▶ **Conduct an organizational audit.** Look carefully at your shared values and common purpose to determine whether your group's, along with the company's, system and structures are in alignment with them. Better yet, do this with your constituents. Start with this question: are the people most respected in your team (company) the ones who are living the values and willing to sacrifice for the common purpose? Do what it takes to make sure that this perspective holds true for your group. Be willing to confront other managers about any areas in which the words and the actions don't go together.

Our studies reveal that even in organizations with very strong cultures, the greatest challenges in maintaining people's focus and commitment have to do with ensuring that the actions and decisions of leaders are consistent with what they say and with what the institution recognizes and rewards. At Levi Strauss, the Total REM 2000 Task Force (for total reimbursement in the year 2000) is making recommendations to make certain that performance management and pay delivery systems support the company's aspirations. For example, three of these recommendations are that all employees (exempt and nonexempt) should be eligible for both annual and long-term incentives, that all of these should have a team component, and that performance evaluation should include continuous improvement and aspirational behaviors along with meeting business and strategic objectives.

▸ *Get everyone to champion values.* At Dreyer's, an ice cream producer with recent yearly revenues of $350 million, the company makes certain that all its managers can champion shared values, or what they refer to as their "grooves." For example, at every monthly managers meeting, a manager's name is randomly selected. Then it is that person's opportunity to share his or her "favorite groove war story." Those coming to the meeting are aware that through the luck of the draw they may have the opportunity to share an occurrence that relates to shared values. In fact, says CEO Gary Rogers, "even when we have our executive committee meetings, just the top seven people, we always start with groove stories. It's now sort of a habit throughout the company; it's rare that a meeting starts without a groove story."

Consider this as the sole topic of your next meeting: how is each of us modeling our values? Be the first to describe what you have done.

C H A P T E R

8

Sustaining Hope

*Really believe in your heart of hearts that your
fundamental purpose, the reason for being, is to enlarge
the lives of others. Your life will be enlarged also. And all
of the other things we have been taught to concentrate
on will take care of themselves.*

Pete Thigpen

Executive Reserves

When leaders act in ways that uplift our spirits and restore our
belief in the future, they strengthen their own personal credibility.[1] Constituents look for leaders who demonstrate an
enthusiastic and genuine belief in the capacity of others, who
strengthen people's will, who supply the means to achieve, and
who express optimism for the future. Constituents want leaders who remain passionate despite obstacles and setbacks.
In today's uncertain times, leaders with a positive, confident,
can-do approach to life and business are desperately needed.

Leaders must keep hope alive. They must strengthen our
belief that life's struggle will produce a more promising tomorrow. Such faith results from an intimate and supportive relationship, one based on mutual participation in the process of
renewal. Frederic M. Hudson, president of the Hudson Institute and founding president of the Fielding Institute (which
provide life/career planning, executive development, and or-

ganizational consultation), offers poignant personal testimony to the power of a supportive relationship in overcoming despair and restoring hope.

> In August 1943, when I was nine years old, I awakened one morning in silent terror. I was unable to move any part of my body except my eyes. My muscles seemed frozen, and my voice was silenced. Although I had gone to bed as a walking, talking, wiggling boy, I woke up the next day paralyzed with polio. Neither my legs nor my arms would respond to my desperate efforts to move, and my neck and jaw were rigid as rocks. Breathing was panicked and pain was everywhere. . . .
>
> The next thing I remember was lying on the back seat of my parents' old automobile as they drove me thirty miles from my home in upstate New York to a hospital in Syracuse. That journey was unbelievably painful. I was sicker than I had ever felt in my life, and I knew the seriousness of the journey. I felt a helplessness and fear never experienced before. . . .
>
> At the hospital, they placed me on a very hard bed (with no pillow) in a quarantined ward. I spent my waking moments staring upward at the ceiling—my only option—and feeling totally helpless. . . .
>
> A wise nurse named Susan spent lots of time with me. Quiet and caring, she visited me frequently and told me many things. Her main message went like this: "Your future, Frederic, is hidden on the ceiling, and you can find it if you look very hard. Look for what you will be doing as you grow up. It's all up there. Will you be a track star, a tennis player, a scientist? Will you be going on trips to faraway places? Will you be making model airplanes and flying kites? Will you be going to summer camps and swimming? Will you go to college and become someone special? Will you marry and have a family? Frederic, all you have to do is to study the ceiling. When you see your future it will start to happen![2]

Hudson then spent his days in the hospital searching the ceiling for his future. The first vision he remembers is of running and playing and being active. He saw himself bouncing through the woods; having friends again; laughing; climbing; going to college; being a husband, father, and doctor. Nurse Susan knew that the only part of little Frederic's body that worked were his eyes, so she projected pictures on the ceiling to aid his imagination. She also projected a checkerboard and taught him to play chess. She read to him, played music, and tutored him on his school lessons.

And then Hudson found he could wiggle his toes. Nurse Susan told him that his visions were being realized and that he was now in training. She rigged a device so he could ring a bell with his toes. Then when his legs became somewhat mobile, she rigged another contraption so he could open and close windows and doors. And on it went. And today, "I now walk, run, play tennis, and live without any noticeable deficit," says Hudson.

Nurse Susan is a role model for anyone who would wish to enliven hope in others. Look at what she did. She took charge of the situation, yet gave of herself. She struggled and worked hard to assist in Hudson's recovery. She inspired positive images to appear in his mind. She filled him with thoughts of future possibilities. She taught him to play games. When Hudson finally began to wiggle just a little, she rigged gear that enabled him to build his strength and mobility. Nurse Susan exemplified hope in action. In short, she was truly a credible leader.

The conditions in which we now live resemble in many ways Hudson's bout with polio. We have awakened to the silent terror of declining economic and social fortunes accompanied by a loss of confidence in our leaders, in our institutions, and even in ourselves. Businesses and societies seem frozen, unable to break free of worker cynicism and citizen alienation. Disaffected and disenfranchised residents have rioted and burned their own neighborhoods. Centuries-old ethnic tensions keep erupting into violence. Corporate boards are revolting, shareholders are protesting, consumers are defecting, and employees are burning out.[3] Old regimes are

enthusiasm, passion, and stamina. Her intensity fuels her and infects all around her. She says, "To me the desire to create and to have control over your own life, irrespective of the politics of the time or the social structures, was very much part of the human spirit. What I did not fully realize was that work could open the doors to my heart."[6] With the doors of her heart open, she has created a market for her natural body care products, expanded her business globally, and (most importantly to Roddick) demonstrated that a business can be successful serving customers, associates, shareholders, and communities while also preserving the environment and contributing to world peace.

But for all her success, Roddick has had her share of setbacks. When first in business together, she and her husband ran a small hotel and a restaurant. Writing about why their Littlehampton restaurant, Paddington's, didn't work out, Roddick explains, "The reason was quite simple—we had done everything wrong. It was the wrong kind of restaurant in the wrong street in the wrong town, launched at the wrong time—in the middle of the Tories' 'three-day week' crisis. We were young, we thought we knew it all and we had certainly not bothered to take any advice. We thought we could impose our will on our customers and sell gourmet food in an egg-and-chips town." But the Roddicks were not down for long: "What saved us, once again, was our willingness to recognize that we were wrong and our ability to move swiftly on to the next idea."[7]

Roddick, like Walton, has an extraordinarily strong will to succeed and an intense desire to be different. She writes:

> The principal forces which motivate a leader are an incredibly high need for personal achievement and a different vision of the world. . . . You don't really have to be charismatic, you just have to believe in what you are doing so strongly that it becomes a reality.
>
> A fundamental shortcoming in much of business today is that the leadership lacks vision and passion—the two most important ingredients to inspire and motivate.

> In The Body Shop we have both in abundance and we possess, in addition, a further secret ingredient: an extraordinary level of optimism, almost amounting to euphoria, which permeates the whole company. We are incurable optimists—and incurable optimists believe they can do anything.[8]

Retailers Roddick and Walton are oceans apart on politics but members of the same crew when it comes to the qualities just described. They see setbacks and defeats as temporary challenges that can be overcome by will and courage. They demonstrate that by defying the verdict, constantly exhibiting courage, and actively tackling the work required—all while maintaining a sense of humor—we can triumph over adversity. And we can inspire others to do the same.

Defy the Verdict

Norman Cousins, former editor of *Saturday Review* and one of the most influential magazine editors of the twentieth century, is a classic example of success in defying the verdict. In *Anatomy of an Illness*, he chronicles how he mobilized his body's healing resources and beat all the medical odds against a rare disease.[9] After a decade of work with the medical community, he then wrote about his and other researchers' quests for proof of the mind's role in healing. In *Head First: The Biology of Hope*, Cousins observes that when presented with a serious diagnosis, some cancer patients "responded with a fierce determination to overcome. They didn't deny the diagnosis. They denied the verdict that is usually associated with it. Was it any coincidence that a substantial number of these patients lived significantly longer than had been predicted by their oncologists?"[10]

Credible leaders behave as the people in Cousins's study. They acknowledge reality but do not dwell on the threat. Instead, they see change as an opportunity for renaissance and learning; they move quickly to mobilize personal and group resources. They believe they can influence the outcome and can turn the tide of events to their advantage. They do not become bitter or alienated; instead, they become engaged and committed. They do not dissolve into despair but resolve to act quickly and zestfully.[11]

Credible leaders are proactive. They do not wait to be told what to do. They believe that it is possible to exert internal control, rather than being controlled externally by others or events. They recognize that they cannot control all of what goes on in life, but they are determined to be in charge of the quality of their own lives. Maybe the company has no overarching vision or plan; for credible leaders, even this barrier is not an insurmountable roadblock. Leaders search for their own chances to make something happen; they also instill this attitude in constituents, creating ways that they can take charge of at least their own responsibilities.

It would be foolish, of course, for us to ignore the fact that we have life-threatening diseases or that our businesses are failing or that our families are troubled. It would be absurd to deny changes in our bodies, organizations, or families. Yet we can be well-informed and deeply understand the peril we face without accepting a prognosis that we are doomed. Reality may mean that we have lost a loved one or that we are disabled; it does not have to mean that we have been sentenced to a life of misery. Though the world may be plagued by poverty, pollution, unemployment, riots, and infectious disease, it does not have to mean that civilized society is coming to an end. The restaurant may not be working, the warehouses may have been destroyed, or restructuring may have cost us our job; however, our companies will not necessarily go bankrupt or our business careers be over.

This is not just a matter of "where there's a will there's a way." This old folk wisdom is only half correct, says psychologist and researcher, Charles R. Snyder. Hope, he has found, "means believing you have both the will and the way to accomplish your goals, whatever they may be."[12] It takes both a will and a way to achieve what Walton and Roddick have. It takes both to thrive in a volatile and dynamic business environment.

Imagine that you have set a goal to develop a pathbreaking new product. For you to hope to be successful, you will need both the boundless energy to accomplish this monumental feat and the business plan and competencies to implement the strategy. Entrepreneurial success goes to the person with the energy and the strategic initiative. Whether it's starting a business, turning around a losing operation, or climbing Mt. Everest, people must possess both the energy for the quest and the means to achieve success.

Before you set out on your leadership journey, then, develop a strategy, and make sure you have the energy to travel the distance. Disappointment awaits those who set out without a map and without the necessary fuel.

Have Courage

Without courage, there can be no hope. People are inspired by leaders who take initiative and who risk personal safety for the sake of a cause. Only those leaders who act boldly in times of crisis and change are willingly followed.

Competing in the new global economy, restoring nations to economic and social health, and bringing peace to a fractious world are chores for the lion-hearted. Great courage, strength of character, and commitment are required. This is not a time for the timid. Leaders must summon their will if they are to mobilize the personal and organizational resources to triumph against the odds. And they must have the boldness to communicate reality honestly to their constituents.

The philosopher Peter Koestenbaum writes, "A courageous leader always claims the power to initiate, act, and risk, for courage means to act with sustained initiative."[13] He tells us that the critical success factor in being courageous is our human freedom: "Claiming your freedom is the ultimate secret for mastering your life. To discover your freedom inside your heart is an exuberant experience of both exhilaration and hope, and that freedom can never be extinguished. Heroes have exercised this freedom at the risk of life itself. True love means to surrender that freedom to another. The greatest gift you can ever give is the surrender of your freedom. That is the ultimate act of love—toward a spouse, a child, a boss, a friend, a nation, a leader, a cause, an ideal, or God."[14]

Koestenbaum tells us that courageous acts are the ultimate acts of love. We are reminded of our research, which reveals that the most admired leaders (people such as King, Gandhi, and Mother Teresa) have given others their freedom. People revere those who have the courage to give up their own liberty so that others can be free.

We often talk about the courage of our convictions, meaning that we are willing to stand up for what we believe. But perhaps the courage of conviction can be better understood as the willingness to risk surrendering our freedom for our beliefs. It would seem that the truest measure of commitment to common vision and values is the amount of freedom we are willing to risk.

Balance Hope and Work

Surrendering freedom is relative, of course. We don't have to risk what King and Gandhi did to show the courage of conviction. Best-selling author and social activist Rita Mae Brown has certainly had her beliefs severely tested. Her good grades got her a scholarship to the University of Florida, but her civil rights activism got her thrown out. Her diligence earned her a doctorate from the Institute for Policy Studies in Washington, D.C., but her questioning attitude got her in trouble. Both the F.B.I. and the C.I.A. kept a file on her in the seventies.

It is no wonder that Rita Mae Brown says, "People are like tea bags; you never know how strong they'll be until they're in hot water. In times of trouble, you not only discover what you truly believe but whether or not you can act on your beliefs."[15] Brown helps us to connect courage and hope with action, everyday actions. She says, "I believe you never hope more than you work. In action, this means I work ten to sixteen hours a day, usually seven days a week. Since I love my work, which is writing, this is a joy. I believe you are your work. Don't trade the very stuff of your life, time, for nothing more than dollars. That's a rotten bargain."[16]

Whatever you hope for—freedom, peace, justice, happiness, quality, progress, clean air, technical superiority, or business success — you have to work for it. And the more hope you have, the more work you put in to get what you want. That's how courage and action are connected. That's what it means to surrender your freedom.

If you hope more than you work, you (and your constituents) are likely to be very disappointed. And your credibility is likely to suffer. But what about balance? Don't good leaders have balance in their lives? Certainly. And balance is relative: we each define it for ourselves. None of us can determine if another's life is out of balance without knowing the weights and measures in that person's life. If a leader, for example, loads up one side of the scale with a ton of hope, the only way his or her life will be in balance is to load the other with a ton of work. Anything less would surely bring disappointment. However, if a leader has only an ounce of hope and loads the scale with a ton of work, the scale is out of balance. The secret seems to be not to overload the scale on either end. When hope and work, challenge and skill, are in equilibrium, that's when you experience optimal performance.[17]

People with high hope are not blind to the realities of the present. If something isn't working or if the current methods aren't effective, they don't ignore it, cross their fingers, or simply redouble their efforts. They assess the situation and find new ways to reach the goals. And if they begin to recede rather than appear closer, people with hope reset them.[18]

Changing the strategy or aiming for another target is not defeatism. In fact, if a leader persists in a strategy that doesn't work or stubbornly pursues one that is blocked, constituents can become frustrated and depressed, leading them to feel defeated rather than victorious. It is better to find a new path or decide on a different destination. Then once that end is reached, set a new, more challenging objective. Credibility is not always strengthened by continuing to do what you said you would do if that way is not working. Admitting that you are wrong and finding a better course of action is a far more courageous and credible path to take.

Enjoy Yourself

Sometimes the best answer is laughter. Credible leaders have a sense of humor; they are able to laugh at themselves and their troubles. Being able to laugh even in the most stressful of times helps people thrive.[19] Norman Cousins attributed his recovery to the funny movies he watched for hours each day. He believed that laughter released the body's natural healing powers, and science is proving him right. Credible leaders find the comic in the tragic. They make it okay to have some fun even when times are tough. They know that laughing—even when you are low—uplifts the spirits. Humorless people who take things too seriously are much more likely to dig themselves deeper into the hole of despair. And to bury us all.

AROUSING POSITIVE THOUGHTS AND IMAGES

To keep hope alive, leaders must inspire constituents to see positive images of the future.[20] As athletes have known for some time, stored mental pictures influence our performance. Unless we can see ourselves as being successful, it is very difficult to produce the behavior that leads to success. Experiment after experiment shows that positive images make groups more effective, relieve symptoms of illness, and enhance achievement in school and the military.[21] We are now beginning to see these discoveries applied to business organizations.

Dutch sociologist Fred Polak has observed, *"The rise and fall of images of the future precedes or accompanies the rise and fall of cultures.* As long as a society's image is confident and flourishing, the flower of culture is in full bloom. Once the image begins to decay and lose its vitality, however, the culture does not long survive."[22] Given the often negative portrayal of businesses in the media and the increasing cynicism of the work force, one might legitimately wonder what the future holds. If what Polak says is true, as individuals and as leaders, we had better begin to paint more affirmative images for ourselves and our constituents.

Reflect Optimism

Because of their expectation that things will work out for the best, optimists look at the future and see attractive possibilities. These motivate optimists to be proactive and to take actions that improve their work performance and their physical and mental health. In contrast, pessimists envision negative scenarios and see probabilities of failure.[23]

The habitual ways that optimists and pessimists explain why events happen differ dramatically. Martin Seligman and colleagues have found that pessimists see failed events as permanent, universal, and personal defeats. They blame themselves for the bad things that happen, and they ascribe the good things to conditions not under their control. Optimists, by contrast, tend to see defeats as temporary and having specific, not universal, causes. They blame circumstances for the bad things that happen. And when good outcomes occur, optimists believe that these things always happen to them, that positive events enhance everything they do, and that good things come from their actions and not the circumstances.

Optimism is essential to strengthening credibility. Leaders with their eyes on an ideal and strong image of tomorrow reflect optimistic outlooks. In expressing their convictions that it will work out for the best and be better than the past, optimists instill confidence in others. Constituents begin to adopt a similar attitude. When they look to the future, they also see the possibilities of success.

Based on Seligman's research, leaders who want to inspire optimism would employ a number of distinct strategies. When a failure or setback occurs, they do not blame themselves or the people working on the project. Instead, they find situational circumstances that contributed to the failure and convey a belief that the situation is likely to be temporary, not permanent. They stress that the failure or setback means a problem only in this one instance and not in everything. When success occurs and milestones are reached, leaders who want to breed optimism attribute success to the individuals in the group. They convey a belief that many more victories are at hand and predict that good fortune will be with them for a long time.

None of this is to suggest that leaders should avoid getting people to accept personal responsibility. Optimism and personal responsibility are not mutually exclusive. People can either accept responsibility for a problem and its consequences with an optimistic attitude that will enable them to persist in solving it, or can view it with a pessimistic attitude that defeats them before they start. Which person would you rather have on your team? Which leader would you rather be?

Although the ledger shows we profit most from optimists, the ones who believe we can do anything may lead us right into bankruptcy. So don't write off the pessimists. We need one or two around to keep us honest, to keep us on our toes, to hold out the caution flag, and to get us to look at ourselves more deeply. Pessimists more accurately judge the amount of control they have over a situation, and they are more accurate in judging their own skills.[24] Because of this they are likely to be the ones to question whether a strategy has worked or will work.

Seligman advises, "At the head of the corporation must be a CEO, sage enough and flexible enough to balance the optimistic vision of the planners against the Jeremiads" of the bureaucrats.[25] Credible leaders are hopeful about the future — and yielding enough to heed words of caution. Seligman refers to such people as flexible optimists.

Struggle to Inspire

Optimism, like hope, does not mean simply waiting for good things to happen; it means acting in ways that create positive futures. But such futures do not always come easily. Sometimes, if not always, struggles and suffering are necessary to achieve greatness. As in athletics, success in business is governed by the rule of "no pain, no gain." Even the hardiest of world-class competitors pull muscles, strain ligaments, tear tendons, and break bones. No one — athlete, business leader, or government leader — ever hopes for injury, but each experiences it. And each has to work through the pain. Leaders who are not willing to suffer personally the pain and strain of high-level competition will find that their credibility quickly diminishes.

For leaders and constituents alike, suffering breeds increased passion for the goal or cause. The myth is that passion comes from joy. It does not. The word *passion* has its roots in the Greek and Latin words for suffering. The most passionate people are those who have suffered the most. They have risked their independence, their fortunes, their health, and sometimes their lives for people and a purpose beyond themselves. Passion earned from suffering is inspiring.

Leaders who are truly inspirational, who demonstrate courage and passion, are the first to suffer. They are the first to step out into the unknown, to confront self-doubt, to suffer defeat and disappointment, and return to triumph. A leader who risks embarrassment and ruin and yet succeeds in maintaining the strength of conviction gives others courage. We are uplifted by those who show us that we will survive. Someone who sits by in comfort while ordering others to suffer is no leader.

When we talk about suffering, we do not mean that leaders have to wear sackcloths and hair shirts. We are not suggesting that they should cut their pay to zero and give up the positions they have legitimately earned through hard work, experience, and education. We do mean, however, that leaders, especially the most senior ones, must participate in the pain like every other member of the organization. Sharing the pain is just as necessary as sharing the gain.

Jim Autry gives testimony to this idea: "I believe that the leader has a great ability to turn people's cynicism into hope, just in the way he or she does the leading." Like many others, Autry's company, Meredith, had to find some ways to cut the cost of operations in the last few years. "Against the grain of what everybody else seemed to be doing out there in American business," Autry took the problem to the employees and got them involved. He reassured them there would be no layoffs but asked them what they thought about freezing salaries for one year. He asked them to figure out ways to cut costs, while constantly looking to the brighter future that would result from their positive collective action.

When the CEO of Meredith had earlier told Autry that the company was thinking about a salary freeze, Autry had replied, "Go ahead as long as you and the chairman of the board and everybody else freeze." They did, and that move saved the company a lot of money. Plus, as Autry told us, there was not "one complaint, no cynicism that the CEO or the chairman would be excluded. We said right up front, 'We're all going to skip a year, and nobody's going to get any special bonuses or any of that.' Because of that honesty and forthrightness and because of getting people involved in the process of cutting costs . . . we had a success. . . . I think I was able to not only overcome, but prevent, a lot of cynicism at a time that I saw my competitors with work forces of people just falling in despair with their cynicism and mistrust of the company."

When leaders share in the pain, as they did at Meredith, they develop compassion for others who are suffering. *Compassion* means "to suffer together." Only those who have suffered with their constituents can genuinely uplift others. Only those who have felt the pain of loss and yearning for fulfillment can truly inspire. It may be that one of the reasons for increased cynicism over the last several years is the perception that those in leadership positions have not suffered along with their constituents, that they are unwilling to risk what they have gained for the sake of the cause, that they care only for themselves. It is ironic that those in power most risk losing everything when they are least willing to give up just a little.

GIVING LOVE AND ENCOURAGEMENT

Anita Roddick has said she believes "all business practices would improve immeasurably if guided by more 'feminine' principles—qualities like love and care and intuition."[26] Patrick Townsend, a retired Marine Corps major, would agree. Now a highly respected quality consultant and author of two books on quality, Townsend wrote about leadership while in the corps and made these observations:

> Perhaps the most obvious thing that leadership and love have in common is the act of caring about the welfare of others—an act that is central to both. One's love for another implies caring for the well-being, physical and mental, of the other. . . . A person who would call himself [or herself] a leader of Marines must be capable of love, of allowing themselves to be loved, and of understanding the awesome responsibilities incurred when one seeks and accepts the love of others. . . . The technical knowledge, the courage, the personal integrity so often discussed are definitely necessary. Love though is what makes it work; it is what makes the followers willingly accept the technical knowledge and treat the courage and personal integrity as something to emulate rather than just applaud.[27]

Autry discusses a similar connection between love and leadership in his book *Love and Profit: The Art of Caring Leadership*.[28] Quite serendipitously, we interviewed Autry on Valentine's Day and asked him about the connection between the two words *love* and *profit*, words we don't often speak in the same breath or see on the same page.

Autry replied, "Creating a caring workplace—a place in which people have friendships and deep personal connections and can grow personally and emotionally, psychologically and spiritually, as well as financially and professionally—is an important aspect of creating profit." As part of that process, Autry recommends, "If you find that you're not liking what you're doing, you should fall in love with it. . . . I started really liking to be a manager, but . . . it was only after developing and evolving a way of doing things in a management style that came to be the love and profit style, the community-building style, that I could see extraordinary fruits." Indeed, these were impressive: in his eleven years as president, the Magazine Group grew from four to sixteen magazines and from $160 million to $500 million in revenue.

The fruitful leadership approaches of Roddick, Townsend, and Autry fit very neatly with what Yale professor Robert J. Sternberg, one of the foremost researchers in the fields of human intelligence and love, and colleague Susan Grajek have found to be the essential aspects of loving relationships. Sternberg and Grajek report that the general factor of love "seems well identified as one of interpersonal communication, sharing and support. Its aspects include especially (a) deep understanding of the other, (b) sharing of ideas and information, (c) sharing of deeply personal ideas and feelings, (d) receipt and provision of emotional support to the other, (e) personal growth through the relationship and helping the other in his or her personal growth, (f) giving help to the other, (g) making the other feel needed and needing the other, and (h) the giving and receiving of affection in the relationship."[29]

Although not all of these elements may be appropriate to every aspect of business, it is striking how many are integral to the six disciplines of credibility. We know from our research that when people believe that another person understands them, they give that person more credibility. Listening to the ideas of another and sharing personal information also increase credibility. Developing others, helping others, increasing others' self-esteem, and expressing genuine concern are all behaviors of credible leaders. Could it be that love is the ultimate act of earning credibility?

Encourage Passion — and Profit

When we talk about what we love to do, gain a deeper understanding of others, share more intimately, and truly enjoy the interaction, our energy and passion are contagious. By caring, loving, and showing compassion, we can release a spirit in people that is unequaled. This is something that we can do in business every day without sentimentality or overbearing flattery. After all, we're not talking about romance here, we're talking about love and profit.

How this process works became crystal clear to us in an executive session of Square D Company's Vision College, a two-day seminar on the company's vision and values. Over a two-year period, this seminar was attended by all of Square D's twenty thousand employees, in groups of twenty-five. During one memorable experience, seminar leader Gail Wilson, actress, acting teacher, and executive educator, asked us to play "passion-compassion."

Here's how it works. People get into pairs. One person chooses to be the presenter and selects a topic about which he or she feels passionately. The other member of the team plays the compassionate role, encouraging expressiveness, listening actively, showing interest or concern, and drawing forth enthusiasm.

Wilson demonstrated the compassionate role for us. A soft-spoken senior executive who had difficulty expressing himself with animation volunteered to be her passionate partner. As the executive spoke about something he loved to do, Wilson would laugh, touch, slap her thighs, say "Uh huh" or "Tell me more about that," open her eyes widely, or gesture encouragingly. Like a dancer, she moved with her partner as he gradually became more animated, energetic, expressive, and uplifting. He slashed the air with his hands, rose up on his toes, spoke with varying intonations and inflections, bounced up and down, and smiled with joy.

In the span of a minute, through her expressiveness and her empathy, Wilson had enabled another human being to display more intensely his feelings about something he loved. Her compassion—and, yes, her love—helped him to demonstrate his enthusiasm. In those brief moments, we saw how readily compassion can benefit both sides of a relationship in all aspects of our lives.

Seek and Give Support

Just having one supportive, stable relationship is an important condition for transcending adversity.[30] Numerous research findings conclude that having friends enables people to live longer and happier lives.[31] Evidence is also mounting that social support is important to the long-term survival of cancer and heart-attack patients. It is growing increasingly clear that social connection and intimacy are necessary conditions for a joyful life at home and at work.

Frederic Hudson, whose story opened this chapter, teaches us another side of hope in action: being open to receiving help and taking charge of one's life. Even the nurse Susans of the world cannot help someone unwilling to accept the gift of support and someone unwilling to act. People who sustain their own hope over time make friends, seek support, and listen to advice. They form caring relationships, and they enjoy others' company. They are thoroughly connected to sources of support and have an extensive network of friends and supporters they can call on to extend a helping hand in times of need.

Credible leaders recognize that their sources of support are vital to them. They also know that it is essential to extend their support to others. Steve Shepstone, a partner in Peckham Shepstone & Associates, an outdoor education company in the United Kingdom, told us about an incident involving one of his most admired leaders, an incident that clearly affected him. During a very competitive rugby match, Steve's physical education teacher and rugby coach abruptly stopped the game, turned to the crowd in the stands, and shouted loudly that the tackle Shepstone had just made was the best he had ever seen. Shepstone was five feet six inches tall at the time. His opponent was six feet six inches.

That best-ever tackle occurred over twenty-five years ago, but Shepstone recalls it as if it were today. He reports that when he was with this admired leader, he felt "proud, confident and wanting to do it again." Imagine wanting to go out again and tackle someone a foot taller than you. The leader's recognition made that possible. Leaders we admire support us and recognize our efforts to tackle big problems. And when they do, we want to tackle even bigger ones.

Whether a spontaneous accolade like this or in a more formal ceremony, recognition does much more than make people feel good. It motivates the person singled out and can educate others (in Shepstone's case, the other players). In a larger sense, it can help in aligning people's actions with shared values. People can then clearly see that effort has made a difference and can make a difference in the future.

FOR HEALTHY LIVES AND SUPERIOR PERFORMANCE: MAKING HOPE A PRIORITY

"Keep hope alive" is more than a political slogan. Hope is essential to achieving the highest levels of performance. People with high hope have a greater number of goals across various arenas of life, select more difficult goals, and see their goals in a more challenging and positive manner than people with low hope.[32]

Keeping hope alive is also essential to an active and healthy life. In some of the most dramatic studies of hope, a group of researchers examined depression and psychosocial impairment among men and women with traumatically acquired spinal cord injuries. They found that patients who exhibited more hope had less depression, greater mobility (despite similar injuries), and more social contacts. In short, "Those with high hope were more adaptive in all realms, regardless of how long they had been injured, whether just a month or 40 years."[33]

Similar links have been made between optimism, a sibling of hope, and health. In a longitudinal study of healthy and successful members of the Harvard classes of 1942 through 1944, researchers examined this link. They conclude that "optimism early in life is associated with good health later in life."[34] Other research reveals that pessimistic college students visited the doctor nearly three times as often as their optimistic peers, and the pessimists were ill more than twice the number of days. Optimists live longer following heart attacks and after the diagnosis of cancer (though the illness itself is the ultimate determinant of the survival rate).[35] Now it may just be that pessimists have habits that are bad for their health. But it could also be that optimism and pessimism trigger some yet unknown biochemical reaction. Whatever the cause, optimism and hope are better medicines than pessimism and despair.

Unfortunately, despite the overwhelming evidence that hope spurs on achievement, the majority of people are not full of high hopes. In one study of more than seven thousand women and men from ages eighteen to seventy, Snyder found that only about 40 percent of people had both the will and the way—the two basic ingredients of hope—to accomplish their goals. About 20 percent believed they could find the means to attain their goals but did not have the will. Another 20 percent said they had the energy to pursue their goals but could not think of ways to achieve them. The rest (another 20 percent) "had neither the will nor the way."[36] This data on hope has some disturbing parallels to findings on cynicism among the work force that we discussed in Chapter Two.

These results point to a potentially serious problem for organizational leaders. If only 40 percent of working-age adults have the energy and the knowledge to achieve their goals, then we do not have even half the hope we need to achieve optimal organizational performance. Some 60 percent of our eligible and existing workers may lack the aspirations, energy, or methods to get extraordinary things done in organizations.

In view of this challenge, it would seem logical to add hope to the human resource development curriculum. But when was the last time you saw a course on leadership by hope offered along with a course on management by objectives? Would it be worth it? Can a pessimist become an optimist, a hopeless person a hopeful one? Are these permanent conditions, or can people change? Can leaders increase hope and optimism? Snyder, Seligman, and colleagues have found that they can indeed be developed. Using videotaped interviews and other learning methods, other researchers have been able to nurture hope in entering college freshmen and the adoption of positive health habits in women.[37] They have been successful in improving performance in teaching, in learning, in sales, in nursing, in management, and in other domains of work and life.[38]

To enliven team spirit, breed optimism, sustain hope, foster resilience, and renew faith and confidence, leaders must learn to look to the bright side. As leaders, we must take charge of the situation and enable others to gain a sense of control over their own lives. We must demonstrate the flexibility to try a new course when the traditional approaches point to a dead end. We must talk positively about the future and selflessly share the success of achieving excellence. We must continuously seek and offer the support necessary to withstand the hardships of the struggle, and we must make the personal sacrifices needed to thrive.

Hope is an attitude in action. It enables people to mobilize their healing and their achieving powers. It helps them to transcend the difficulties of today and envision the potentialities of tomorrow. Hope enables people to find the will and the way to aspire to greatness. Hope is testimony to the power of the human spirit.

SUSTAINING HOPE:
FIRST STEPS/NEXT STEPS

We know the realities of today's economy — social uneasiness, political unrest, governmental instability around the globe — and the gloomy forecasts for the days ahead. Sustaining hope through such times will be a major task, even for natural optimists. What steps can we take to rise to the challenge and to help those we lead to rise and hope, as well?

▸ **Exercise.** If you're feeling depressed, don't sit around moaning; you'll only get further depressed. Instead, exorcise the blues with some physical exercise. Choose an activity you like, and put some energy behind it.

Optimistic and resilient people have healthier life-styles.

They eat better, exercise more, and don't abuse their bodies. If you want a group of constituents who believe in the future, be proactive about promoting exercise and other good health habits. As one step, take a five-minute "energy" break during your meetings and training programs. Participants and faculty in the summer Executive Programmes at Queen's University in Kingston, Ontario, exercise at their places for a few minutes each morning and afternoon. The leaders make it fun. We have taken imaginary exercise trips across Canada and done aerobics to 1950s pop music. Why not try this at your weekly meetings?

▶   *Write your vision of the future.* In Chapter One, we reported that constituents expect their leaders to be forward-looking. Leaders have a sense of direction and a positive ideal image of tomorrow's common good. Leaders also engage in dialogue with others about what others see across the horizon of time, seeking a common vision that all can share. Compelling visions distinguish credible leaders from other credible individuals.

Positive and unique mental images of the future are also necessary for sustaining hope. Being hopeful means finding the future in the cracks in the ceiling, as Frederic Hudson did. It means staring out into the unknown and imagining the possibilities. It means visualizing the future in detail. It means being creative about options. To increase your credibility, share your vision with your constituents.

In our book, *The Leadership Challenge,* we devoted two chapters to inspiring a shared vision and offered a dozen exercises to get you started in envisioning the future and enlisting others.[39] Here's one from that list that you might want to try again or for the first time.

Ask yourself this question: "Am I in this job to do something, or am I in this job for something to do?" Your answer will most likely be "to do something." That being the case, take out a piece of paper, and at the top write, "What I want to accomplish." Now make a list of all the things that you want to achieve during your tenure in that job. Then consider each entry, and ask yourself, "Why do I want this?" Keep on asking why at least five times. By doing this exercise, you are likely to discover a few higher-order, long-term values that are idealized ends for which you strive.

▶   **Set goals and make a plan.** Hopeful and optimistic people have more than positive images of the future; they have goals and plans for how they will achieve them. Take your vision statement, break it down into projects, set goals for each, and make a plan to achieve them.

The best goals are SMART: Specific, Measurable, Attainable, Results-oriented, and Time-bounded. Use these criteria when making your plans. What exact outcomes will you accomplish? How will you know when you reach them? How will you measure your success? How will you know if the objectives are within your and the group's reach? By when will you have accomplished them?

Take another tip from the optimists, and plan small wins.[40] As discussed earlier, awesome challenges and wrenching changes can overwhelm people. Major social and economic problems can seem impossible to solve. Leaders know that the most effective change strategies are processes of accumulating little incremental victories — even when the ultimate goal is a complete overhaul of the system. This ultimate objective should be a stretch. But as you plan for it, set smaller incremental objectives that are easily achievable. To sustain hope, divide tasks up, reduce them to their bare essentials, make things manageable in brief time periods, experiment continuously, and move with the natural innovation adoption cycle.

And if you find that you are not meeting your plan, don't frustrate yourself and your group. Be flexible and change the plan or reset your targets.

▶   **Choose flexible optimism.** As Seligman points out, the better leaders are flexible optimists. Credible leaders pay attention to both optimists and pessimists and choose optimism appropriately. Seligman offers these guidelines:

- If you are in an achievement situation (getting a promotion, selling a product, writing a difficult report, winning a game), use optimism.
- If you are concerned about how you will feel (fighting off depression, keeping up morale), use optimism.
- If the situation is apt to be protracted and your physical health is an issue, use optimism.
- If you want to lead, if you want to inspire others, if you want people to vote for you, use optimism.
- If your goal is to counsel others whose future is dim, do not use optimism initially.
- If you want to appear sympathetic to the troubles of others, do not begin with optimism; although using it later, once confidence and empathy are established, may help.
- If your goal is to plan for a risky and uncertain future, do not use optimism.[41]

We are not suggesting, of course, that you should choose pessimism in any of these circumstances. The point is to temper your approach from unalloyed optimism.

▶ *Suffer first.* If you are planning a change that will cause hardship to others, think about what you can do to share visibly in those hardships or what you might do to deny some of the privileges of rank. Be the first to accept some hardship yourself, as the executives at Meredith Corporation did. Your example will show others that you are participating with them in sharing the pain. Your willingness to participate demonstrates your passion for the cause and inspires others. Such actions create a stronger sense of community between leaders and constituents and breed more confidence in the leader.

▶ *Nurture optimism and passion.* Emotions are contagious — literally. Moods are social viruses, and you can catch a bad one as easily as a bad cold. You can also catch a good mood.[42] So make a conscious effort to avoid the naysayers and to seek out the "can-doers."

Go to a comedy club. Or try watching a funny movie or television program regularly. As banal as they are, shows like *America's Funniest Home Videos* will make you laugh. And laughter is very good medicine. A good belly laugh improves blood circulation, increases oxygen in the blood, and just plain makes you feel good.

Try playing Gail Wilson's passion-compassion game. Find some partners, and ask them one at a time to talk about something they just love. Encourage them to be as expressive as possible. Mimic their gestures, draw them out, laugh with them. Everyone will feel better. Try this as a way to start a meeting. Instead of the usual "okay, let's get down to business" opening, begin with five minutes of fun. We bet you'll enjoy the meeting more, and you are much more likely to achieve good results.

▶ *Go visiting.* We have learned that support generates hope. We have also learned that getting to know other people adds to their trust in us. By increasing human interaction, we increase optimism and credibility. Make a commitment to start your day by chatting with your constituents. Stop by your colleagues' offices or cubicles, and ask them how they are doing. Inquire about what they did last night, what good news they might have to share, or what problems you might be able to help them with. With each person, find out something you didn't know before. Be frank about your own self, and let others know about the things that bring joy to your life.

Let's say you have fifty constituents you ought to see each week. That's ten each work day. At five minutes each, that's just under one hour each day. If strengthening credibility is the goal, there is no more productive way to spend that hour than talking one on one. Assuming, of course, you do it with good cheer. If you wake up on the wrong side of the bed and feel grumpy, you're likely to make others feel the same way. So turn on a funny tape, and get yourself in a good mood before you go talk to people.

▸ ***Dispute your negative beliefs.*** Seligman suggests that to become more optimistic, you have to learn to dispute your negative explanations of the bad things that happen to you. He calls this technique the ABCDE model (Adversity, Belief, Consequences, Disputation, and Energization). Seligman explains, "When we encounter adversity, we react by thinking about it. Our thoughts rapidly congeal into beliefs. These beliefs may become so habitual we don't even stop and focus on them. And they don't just sit there idly; they have consequences."[43] If, when you encounter adversity, you tend to explain it in the form of personal, permanent, and pervasive factors, you are likely to give up and become paralyzed. If, however, you view adversity as a temporary hurdle, you become energized.

How do you get from the consequences of your beliefs to energy? The first step in becoming more optimistic is to be reflective: record specific adversities, your beliefs about them, and the consequences of your beliefs. Identify those adverse circumstances that you explain with negative beliefs. Now dispute them. Find an optimistic explanation for adversity, one that will make you hopeful about the future and cause you to feel less overwhelmed, more relaxed, and better about yourself. Try discrediting your own negative beliefs. Then try the same technique with your group. Look for explanations that will evoke positive energy in the group and spur it on to higher levels of achievement.

▸ ***Reclarify your values.*** A consistent theme we have presented is that earning credibility begins with the clarification of personal values. This process also contributes to the ability to bounce back after a failure. Values are a gyroscopic force, providing a stable directional reference even in stormy seas. Credible leaders clarify their own values, help others clarify theirs, and affirm shared values.

We prescribed values clarification in Chapter Three as the first step in strengthening credibility. We also recommend it as a final step in the process. If you've already written your leadership credo, do it again. And again. Make sure that the principles that you believe should guide your organization are clear to you and to others. Try another exercise we listed in Chapter Three. If you've tried them all, then invent a new one of your own. Take every possible measure to clarify your values.

9

The Struggle to Be Human

Credibility is not simply something I decided to have.
It is something that I struggle for.
I struggle for the consistency—
in my managerial life and throughout my life.
Kirk O. Hanson
The Business Enterprise Trust

Uncertainty is on the rise. Once unquestioned, many organizational purposes, now in flux, seem ill-defined and inconsistent. More and more people are asking, Where are we headed? What's our vision for the future? In the new global marketplace, old processes do not work anymore, so organizations purge the old and wasteful ones, experimenting with bold and more intelligent systems. Trial and error becomes the norm, even when the goal is total quality. Constituent diversity multiplies, barriers to collaboration tumble, and functional and departmental boundaries become less well defined. Contemporary organizations cannot be depicted by those inflexible boxes on the old organization charts—if indeed organizations ever fit that model.[1]

How should we restructure our organizations? Which values should guide organizational decision making? There is no consensus; we face uncertainty. We don't know what the impact of the multicultural work force will be upon our organizations and communities. We don't know precisely what skills we'll need for the twenty-first century, and we have no clear educational policies to help develop them. We don't know what levers to pull to fix our domestic and global economies. We don't know the true impact of global interdependence upon the nature of our organizations.[2]

These conditions make it imperative that leaders increase their credibility with their constituents. They also make it extraordinarily difficult to do so. Credibility is earned, we have said repeatedly, when we do what we say we will do. But if things won't hold still long enough for us to be consistent in word and deed — or even appear to be consistent — how can we be seen as trustworthy? If we don't know what variables will influence the outcome, how can we be seen as competent? If we have to keep experimenting with new approaches, how can we be seen as enthusiastically committed to our beliefs?

We wish we had an easy answer. We don't. We suggest that you be very skeptical of anyone who claims to. We do know for certain that credibility is the foundation of leadership. Act in ways that increase people's beliefs that you are honest, competent, and inspiring, and people will be much more likely to want to follow your direction. In the preceding chapters, we have presented six disciplines that our research suggests will help you do that. But there are no guarantees. In fact, now that you have read this far we want to offer you a warning: you can perfectly execute everything we have prescribed and still get fired.

Organizational life is full of struggles and tensions. These may stretch every one of us to our limits, and we may not be quite sure if we are up to it. Not only that, the realization is setting in that this uncertainty will probably continue for the rest of our careers. We are not talking about recession. We are experiencing a fundamental restructuring of the economy and of society. There are constant tightenings and loosenings, pushings and pullings. Companies are likely to seem more like organized anarchies than like the bureaucracies that typified the public and private sector in previous decades.

Leaders feel these tensions acutely because of their responsibilities to set the example and inspire others to work collaboratively toward a shared vision of the future. Leaders who are the most in touch with their constituents—and therefore likely to be the most credible—experience the pain most intensely. We acknowledge these tensions; further, we suggest that leaders would do well to learn to love the struggles. Without tension, there is no energy, without energy there is no movement, and without movement there is no progress. And making forward progress is the measure of leadership. So let us wrestle with some of the tensions and dilemmas that leaders experience as they stretch to strengthen credibility.

THE TENSION BETWEEN FREEDOM AND CONSTRAINT

Organizational consultant Neale Clapp once told us that he believed the fundamental tension for people in organizations was that between freedom and constraint. When do we delegate, and when do we decide? When do we accept another's authority, and when do we rebel against it? When do we empower others, and when do we use position power? When do we set limits, and when do we break the rules? When do we listen, and when do we tell?

To say that leaders should always increase freedoms and relax all constraints is intellectually dishonest and totally unrealistic. To say that constituents should always accept the constraints and never challenge the status quo is equally dishonest and unrealistic. We can count on people to strive to be free. We can also count on organizations to exert constraints. Part of a leader's job is to engage people in grappling with the tension between freedom and constraint.

We see this wrestling in experiments with flex-time, telecommuting, in-company day care, parental leave, quality programs, and self-directed work teams. We see it in the empower-ment movement, which is essentially a dialogue about freedom and constraint. More freedom is becoming the norm. But it would be foolish and irresponsible to expect organiza-tions to abandon all constraints. Institutions must have limits; the question is not whether these exist, but how many, how much, and of what type.

Strengthening Credibility

What does the tension between freedom and constraint have to do with strengthening credibility? In Chapter Two, we said that leaders demonstrate their commitment to a consistent set of expectations by clarifying meaning, unifying constituents, and intensifying actions. This process, repeatedly followed, earns and sustains credibility over time.

As you begin to engage actively in the process of clarify-ing, unifying, and intensifying shared meanings and actions, be aware that you are tugging at an uneasy tension between liberty and limits. The credibility process implies more choice than most, yet it does result in restrictions. It still draws a line in the sand. In tandem with the credibility-strengthening pro-cess, then, you are trying to determine what autonomies and what controls are collectively needed in order to create your ideal organization. Be clear about the fact that people will have choices, but be equally clear that these have limits. They are constrained by the owners, the shareholders, the customers, the economic system, the idiosyncrasies of the founders, the executives in power, the people in the room at the time, and a host of other unseen forces.

It is the responsibility of the leaders to make sure that everyone has the opportunity to express his or her opinion and to get a fair hearing. Leaders must provide the forum for discussion, debate, and reconciliation. Don't ram credos through just for the sake of expediency.

Values discussions should be intense. We cannot imagine talking in hushed tones about something as important as the principles by which we are expected to live for most of our waking hours. If there isn't energy and passion in the discussion, then you should be skeptical about what is being said. Of course, not everyone has to pound the table, but it does mean that you should all be able to feel the emotion when anyone in your group speaks about what they believe.

But organizational leaders should not pretend that listening is the same thing as agreeing. They should not make it seem that a constituent group will get everything it wants or that people will be allowed to "do their own thing." They should also not pretend the process goes on forever and that every time a new person joins the organization they will go through the consensus-building process all over again. Timetables must be set, decisions must be made, and people must get on with it. There comes a time when the group must agree to live by certain values, at least for the foreseeable future. An organization needs to have its foundation solidly in place for a period of time in order for it to build. A constantly shifting foundation does serious structural damage to an organization. No enterprise can afford that.

What should people do if they find that the shared values are inconsistent with their personal ones? The first responsible action is to ask for clarification. Ask, What does this really mean? If there is still conflict, then manage the disagreement. Ask, What can we do so that the organization can keep its integrity and I can keep mine? Usually either the process of clarifying or the process of negotiating will reconcile the dilemma. If you have clarified and negotiated and conflict still exists, there are at least two other choices: withdrawal or rebellion. But if you choose the latter, do so with the understanding that the organization will deal with the rebellion as a challenge to the community and to the shared values and norms that make it whole.

Taking Personal Responsibility

The decision to sign on, get out, or rebel is an issue of personal responsibility. This is a major topic these days; managements, human resource professionals, politicians, and self-help gurus tell us we need more of it. But what does it really mean to be responsible?

Dictionaries, management texts, and psychology books are of little help. To appreciate fully the significance of personal responsibility, we must turn to philosophy. We looked up "responsibility" in *The Great Ideas: A Syntopicon of Great Books of the Western World*; the index directed us to "punishment," "sin," and "will."[3] From Aeschylus and Sophocles, to the Old and New Testaments, to Hegel and Kant, the personal responsibility discourse has been about whether people freely choose their actions or whether they are divinely predestined to act in certain ways. Hence the term *free will*. Freely choosing to do something is an indispensable condition for empowerment. Free choice is also an indispensable condition for the punishment of civil misdeeds or of religious sin.

Personal responsibility can exist only if people have free will and if they exercise it. Personal responsibility cannot exist independent of choice. In personally choosing to act, individuals are saying explicitly or implicitly, "I will accept the consequences of my actions." The credibility-strengthening process hinges upon the belief that we human beings are personally accountable for our own actions. People are held accountable against the standard of shared values upon which we have agreed. Ignoring this precept, as many leaders have in not accepting the consequences of their own actions, contributes to people's increased cynicism.

Let us therefore all acknowledge that in setting out on a course to strengthen credibility, we are embarking on an ancient philosophical quest. We are seeking to understand the powers and limitations of our humanity. The tension between freedom and constraint will be felt in every choice we make. But the overriding decision for each of us is whether we are willing to take personal responsibility and be held accountable for the path we choose.

THE TENSION BETWEEN LEADING AND FOLLOWING

Though each of us is regularly a leader and a follower in the same organization at the same time, there are times in our careers when the two collide. Take the case of a friend of ours, a former senior vice president of marketing for a large packaged-goods company. Several years ago, he faced a critical leadership challenge. New technology made it possible to introduce a substitute for his company's food product. Major customers were shifting to the food substitute. His market studies clearly indicated that the future of the industry lay in the new product. He was convinced that his company had to revise its long-range plans and develop its own entry into the market or suffer disastrous consequences.

He took his studies to the board and urged development of a market entry. The board did not share his point of view. It authorized its own independent investigations by two prestigious management consulting firms to determine market trends and technical feasibility of producing the product. To the board's surprise, the consulting reports supported the senior vice president's sense of the market. Still unconvinced but now a bit worried, the board asked two law firms to determine whether entry into the new market would pose any antitrust issues. Both sets of lawyers agreed there would be no problem.

Despite the overwhelming evidence that the senior vice president's strategic vision was clear and attainable, the board sought the opinion of yet a third law firm. This one gave the board the answer it apparently was looking for all along. This third law firm thought there might be a chance of some legal problems, so the company abandoned the pursuit of the new product. The senior vice president, however, could not in good conscience go along with the decision—to him it was a matter of integrity. He felt so strongly about his vision for the industry that he continued to pursue it. But despite an untarnished reputation and a superb track record, he could not persuade his management to undertake a new strategic direction. The board won out, and he subsequently left the organization.

This critical incident illustrates another dilemma people experience in organizations: when do I lead, and when do I follow? No matter what the level, the problem is ever present. There are distinct differences between what people expect of leaders and what they expect of colleagues and teammates: these expectations are in dramatic conflict.

Contrasting Expectations

During the course of our research for this book, we asked people to complete a checklist of the characteristics they looked for and admired in a colleague, someone they would like to work alongside as a team member on a project. We used the same instrument (introduced in Chapter One) that we had used in asking people to rate their admired leaders. As we had with respect to the leader qualities, we asked people to select those seven that they most looked for and admired.

The leader-colleague comparisons reflect some extremely important similarities as well as some significant differences. The expectations for U.S leaders and colleagues are set forth in Table 9.1, with characteristics listed in rank order. What similarities and differences do you spot?

In virtually every survey we have conducted, honesty has always ranked first on all lists. Competence has also received votes from a majority of respondents. Honesty and competence, you will recall, are the two most important elements of source credibility. We want to know that our leaders and our colleagues are worthy of our trust, and we desire that our leaders and our colleagues be capable and effective. This finding reinforces the importance of credibility in every working relationship. Whether the person is in the role of a team member, a constituent, or a leader, people need to believe in that individual. This is why we have concluded that *credibility* is the *foundation* of *all* working relationships — and of all relationships that *work*.

Notice also the striking differences in these lists. The contrasts between what we desire in a leader and what we look for in a colleague help us to understand better one of the most basic dilemmas facing any person who would be a leader: the tension between when to assent and when to dissent, when to cooperate and when to initiate.

We have noted that people expect their leaders to be

Table 9.1. Most Desirable Characteristics.

Leaders:		Colleagues:	
Characteristic	Percentage of people selecting	Characteristic	Percentage of people selecting
Honest	87	Honest	82
Forward-looking	71	Cooperative	71
Inspiring	68	Dependable	71
Competent	58	Competent	70
Fair-minded	49	Intelligent	46
Supportive	46	Supportive	43
Broad-minded	41	Straightforward	37
Intelligent	38	Broad-minded	35
Straightforward	34	Imaginative	32
Courageous	33	Inspiring	31
Dependable	32	Forward-looking	27
Cooperative	30	Fair-minded	25
Imaginative	28	Ambitious	20
Caring	27	Caring	19
Mature	14	Determined	19
Determined	13	Independent	19
Ambitious	10	Loyal	16
Loyal	10	Courageous	14
Independent	5	Mature	13
Self-controlled	5	Self-controlled	7

forward-looking, to have a sense of direction and a concern for the future of the organization. People also expect leaders to be inspiring—to be energetic and positive about the future. Leaders must be able to communicate their visions in ways that uplift and encourage people to enlist. In combination, being forward-looking and inspiring make a leader visionary and dynamic. They make a person attractive to others. They point people in pioneering directions and give them energy and drive. They get people focused on and enthusiastic about building the organization of the future, putting today's actions in a strategic context. Add to this the rest of the foundation of credibility (honesty and competence) and you would think you would have an unbeatable formula for success.

But look again. The qualities of forward-looking and inspiring are conspicuously absent from the qualities we most want from our colleagues. Instead, people prefer that colleagues be dependable and cooperative. People want to know that they can count on their colleagues to be responsible team players. They wish everyone can work together collaboratively and to subordinate individual needs to group goals.

Having dependable and cooperative colleagues is absolutely essential to accomplishing even the most mundane tasks in organizations. People must be able to rely on each other, to get along with each other, and to set aside personal agendas for the good of the organization. Without dependability and cooperation, no group task would ever get done, and politics would be rampant.

But here's the rub. Being forward-looking and inspiring is often not harmonious with being cooperative and dependable. Let's say that you envision a new product or service that will take the organization in new directions. You have done your homework, and you are convinced that the market is going to demand what you envision. The trouble is that your team has invested time, energy, even careers in pursuing the current strategic vision of the organization. You are listened to politely and then told to get back to getting the gang fired up about the existing plan. But your personal integrity and your energy will not allow you to just forget it, so you persist. You sell even harder. Pretty soon, people start to wonder what happened to the loyal team player. Why isn't she getting on board? Why isn't he cooperating? Despite pleadings for more effective leadership, there are times when people would be just as pleased to have a better team player.

That is what happened in the case of the senior vice president of the packaged goods company. He did his homework. He knew his job. He was competent. He looked ahead and knew that the organization had to change its strategy. He was being forward-looking. With the vigor and enthusiasm of the long-time salesman that he was, he got excited about the future possibilities. So he gave it his best sales pitch. He was being inspiring. His integrity demanded that he stand up for his point of view. After all, we want leaders who are honest. He gave his colleagues on the board as accurate an image of the future as possible. But his strategic vision did not fit with the company's. Despite his honesty, competence, vision, and inspiration, he was branded "not a team player" when he clashed with management on this important issue and knew that his career with the company was over.

The norms of cooperativeness and dependability dominated this struggle. And as essential as they are to teamwork, in this case and in many others, they can also inhibit organizational change and growth. Too rigidly adhered to, they can result in faithful allegiance to the status quo and unquestioning loyalty to the party line. They can also inhibit the development of the leadership skills we so need in business today. The company in this story did miss a significant market opportunity and suffered financially.

If your vision of the future is opposed to that of your hierarchical superiors or your teammates, you may be perceived as uncooperative and disloyal even if your view is *correct*. Persistently selling a point of view may only reinforce this perception and may diminish the support of colleagues and managers alike. It may lead to being branded a renegade. It may even result in being fired, transferred, or asked to depart "voluntarily."

No Easy Path

There is a crucial difference between a pioneering leader and a dependable colleague. Though success in both is founded on personal credibility, leadership requires the realization of a unique and ideal image of the future. Teamwork requires cooperation and reliable adherence to that common vision. Leadership and teamwork are certainly not mutually exclusive—in fact, exemplary leaders foster collaboration—yet there is a dynamic tension between them. Sometimes, when an individual's vision is in conflict with the existing strategic vision of an organization, a choice is demanded: do I lead, or do I follow? Do I work with the group in the direction we've agreed, or do I set off on a new course?

There is no easy path for leaders to take. As Warren

Bennis, author of several books on leadership, has observed, "Within any organization, an entrenched bureaucracy with a commitment to the status quo undermines the unwary leader. To make matters worse, certain social forces—the increasing tension between individual rights and the common good, for example—discourage the emergence of leaders." Bennis also states that people "seem unwilling to embrace any vision but their own—a narrow one that excludes the possibility of sacrificing a little bit today to gain something better tomorrow."[4]

If individuals cannot learn to subordinate themselves to a shared purpose, then no one will follow, and selfishness and anarchy will rule. Yet in order to grow and improve, organizations must create a climate that fosters leadership; they must encourage the honest articulation of fresh strategic visions of the future.

In these uncertain times of business transformation, it is absolutely necessary for executives to encourage and tolerate more internal conflict than has been allowed in the past. If organizations expect people to show initiative in meeting today's serious business challenges, then they have to relax their expectations of abiding devotion. Instead, they must support efforts of honest and competent people to find solutions to the problems that are confronting their companies. In short, they must develop the leader in everyone.

PERCEPTION OF SUCCESS

At a recent workshop, we used a video case featuring Pat Carrigan at the Bay City, Michigan, General Motors parts plant that she managed until 1990.[5] People talked about how Carrigan fostered collaboration and strengthened others and how her actions contributed to a significant improvement in plant performance and work attitudes. There seemed to be consensus that Carrigan was a model of credible leadership.

But then one workshop participant said, "I don't think she was a very good leader." We asked that he elaborate.

"General Motors has not adopted her style of leadership throughout the company. If she were really as good a leader as you say, then she should have been able to influence other plants to change."

This comment sparked a debate among participants about the criteria for leadership success. Is success defined in terms of the scale and scope of influence? Is the ultimate objective of leaders to have the largest number of constituents? Are leaders successful only if they can spread their influence beyond the plant or department to the company? Or beyond the company to the country? Is it possible to be judged a credible and successful leader if you guide only twelve people to places they have never been before? Or must it be 1,200, 12,000 or 120,000? Is it the responsibility of successful leaders to enlist ever-greater numbers of constituents in their vision and values? Can leaders be said to be extraordinarily successful if they choose to lead a small organization for their entire careers?

What of the neighbor who organizes a local fundraising drive for the homeless, or the line employee who starts the company's recycling program, or the student who starts a campaign to get kids off drugs? Are these people not leaders? Is the leadership label reserved only for people in exalted positions?

The scale measure pervades a lot of discussions about success. The more constituents you have, the better at leading you must be. The argument is easy to understand. It takes extraordinary talent and energy to lead a large company, country, or movement, particularly over time. Outstanding skills are necessary. Certainly there is a level of superior competence involved.

But taken to its logical extreme, no leader could be judged entirely successful, even those who have influenced millions. Judaism, Islam, Buddhism, and Christianity, for example, have thrived for centuries. Moses, Mohammed, Siddhartha Gautama, and Christ are considered by many to be extraordinary leaders. But in their lifetimes, they did not convert every soul to their beliefs. Not everyone has been converted to this day.

Or take another person on the list of most-admired leaders, Mother Teresa. Her ceaseless compassionate work on behalf of the poor around the world has won her a Nobel Prize. Yet she has very few constituents by comparison to many corporate presidents. Does that mean she is not as good a leader as they are?

And what about Mikhail Gorbachev? The changes in the former Soviet Union brought about during his tenure were not even imaginable prior to his assumption of the leadership role. Yet he failed to retain the support of his constituents and was replaced. Was Gorbachev therefore not a credible leader?

People often ask a related question about Carrigan and other leaders we use as examples. "What happened after she left? Is the plant still operating by the same principles, or was it only possible when she was there?" If the plant operated by Carrigan's principles only while she was the plant manager and then adopted some new ones when the new plant manager arrived, would that make her less of a leader? And what does that say about the willingness to allow others the opportunity to make their unique contributions? If the next plant manager made significant changes, would that negate what Carrigan had done?

These issues of scope and endurance reflect values. If we value bigger, more grand, and longer, then we are likely to be disappointed in most leaders and in ourselves and to limit to a very few the number of people who can lead. In our view, leadership is both local and global. Acts of credible leadership come in all sizes. You can lead people to change the world, or you can lead yourself to change your own work space. Leadership is also transitory, and most often lasts for only a relatively short time. There are those whose influence has spanned centuries and crossed continents, but they are not the only ones who have led. Those whose influence has spanned only a few days and a few blocks can still have taken people to places they have never been before.

So what defines success? When it comes to leadership,

perhaps the most appropriate response we can give is that we should all adopt the Sierra campsite dictum. Whether your leadership is confined to your own 25 square feet or extends to the plant's 250,000 square feet or to the corporation's 2,500,000 square feet, success is leaving the area a better place than when you found it.

FROM EXCELLENCE TO EXCESS

In this book, we have offered the six disciplines of credibility as the means for building the foundation of leadership. We have prescribed methods and techniques we believe everyone can use to achieve mastery over the fundamentals of leader-constituent relations.

Excellence is a noble goal. To be preeminent in one's profession is a worthy pursuit. To surpass the average and to become superior is what makes for high-quality services and products. But one can go too far. One can go beyond excellence to excess. We do not mean an excess of excellence, but too much focus on each credibility discipline for the sake of perfecting the method instead of producing the intended result. Excessive emphasis on the disciplines can mean the triumph of technique over purpose.

It may be hard to imagine how we can have too much self-knowledge, appreciation, affirmation, mastery, service, or hope. But we can indulge in each discipline beyond what is necessary and sufficient and end up with negative characteristics that can damage credibility. The line between excellence and excess is often a fine one. We offer a few caution signs to watch for on your leadership journey and antidotes for overindulgence in any of the disciplines. These signs and antidotes are summarized in Table 9.2.

From Self-Discovery to Arrogance
We have learned that discovery of self, self-knowledge, is essential to credible leadership. People do not trust someone

Table 9.2. From Excellence to Excess.

Discipline	Excess leads to	Antidote required
Discovering your self	Arrogance	Openness
Appreciating constituents	Fragmentation	Complexity
Affirming shared values	Rigidity	Challenge
Developing capacity	Vanity	Humility
Serving a purpose	Subjugation	Independence
Sustaining hope	Dependence	Action

who is not clear about personal beliefs and continues to shift from position to position based upon the latest opinion poll. But we must watch out for those who are so persuaded that their values are the right values that they become moralistic, judgmental, arrogant, and self-righteous. People like this become overbearing and boorish. They are not interesting to us because they are not interested *in* us. We do not want to be around them, much less follow them.

Overconfidence is another danger of excessive self-knowledge. Much as it is critical that we believe in our abilities to succeed, we may become blind to the limits of our competencies. This myopia occurs especially when the environment changes and the skills that worked for us before may not continue to serve us well. Overconfidence can lead to cockiness, poor judgment, and insensitivity to the situation or to others.

The antidote to arrogance is openness. When leaders stay open to others, they avoid the hubris that sometimes comes from being in charge. Trust is maintained when people see that we are not "know-it-alls" and are interested in learning from others. It is also maintained when others see that we are willing to admit our own mistakes and learn from them, instead of dismissing them as someone else's problem.

From Appreciation to Fragmentation

Listening to constituents is essential to success in leadership. When constituents believe that their leaders have everyone's best interests at heart, they are more likely to trust them. In contrast, people will not willingly follow those who are interested only in advancing their private agendas. Leaders, therefore, must listen to all their constituents.

There is ample evidence that diversity is good for business. As we discussed previously, it increases innovation. It improves the probability that decisions will reflect the broadest constituency. It enhances the chances of success in a multicultural marketplace with a multicultural work force. But in the process of coming to appreciate the diverse values of others, leaders must guard against vacillation and fragmentation. There may be so many constituent groups and their points of view so divergent that leaders may oscillate between one significant need and another. Or they may make promises to every group.

This tendency is especially true in politics. Every special-interest group lobbies for its needs by appealing to one established value or other, from freedom to security to justice to equality to competitiveness to peace. None of these values can be denied their fair hearing. Yet in appreciating the diversity of these cherished principles, the system gets bogged down, decisions don't get made, and constituents become frustrated and angry.

Of all the dilemmas faced by political leaders—and all leaders for that matter—this is perhaps the most disillusioning. Legitimate leaders promote choice and do not dictate values; however, coming to a decision that motivates the largest possible constituency appears increasingly difficult. The diversity of interests makes decision making extraordinarily taxing. By honoring too many differences, leaders may create false hopes or protests of resentment. By encouraging all voices to speak, leaders may create a Tower of Babel where no one understands anyone else. There has to come a point when listening stops and choosing starts.

Organizations are social constructions, born of collective imaginations. Part of leading, then, is emphasizing what is held in common, not just the different. Instead of creating factions, leaders must learn to reconcile value choices into new values combinations.

Most of us tend to view problems and events through a very narrow frame. The everyday term *simple-minded* indicates a commonsense understanding of this phenomenon. Research suggests, however, that people who are more cognitively complex—who are able to see and understand their environments from several different perspectives—are more effective as leaders and managers. They are more tolerant of ambiguity, less prejudiced, better able to resolve conflicts cooperatively, and better able to make moral judgments.[6] So, in the words of University of Michigan professor Karl Weick, "complicate yourself" as an antidote to fragmentation.[7] The ability to take a 360-degree view helps us to know that our decision is credible, even if it may not agree with a powerful constituency. Diversity complicates a leader's job, but those who can handle the complexity make better leaders.

From Affirmation to Rigidity

Our research indicates that shared values make a difference to the leader, to the constituents, and to the organization. A leader must build consensus around core beliefs and then publicly affirm what has been agreed. Leaders find common ground, build a sense of community, and resolve dilemmas on the basis of principles, not positions.

Shared values are an attribute of a strong-culture company.[8] And strong cultures can produce strong performance. Yet as Harvard professors Kotter and Heskett have documented, they can also produce weak results. They point to data from 1977 to 1988 showing that some firms with very high scores on culture did poorly on measures of new income growth, return on capital, and growth of stock price. "These cases," they conclude, "suggest that one criticism of the strong-culture theory—that the cultural drummer can lead a firm into decline as well as into success—may be valid. . . . Strong cultures can lead people—even reasonable, thoughtful people—astray."[9] Shared values can become straightjackets.

A principle that was once a cornerstone of the corporate foundation can become obsolete. Kotter and Heskett observe that a "strong culture can easily become somewhat arrogant, inwardly focused, politicized, and bureaucratic."[10] In today's rapidly changing world, these characteristics undermine corporate performance.

Consensus on norms and values also makes people subject to "groupthink," as researcher Irving Janis has called it.[11] The strong desire to maintain harmony among group members, and an understandable need to maintain their own self-esteem, inclines them to avoid creating discord. They choose not to bring up contrary points of view and censor themselves from raising doubts about a policy decision. The results can be disastrous. According to Janis, groupthink contributed to some extent to many historical fiascoes, including Prime Minister Neville Chamberlain's appeasement of Hitler during 1938, the failure of Admiral Kimmel's inner circle to respond to warnings about the invasion of Pearl Harbor, and President Kennedy's advisory group's decision to launch the Bay of Pigs invasion.[12]

Communities can become cults, which limit free choice and reward only blind obedience. Such conformance can be deadly (as in the case of Jim Jones's cult at Jonestown) or it can be simply numbing. Communities can also become country clubs, emphasizing the needs of the members over the needs of the larger constituencies, such as customers and shareholders. This country-club norm can quickly cause a group to lose touch with the outside world.

The antidote to rigidity is challenge. To keep the organization from becoming inflexible, leaders must consciously induce a challenge to the established values. They should take a periodic look at these to see if they are still legitimate and to determine what to do about it if they are not. The Saskatchewan Public Service Commission conducts a semiannual values audit with these points in mind. Its purpose, according to Jim McKinlay, former executive director, Staff Development Division, is twofold: to assess the degree to which staff is truly living the values and to assess their continuing validity. For example, as a result of an audit, the commission rewrote one of the six values because it recognized that employees *"could not live it the way it was written."*[13]

From Development to Vanity

Credible leaders encourage people's capacity to deliver. They give people choices and latitude; they educate and build confidence. In the credible organization, everyone is a leader, everyone is master of his or her own fate.

Yet excessive self-development can lead to vanity. It can lead to the leadership and organizational equivalents of the posers on Muscle Beach who strut around flexing their biceps. Their sole purpose is to look good, not to do good. The focus can become the right cars, carpets, paintings, clothes, restaurants, clubs, gadgets, trophies. Competitions to win quality awards have the potential to become the latest in organizational vanity. What do they have to do with becoming the best? As psychologist George Leonard, author of nine books and holder of a third-degree aikido black-belt, points out, "If you're always thinking about appearances, you can never attain the state of concentration that's necessary for effective learning and top performance."[14]

Excessive self-improvement can lead to a continuous striving for perfection. Mastery experiences are essential to developing confidence; however, striving for perfection is not part of the process. Leonard writes, "Mastery is not about perfection. It's about a process, a journey. The master is the one who stays on the path, day after day, year after year. The master is the one who is willing to try, and fail, and try again, for as long as he or she lives."[15]

Perfectionism makes people continuously dissatisfied with their own performances and those of others. It causes them to interfere with the learning of others—"Oh, here, let me show you how to do that"—and to become intolerant of mistakes. Perfectionists never let others shine in their own way. Leaders who strive for perfection are likely to become tyrants. Vanity and perfectionism contribute to an arrogance that can ultimately be the undoing of excellent companies and of excellent leaders.

Excessive emphasis on individual mastery can also lead to valuing personal control over organizational purpose. If everyone is master, where are the servant leaders? By developing everyone to be a leader, we are likely to increase the tension between freedom and constraint, between the rights of the individuals and the common purpose of the institution. We should all keep in mind that if everyone is a leader, everyone must be a servant as well.

The antidote to vanity is humility. Leaders need to be aware of their own and their organization's shortcomings and be willing to admit to them. They need to encourage and support others in admitting they are wrong without fear of punishment or reprisal. People who work in organizations emphasizing humility are proud, yet they do not allow pride to consume them. One of the most successful retailing operations of modern times, Wal-Mart, still functions out of unimposing headquarters in Bentonville, Arkansas. Lack of pretension may have a great deal to do with its success.

From Service to Subjugation

Leaders serve a purpose and the people who have made it possible for them to lead. The credible leader is one who puts the purposes and principles of organization ahead of all else. To remain credible as a servant, leaders must stay in touch. They must go first and not ask anyone to do anything they are unwilling to do. Leaders ask questions, keep promises, hold themselves accountable, and atone for their mistakes.

But emphasizing the servant nature of leadership raises a very fundamental question: when do I respond to my constituents, and when do I act on my own principles? A leader is often faced with having to subordinate one's self for the common good. But there is an important distinction between subordinating and losing one's self.

Not too long ago, a member of a county board of supervisors posed this problem to us: "What should elected officials do if they believe personally that something is in the long-term best interests of their constituents, but know that right now the constituents won't support it? Should we respond to what people say they want today without regard for the future of the community? Should we be governed only by polls? Aren't we elected to think?"

There are no easy answers to these questions. Listening is important to earning credibility, as is taking a stand: we have to acknowledge the tension. Leaders have to listen to those whom they serve. But not everyone will agree, and decisions must be made. Too much listening and too much polling of people's opinions can turn to inconsistency; it can become just trying to please, not trying to lead. If you are the leader of a group and you have developed your credo, competence, and confidence (like Pat Carrigan, for instance), should you not have some say over what the plant values should be?

Similarly, if you feel strongly about the environmental legacy you are leaving your children, then should you not act on that belief? Gail Mayville did just that while an office manager at Ben & Jerry's Homemade. The socially conscious company was creating some environmental problems of its own by overloading the Waterbury, Vermont, sewage treatment facility with its ice cream factory's liquid garbage. The Ben & Jerry's factory was in danger of being shut down if something could not be done about the mess. Without being asked, Mayville took the leadership initiative and came up with a creative solution. She determined that the waste could be recyled organically by feeding it to pigs. She had Ben & Jerry's provide the waste—and the pigs—to a local farmer who was willing to participate.

Mayville feels strongly about the importance of making a difference and acting on your convictions: "You have to be a risk-taker. I know it's scary to head off in a whole new direction, but trust your intuition. It's valid. And don't get discouraged...expect to run into resistance...expect to run into walls. Every time someone told me, 'No,' I'd get this vision of water running in a brook and hitting a stone. The water goes over it or around it or under it."[16]

There is nothing inherently contradictory about being a servant-leader and acting on one's own beliefs. Leaders serve others when they respond to their constituents' expectation that they have a vision of the future. We have devoted this entire book to the foundation of leadership—credibility—but we do not want you to ignore the factor that differentiates leaders from other credible people: being forward-looking. A clear sense of direction is something constituents want and expect from a credible leader.

Mayville and Carrigan, like the other leaders described in this book, are proactive people with strong beliefs. Being of service to others does not mean waiting for constituents to ask before you act. Nor does it mean simply reacting to every demand. It means being proactive on behalf of your constituents, and very often that means anticipating their needs or those of their organizations. This ability to anticipate and commit to the future is the real test of leadership.[17]

Leaders must therefore develop a superior ability to anticipate what their constituents will require. Excellence in anticipation can pay off handsomely. Next time you are out strolling or jogging through your local park, notice how many people are wearing headsets and carrying portable tape players strapped to their waists. Did a customer ask for the first Walkman? No. The idea did not come from a customer. Did an employee ask for the first personal computer? Did shareholders ask for the first airplane? Most innovations that significantly changed the world came from the visions of a few crazy entrepreneurs who anticipated what people would want—if they only knew.[18]

This is not to suggest that the leader is always right and the constituents are always wrong. It is only to acknowledge that it is too simple to say "serve others" and everything will magically be in harmony. The process is more complex. Sometimes you should listen to your conscience and your intuition, instead of to your constituents. To have integrity—to be at one with the person you are both in your private heart and in public places—leaders have to be true to themselves. Integrity demands that you vote your conscience. As long as your overall credit rating remains high, your constituents will still give you a loan if you are occasionally a step or two ahead of them on some issues. But if your credit is all used up and you only use your own convictions and not theirs, they are very likely to call in the note.

The antidote to subjugation is independence. To counteract the effects of losing one's self to the cause, leaders must forge their own identities outside of the organizations they lead. They must find something that defines them besides their work. The most expressive and successful leaders we have encountered in our decade-long study have been those who took their self-knowledge and applied it to something other than their constituents. They had an abiding outside interest: they sailed, played the piano, performed in plays, or wrote poetry, as a few examples. This fact brings us back to the first discipline of strengthening credibility: discover your self. In order to serve others, you must also look after yourself.

From Hope to Dependence

Credible leaders look on the bright side. They are optimistic and full of hope. Credible leaders go forth with love and courage. They inspire positive images and action. They seek and give the support and recognition that enable others to excel.

But too much optimism can result in damaged credibility. Optimism is inappropriate as an initial response if the risks are too high, if the future is dim, or if a person is in need of sympathy. Being overly upbeat can blind one to the realities and to the risks; if promises are not fulfilled, people will be disillusioned and less willing to grant credit in the future. A leader thus needs to define reality.

Providing too much support can foster dependency. If we want self-reliant, self-directed constituencies, leaders can't be expected to offer comfort all the time. They cannot be expected to be available twenty-four hours a day and still maintain their personal health and their worth to the organization.

Pay and recognition are often billed as motivators. But pay is indiscriminate: it covers everything one does, well and poorly. Formal and informal recognition lose their power to motivate if given routinely. People must be able to tell which behaviors contribute to the company's goals and which do not. Raises and recognition must be earned, rather than expected, for an entitlement mentality can deaden performance just as easily as the absence of respect and recognition can.

The antidote to dependence is action. To retain freedom, we must maintain faith in our will and capacity to act. If people feel helpless and victimized and believe they don't matter, they may become dependent on the organization for hope and support and surrender themselves to it.[19] Leaders must be alert that neither they nor their constituents make the institution a substitute for the self.

RENEWAL: NEW BEGINNINGS FROM THE OLD ENDING

People run down. Energy runs out. Talent gets stale. Organizations get stuck. Challenges continue and threats mount, but the old ways of doing things do not work anymore. If we persist in operating by the rules of the past, we cannot hope to have new visions of the future. If anxiety grips the work force, action is strangled. The forward movement that defines the very nature of leadership comes to a halt.

Leaders and constituencies must first acknowledge that what once worked no longer does, and then they must be able to enter into a zone of uncertainty that is at first frightening but from which they emerge reenergized and renewed. And unless people, organizations, and communities are renewed, they are overtaken by the chaos of decline and decay.

The engine of renewal is fueled by learning—or, more accurately, unlearning and then learning anew. In 1973, Donald N. Michael, professor of planning and public policy at the University of Michigan, defined the characteristics of the new competence of learning for changing times. His observations are perhaps even more relevant today than then. He states, "I think *we have no choice* but to try to be competent in ways that are appropriate for coping with systemic turbulence, complexity, and ambiguity. This means that as persons seeking meaning in our lives, worthiness in our efforts, we have no choice but to take the risks, and accept the pain, the excitement, and the exhilaration of *becoming learners* [emphasis his]."[20] Michael asserts that people must find it rewarding to become learners if they are going to change toward an organization that responds to the future rather than reacts to the past. His characteristics of the new learning competence are the following:

- Acknowledging very high levels of uncertainty, and learning to live with the stress of unstable situations

- Embracing error, and using mistakes as learning opportunities

- Accepting responsibility for the future, and evaluating the present in the light of anticipated futures

- Developing interpersonal competence so we can learn from others

- Knowing ourselves

- Creating support groups for ourselves[21]

As we consider the people who earned the respect of their constituents, Michael's description of a learner is apt for each of them. They acknowledged and shared that they did not have all the answers, that they were not always in control, that they were vulnerable. In so doing, they embraced their mistakes and asked what could be learned from them. They looked ahead and wondered what the world would be like in the future, especially if the visions they held were fulfilled. And they wrestled with the values issues revealed by these explorations. They were highly skilled interpersonally, always asking questions and listening to advice. They knew their values and beliefs, their strengths and weaknesses. And they all had broad networks of support.

John Gardner certainly fits this description. He has served six presidents of the United States in various capacities. He was founding chairman of Common Cause and co-founder of the Independent Sector; he has also been president of the Carnegie Corporation and chairman of the National Urban Coalition. He has written seven books and edited two. One of them is *Self-Renewal*. It is hardly a surprise that at age seventy-seven, Gardner began another career as a Stanford University professor.

Gardner believes that learning and relearning are essential to all people; he certainly practices what he preaches. And, he believes, leaders have a special responsibility to renew their institutions: "The pace of change is swift. Institutions that have lost their capacity to adapt pay a heavy price. Yet the impulse of most leaders is much the same as it was a thousand years ago: accept the system as it is and lead it. That is rarely possible any longer. Continuous renewal is necessary. Leaders must understand how and why human systems age, and must know how the processes of renewal may be set in motion."[22]

In advising leaders who wish to set renewal in motion, Gardner urges, "*The consideration leaders must never forget is that the key to renewal is the release of human energy and talent* [emphasis his]."[23]

And so we have come full circle. We have said that credible leaders first discover their own selves and then appreciate the diversity of others. First they find their own energy and talent, and then they find them in others. From time to time, this human energy and talent need to be refreshed. And so does credibility.

Renewing credibility is a continuous human struggle and the ultimate leadership struggle. Strenuous effort is required to build and strengthen the foundation of working relationships. Constituents do not owe leaders allegiance. Leaders earn it. The gift of their trust and confidence is well worth the struggle.

A P P E N D I X

Studies on the Impact of Credibility and What Constitutes Credible Behavior

To understand the genesis of our interest in credibility, we must go back to when we began our first series of investigations into the leadership process, more than a decade ago. Before the notion of benchmarking had entered the organizational lexicon, we had begun asking people to tell us about their personal best experiences as leaders—times when they had accomplished extraordinary things in their organizations. The more stories we heard of these "best practices," the clearer it became that leadership was not "some gift from the gods" (as *charisma* is defined) but a set of identifiable (and hence learnable) practices, strategies, and behaviors. Then, in a management development seminar at Santa Clara University, after forty senior managers had shared in small groups their own personal bests, it hit us all: there were tremendous similarities between the processes adopted by leaders, regardless of such factors as discipline or function, location (geographical or hierarchical), gender, age, experience, profit orientation, education, and so on.

We followed up that observation with a series of systematic studies, involving personal interviews and case studies with over one thousand managers, and empirical investigations now involving more than forty-five thousand people from around the globe. Our original findings formed the basis for our earlier book, *The Leadership Challenge: How to Get Extraordinary Things Done in Organizations.*[1]

We realized early on that knowing about leadership from the leader's perspective was (at best) only half of the story. After all, no one had achieved anything very extraordinary by themselves. In recognition of this, Chapter Two of *The Leadership Challenge* was titled "What Followers Expect of Their Leaders: Knowing the Other Half of the Story." We concluded that chapter by saying, "Managers, we believe, get other people to do, but leaders get other people to want to do. Leaders do this first of all by being credible. That is the foundation of all leadership. They establish this credibility by their actions."[2] And we went on to describe which actions of leaders made others want to follow them. As we continued our investigations, however, we came to appreciate more fully the reciprocal nature of the process and how leadership depends on the eye of the beholder.

We also realized that although there has been a great deal of research on credibility, most of it is scattered across the academic landscape (in psychology, sociology, communication, marketing, political science, and law, for example); very little of this research has appeared in the managerial literature. In his impressive book, *Persuasion: Theory and Research*, University of Illinois professor Daniel O'Keefe cites 750 studies, but fewer than 1 percent (6) are in business journals.[3] Similarly, of the 176 references in the bibliography of social psychologist Robert Cialdini's book, *Influence: How and Why People Agree to Things*, only one citation is from the management literature.[4]

There are two notable exceptions. The first is Harvard Business School professor Rosabeth Moss Kanter's 1977 treatise on *Men and Women of the Corporation*. The executives in her study, when asked to define the characteristics of effective managers, agreed that "credibility was more important than anything else."[5] The second is University of California, Berkeley, professor Charles O'Reilly's 1984 paper based upon data from employees in several high-technology firms.[6] He has found that top management credibility is clearly related to increased involvement and commitment levels among employees. O'Reilly states, "When employees perceive management to be trustworthy and to have a coherent philosophy, they also report higher levels of identification and value congruence."[7] He also notes the dearth of research on credibility and commented that this subject had not been widely studied in the context of modern corporations.

In Chapter One, we described our own investigations into the characteristics most admired in leaders. Recently completed replications (ten-year followups) of our original studies involving executives from both the public and private sectors reveal a remarkable consistency over time.[8] Honesty continues to hold the top ranking, with competency and the ability to be inspirational close behind. O'Keefe affirms that these three characteristics have consistently emerged in "factor-analytic investigations of communicator credibility."[9] Based upon these findings from the literature and our earlier awareness of the "other half of the story," we designed a series of studies over the past few years to investigate both the impact of credibility and the identification of the behaviors that make up credible leadership behavior. Here we describe each of those empirical studies in turn.

STUDY ONE

Our investigations began by looking at the general relationship between credibility and key employee outcomes (for example, commitment, satisfaction, teamwork). The sample included 186 working professionals involved part-time in an M.B.A.

program. These respondents averaged seven years of work experience. Most of them (87 percent) were currently employed, and 42 percent held managerial positions. By function, they represented accounting/finance (26 percent), engineering (23 percent), manufacturing/operations (19 percent), marketing/sales (14 percent), human resource management (3 percent), research and development (2 percent), and management information systems (2 percent). Men comprised 70 percent of the sample.

Credibility of managers was measured by both a global (one-item) scale, as well as a scale consisting of three one-item statements about the extent to which their manager was honest, competent, and inspiring.[10] The correlation between the two scales was .83 ($p < .001$; the average correlation between the global scale and the three separate statements was .68; $p < .001$). Employee attitudes were assessed along seven dimensions (see Table A.1). All items were measured on seven-point Likert scales (with one being "strongly disagree" and seven being "strongly agree").

The sample was divided into high and low managerial credibility groups based upon the mean scores on the global credibility scale. Comparisons between these two groups demonstrated that employees who perceived their managers as having high credibility felt significantly ($p < .001$) more positively about and attached to their work and organizations than those who perceived their managers as having low credibility.

This study confirmed that the credibility construct had an important impact on employee attitudes. It also supported the conceptualization of credibility along the lines suggested by the previous literature (namely, being honest, competent, and inspiring). Subsequent discussions with respondents revealed a clear understanding of the credibility concept, its components, and the interpersonal and organizational impact of credibility. Further analysis revealed no systematic differences in results due to gender, years of work experience, functional background, or managerial position.

Table A.1. T-tests of Employee Attitudes by Managerial Credibility
($N = 186$).

	Credibility	
Employee Attitudes	Low	High
Has personal values consistent with company's	4.05	5.11*
Is willing to work long hours	4.01	5.19*
Is proud to tell others where employed	4.59	5.48*
Feels a sense of ownership in this company	3.39	4.51*
Credits work group with strong sense of team spirit	3.62	4.97*
Feels personally involved with work	4.73	5.27*
Intends to work for this company in two years	2.63	3.90*

*Differences between low and high groups were statistically significant at $p < .001$.

STUDY TWO

We organized five separate focus groups to identify behavioral statements and actions that enacted the traits of being honest, competent, and inspiring. We were interested in understanding how employees would actually know whether their managers were honest, competent, and inspiring. We also explored how employees would know when their managers were not credible. We found that being credible and not being credible were not always at opposite ends of a behavioral continuum. Although credible people were almost always viewed as possessing these three characteristics, those people considered less (or not) credible were not necessarily seen as totally dishonest, incompetent, or uninspiring. Being credible generally required evidence (beyond some minimum threshold) of all three characteristics; not being credible could result from a deficiency in any one of the three characteristics.

The focus groups generated numerous statements indicating which managerial behaviors and actions created credibility in the minds and hearts of employees. Respondents from two focus groups received follow-up correspondence with suggested key summary statements for their review. Based upon their feedback, an eighteen-item measure was developed, with six items measuring each of the three proposed conceptual scales.

Separate administrations of this measure were conducted with managers from three different organizations: a government defense contractor ($N = 24$), a high-technology computer firm ($N = 64$), and a statewide law enforcement agency ($N = 96$). In each sample, the managers were randomly split into two equally sized groups. Half of the respondents were asked to think about an individual with whom they had worked and whom they would describe as a very credible person. The other half were to think about an individual with whom they had worked and whom they would describe as not a very credible person. Then they were asked how descriptive each of the eighteen statements were with respect to that individual. Responses were on five-point Likert scales with one being "not very descriptive" and five being "very descriptive."

T-tests between these two groups (credible person versus not credible person) revealed significant differences ($p < .01$) on all eighteen items (results not shown). The groups were also significantly different ($p < .001$) when items were placed into the separate scale measures (six items each) of being honest, competent, and inspiring. Internal reliability coefficients for these three measures were strong both within the separate samples and across the three organizations. Coefficient alpha was .93 for both honest and competent and .86 for inspiring.

STUDY THREE

The primary purpose of this study was to ascertain the test-retest reliability of the credibility measure. The sample involved fifty-one working professionals enrolled in an M.B.A. program. These respondents averaged nearly eight years of work experience. More than 75 percent were currently employed; of these, more than 50 percent were in managerial positions. Just over 60 percent of the sample were men.

Separate administrations of the instrument over a five-day period showed statistically significant ($p < .001$) test-retest correlations. The test-retest correlation was .83 for honest, .90 for competent, and .86 for inspiring. Internal reliability correlations (coefficient alpha) ranged from .61 to .79 in the first administration and from .76 to .84 in the second administration. These results suggest that neither the credibility construct nor measure is ethereal, and they are tapping into some identifiable and understandable phenomenon.

STUDY FOUR

In this study, surveys were distributed by thirty-nine working professionals involved in an M.B.A. program. These people, all representing different organizations, were asked to distribute randomly a short survey to several people in their company. These surveys were returned directly to the researchers in stamped, preaddressed return envelopes. One hundred and thirteen surveys were returned (for a 53 percent response rate). Respondents had an average of ten years of work experience and approximately 43 percent were currently in managerial positions. Of the respondents, 55 percent were men.

For this administration of the credibility measure, the three variables were assessed on six-point Likert scales ranging from one (for "strongly disagree") to six (for "strongly agree"). Internal reliability coefficients for the three scales was strong, with coefficient alphas of .92 for honest and for competent and .88 for inspiring. Each scale was also significantly correlated with a global credibility measure composed of three one-item assessments of their manager's honesty, competence, and ability to be inspiring (with a coefficient alpha of .72). These correlations ranged from .74 to .78 ($p < .01$).

In addition, as with Study One, respondents indicated the extent to which they had positive work attitudes: strong

Table A.2. T-tests of Employee Attitudes by Low and High Groups on Honest, Competent, and Inspiring (N = 113).

	Honest		Competent		Inspiring	
	Low	High	Low	High	Low	High
Credits work group with strong sense of team spirit	3.96	5.28*	4.10	5.15*	4.06	5.42*
Has personal values consistent with company	4.52	5.42*	4.53	5.39*	4.55	5.56*
Is proud to tell others where employed	5.42	5.97	5.25	6.02*	5.31	6.22*
Intends to work for this company in two years	4.02	5.20*	4.04	5.16*	4.02	5.44*
Has positive work attitude overall	4.48	5.47*	4.51	5.43*	4.48	5.66*

*Differences between low and high groups were statistically significant at $p < .001$.

sense of teamwork, pride in the company, organizational commitment (willingness to remain with the company), and alignment of personal and organizational values. Each of these attitudes was measured on seven-point Likert scales (with one indicating "strongly disagree" and seven indicating "strongly agree"). An overall positive work attitude measure was created as a linear combination of these four items (with a coefficient alpha of .73). Table A.2 shows the comparisons between high and low groups (formed above and below the mean scale score) on each of the three dimensions of credibility and these work attitudes.

As the data in Table A.2 reveal, these three credibility variables were each significantly associated with important work attitudes by employees in a variety of different companies. The overall positive-work-attitude scale showed statistically significant differences ($p < .001$) for each of the separate scales. Respondents who felt that their manager was honest, competent, and inspiring were significantly more likely to feel a strong sense of teamwork, organizational values alignment, and organizational commitment than were those who found their managers as less honest, competent, and inspiring. Their manager's competence and ability to inspire significantly affected feelings of organizational pride as well, whereas the differences in honesty were not statistically significant.

In addition, analysis by demographic characteristics failed to reveal any significant relationships. Neither gender, work experience, or managerial capacity (yes or no) was significantly correlated with any of the credibility measures.

STUDY FIVE

In addition to looking at credibility, as measured by honesty, competence, and ability to be inspiring, in this study we examined if the six disciplines of credibility (described in this book) could be used to measure leadership behaviors that build credibility and how such actions would affect work attitudes. As with Study Two, we began with several focus groups (consisting of experienced managers), identifying which behaviors and actions of managers demonstrated that they were honest, competent, and inspiring. More than 150 different behavioral statements were generated through these discussions. A panel of three academics, eleven executives and senior human resource managers, and five consultants familiar with research on credibility and on leadership sorted these statements into the six credibility disciplines (discovering, appreciating, affirming, developing, serving, and sustaining). The top seven statements (those with the greatest amount of agreement among the raters regarding their importance to credibility) within each discipline were retained for the next stage of analysis (resulting in forty-two items). Internal reliabilities for these six scales ranged from .85 to .93.

Two different samples were available for this study. The first included 101 senior health care administrators from across the United States who were participating in a national conference. These respondents were highly educated (80 percent had postgraduate degrees), in their late forties, and mostly CEOs, presidents, or senior vice presidents in their organizations. The second sample involved 640 professionals and managers from a large public service company. About one-third of these respondents were in management positions. Participation in both studies was voluntary and confidential.

Respondents were asked to think about their current manager in describing the frequency with which this person engaged in these various credibility practices. Five-point Likert scales were used with one indicating the statement "does not at all describe this person" and five indicating "completely describes this person."

In addition, respondents were asked to assess their manager's overall credibility, honesty, competence, ability to be inspiring, and leadership. They also indicated the extent to which they themselves (1) were proud to tell others that they work for this organization, (2) felt attached and committed to this organization, (3) belonged to a work group with a strong sense of team spirit, (4) experienced a sense of ownership for their organization, and (5) found their personal values in alignment with those of the organization. Each statement in this section was asked using five-point Likert scales, anchored by one (for "strongly disagree") and five (for "strongly agree"). A work-attitude scale was created based upon responses to these five statements (coefficient alpha was .85).

Using a linear combination of their responses to the three statements about their managers' honesty, competence, and ability to inspire, respondents were divided into a high or low (average split) group on managerial credibility. This credibility scale had an internal reliability of .84 and a correlation of .85 ($p < .001$) with the overall credibility item.

When these two groups were compared on the six disciplines of credibility, we found consistent differences. Managers who were seen by their constituents as having credibility engaged in each of these six disciplines significantly more than did those managers who were viewed as having less credibility, as shown in Figure A.1.

Figure A.1. High Versus Low Credibility Behaviors.

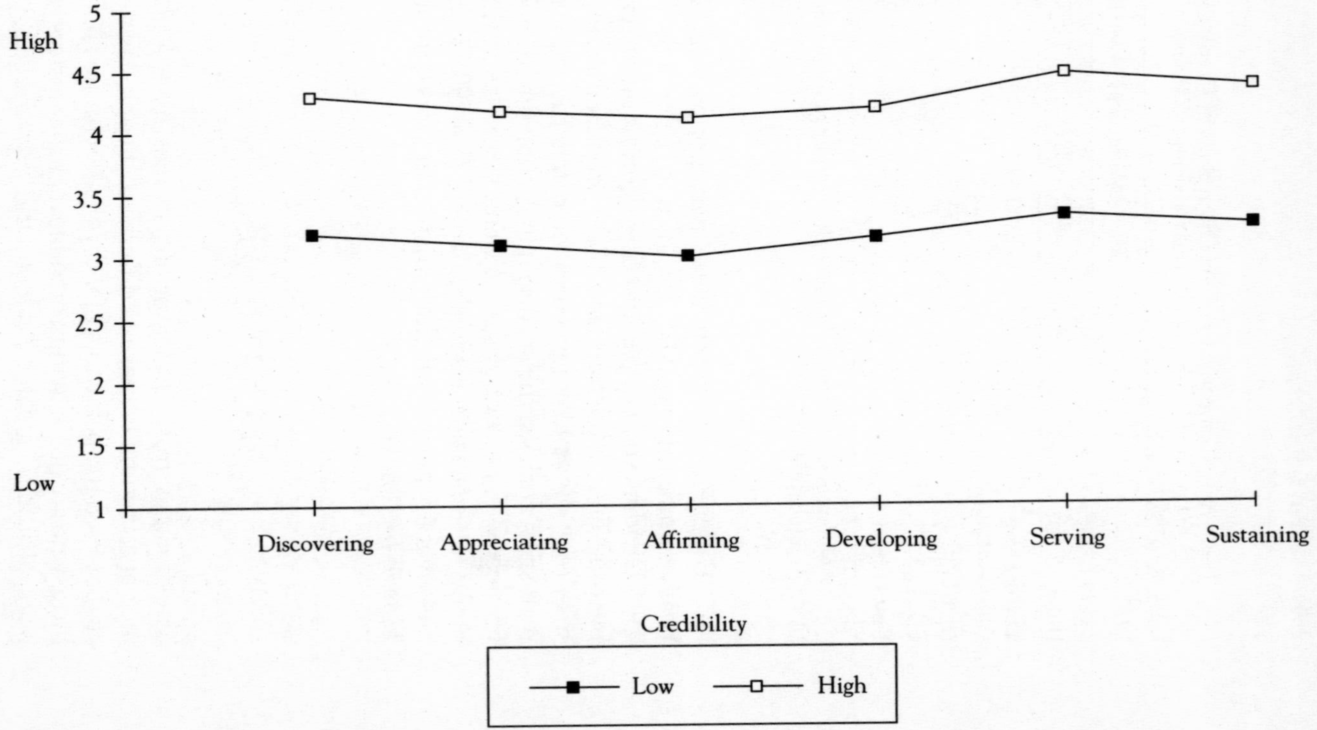

Table A.3. Comparisons of Six Disciplines of Credibility by
Low and High Managerial Credibility Groups.

	Managerial Credibility	
	Low (N = 423)	High (N = 313)
Discovering	21.71	29.68*
Appreciating	20.58	28.64*
Affirming	20.24	28.27*
Developing	20.65	28.98*
Serving	22.26	30.50*
Sustaining	21.50	29.43*

*Differences between low- and high-credibility groups were all statistically significant at $p < .001$.

Differences between these two groups were all statistically significant ($p < .001$), as shown in Table A.3.

Dividing the sample into three groups on the credibility measure (low, moderate, and high) produced equivalent results (not shown). When considered together in a multiple regression analysis, the six disciplines of credibility accounted for nearly 72 percent of the explained variance in the assessments of managers' leadership ability ($F = 299.23$, $p < .0001$) and over 55 percent of the variance in work attitudes ($F = 123.64$, $p < .0001$).

CONCLUSION

The findings from these various studies have a consistent message: credibility makes a difference. People can differentiate between the behaviors of individuals who are credible and those who are not. Having a credible manager fosters favorable work attitudes: greater pride in the organization, stronger spirit of cooperation and teamwork, more feelings of ownership and personal responsibility, and better alignment between personal and organizational values. The six disciplines of credibility—discovering, appreciating, affirming, developing, serving, and sustaining—reliably measure actions that build the foundation of leadership; they distinguish between those individuals who can lead others to new visions of the future and those who cannot.

N O T E S

Preface

1. For a sampling of survey results, see *American Electronics Association 1992 Productivity Survey Management Summary* (Mountain View, Calif.: Pittiglio, Rabin, Todd & McGrath and KPMG Peat Marwick, 1992); R. M. Kanter, "Transcending Business Boundaries: 12,000 World Managers View Change," *Harvard Business Review* 69 (3) (May–June 1991): 151–164; B. Z. Posner and W. H. Schmidt, "The Values of American Managers: An Update Updated," *California Management Review* 34 (3) (1992): 80–94; *An International Survey of Consumers' Perceptions of Product and Service Quality* (Milwaukee, Wis.: American Society for Quality Control, 1991); "What

Keeps You Up at Night?" *INC.* (July 1992): 12; "The Quality Imperative," *Business Week,* 25 Oct. 1991, 10; *International Quality Study* (Cleveland, Ohio: Ernst & Young/American Quality Foundation, 1991).

2. In fact, Malcolm Baldrige National Quality Award judge W. Kent Sterett says that leadership is one of the four key elements in successful Baldrige-winning companies. Quoted in the *Wall Street Journal,* 14 Mar. 1991, B1.

Chapter One

1. Unless otherwise noted, all quotations from leaders are taken from personal interviews, from personal written cases, or from public stories told by the leaders and analyzed by the authors. The titles and affiliations of the leaders in this study may be different today than at the time the manuscript was submitted for publication.

2. J. A. Autry, *Love and Profit: The Art of Caring Leadership* (New York: Morrow, 1991), 71.

3. Xerox Corporation, *Leadership Through Quality* (Xerox Corporation, 1990), 11.

4. R. Howard, "Values Make the Company: An Interview with Robert Haas," *Harvard Business Review* 68 (5) (Sept.–Oct. 1990): 136.

5. S. Zuboff, *In the Age of the Smart Machine: The Future of Work and Power* (New York: Basic Books, 1988), 394.

6. P. A. Allaire, "Beyond Quality," presentation to the conference entitled "Designing and Sustaining World-Class Organizations." Carnegie Mellon University, 31 May 1991.

7. J. W. Gardner, *On Leadership* (New York: Free Press, 1990), 28–29.

8. V. A. Zeithaml, A. Parasuraman, and L. L. Berry, *Delivering Quality Service: Balancing Customer Perceptions and Expectations* (New York: Free Press, 1990), 15.

9. Portions of this section first appeared in J. M. Kouzes and B. Z. Posner, *The Leadership Challenge: How to Get Extraordinary Things Done in Organizations* (San Francisco: Jossey-Bass, 1987).

10.   W. H. Schmidt and B. Z. Posner, *Managerial Values and Expectations: The Silent Power in Personal and Organizations Life* (New York: American Management Association, 1982). Also see B. Z. Posner, J. M. Kouzes, and W. H. Schmidt, "Shared Values Make a Difference: An Empirical Test of Corporate Culture," *Human Resource Management* 24 (3) (1985): 293–309; B. Z. Posner and W. H. Schmidt, "Values and the American Manager: An Update," *California Management Review* 26 (3) (1984): 202–216; B. Z. Posner, "Person-Organization Values Congruence: No Support for Individual Differences as a Moderating Influence," *Human Relations* 45 (4) (1992): 351–361.

11.   B. Z. Posner and W. H. Schmidt, "Values and Expectations of Federal Service Executives," *Public Administration Review* 46 (5) (1986): 447–454.

12.   Korn/Ferry International and Columbia University Graduate School of Business, *Reinventing the CEO* (New York: Korn/Ferry International and Columbia University Graduate School of Business, 1989), 41.

13.   As a few examples of this variation, 93 percent of U.S. executives rated ethical behavior as highly important now, and 96 percent responded that it will be highly important in the year 2000; 79 percent and 76 percent were the ratings from Japanese executives; 78 percent and 81 percent were from those in the Western European community. Korn/Ferry and Columbia University, *Reinventing the CEO*, 89.

14.   These numbers varied by country. For example, being honest, upright, and ethical were very important to 87 percent of Canadian office workers, to 80 percent of workers in the European Economic Community, and to 72 percent of those in Japan. Steelcase, *Worldwide Office Environment Index Summary Report* (Grand Rapids, Mich.: Steelcase, 1991), 7.

15.   P. Jordan (producer), *The Credibility Factor* (Carlsbad, Calif.: CRM Films, 1991) (videotape). This video features James M. Kouzes and Barry Z. Posner, coauthors of this

book, and provides case examples of the principles and practices described herein.

16. Jordan, *The Credibility Factor*.

17. Korn/Ferry and Columbia University, *Reinventing the CEO*, 90.

18. Korn/Ferry and Columbia University, *Reinventing the CEO*, 89.

19. Jordan, *The Credibility Factor*.

20. Kouzes and Posner, *The Leadership Challenge*.

21. W. H. Schmidt and B. Z. Posner. "The Values of American Managers: An Update Updated," *California Management Review* 34 (3) (1992): 80–94; B. Z. Posner and W. H. Schmidt, "An Updated Look at the Values and Expectations of Federal Government Executives," *Public Administration Review* (1993): in press.

22. See, for example, D. K. Berlo, J. B. Lemert, and R. J. Mertz, "Dimensions for Evaluating the Acceptability of Message Sources," *Public Opinion Quarterly* 33 (1969): 563–576.

23. M. De Pree, *Leadership Is an Art* (New York: Doubleday, 1989), 9.

24. *Business Week*, 20 Apr. 1992.

Chapter Two

1. See J. M. Kouzes and B. Z. Posner, *The Leadership Challenge: How to get Extraordinary Things Done in Organizations* (San Francisco: Jossey-Bass, 1987), 282–290, for a discussion of how we learn to lead.

2. I. Federman, remarks to the Leavey School of Business and Administration, Santa Clara University, 2 Apr. 1991.

3. As discussed in the Appendix, this phase of our research built upon earlier work by C. A. O'Reilly, "Charisma as Communication: The Impact of Top Management Credibility and Philosophy on Employee Involvement," paper presented to the annual meeting of the Academy of Management, Boston (Aug. 1984).

4. D. L. Kanter and P. H. Mirvis, *The Cynical Americans:*

Living and Working in an Age of Discontent and Disillusion (San Francisco: Jossey-Bass, 1989), 9–10.

5. P. H. Mirvis, personal correspondence, Jan. 1992.
6. Mirvis, personal correspondence.
7. Steelcase, *Office Environment Index: 1989 Summary Report* (Grand Rapids, Mich.: Steelcase, 1989), 5.
8. Steelcase, *Worldwide Office Environment Index Summary Report* (Grand Rapids, Mich.: Steelcase, 1991).
9. B. S. Morgan, senior director, Opinion Research Corp., personal correspondence, Aug. 1992.
10. H. Taylor, "Confidence in Military Is Up While Confidence in the White House Falls," Harris Poll, press release, 22 Mar. 1922.
11. Mirvis, personal correspondence.
12. Taylor, "Confidence in Military."
13. J. Schmalz, "Words on Bush's Lips in '88 Now Stick in Voters' Craw," *New York Times*, 14 June 1992, 16.
14. Kanter and Mirvis, *The Cynical Americans*, 24.
15. W. Greider, *Who Will Tell the People: The Breakdown of American Democracy* (New York: Simon & Schuster, 1992), 22.
16. Schmalz, "Words," 16.
17. "What Can Restore Fading Loyalty?" *Industry Week*, 4 Feb. 1991, 50–51.
18. B. Davis and D. Milbank, "Employee Ennui," *Wall Street Journal*, 7 Feb. 1992, p. A1.
19. G. S. Crystal, *In Search of Excess: The Overcompensation of American Executives* (New York: Norton, 1991), 27.
20. J. Nelson-Horchler, "The Pay Revolt Brews," *Industry Week*, 18 June 1990, p. 29.
21. "Executive Pay," *Business Week*, 30 Mar. 1992, p. 52.
22. J. Delacroix and S. M. Saudagaran, "Munificent Compensations as Disincentives: The Case of American CEOs," *Human Relations* 44 (7) (1991): 671.
23. American Society for Quality Control, *A Survey of Employees' Attitudes Toward Their Jobs and Quality Improvement Programs*, Milwaukee, Wis.: American Society for Quality Control, 34–36.

24. S. M. Lipset and W. Schneider, *The Confidence Gap: Business, Labor, and Government in the Public Mind* (New York: Free Press, 1984), 378. At its worst, say Lipset and Schneider, suspicion of power makes people susceptible to conspiratorial theories. The popularity of Oliver Stone's films *Wall Street* and *JFK* might be accounted for by our desire to find the "corrupt" leaders who are out to swindle the "honest" people.
25. Schmalz, "Words," 16.
26. "USA to Clinton: Get Us Jobs," *USA Today*, 13 Nov. 1992, 6A. Based on a USA/CNN Gallup telephone poll of 1,004 adults nationwide, taken November 10–11, 1992 (margin of error: plus or minus four percentage points). The *New York Times* reported that Clinton's October 27–29, 1992, rating on the question of whether he could be trusted to deal with all the problems of a president was 40 percent. J. Schmalz, "Americans Are Sadder and Wiser, But Not Apathetic," *New York Times*, 1 Nov. 1992, 4-1.
27. "A Ground Swell Builds for 'None of the Above,'" *Business Week*, 11 May 1992, 34.
28. Steelcase, *Worldwide Office Environment Index*, 7.
29. Lipset and Schneider, *The Confidence Gap*, 399.
30. Mirvis and Kanter, *The Cynical Americans*, 177.
31. V. Polk and J. Rodgers (producers), *The Leadership Alliance* (Schaumburg, Ill.: Video Publishing House, 1988) (videotape).
32. For a discussion of how driven managers function, we suggest R. E. Kaplan, with W. H. Drath and J. R. Kofodimos, *Beyond Ambition: How Driven Managers Can Lead Better and Live Better* (San Francisco: Jossey-Bass, 1991).

Chapter Three

1. P. Jordan (producer), *The Credibility Factor* (Carlsbad, Calif.: CRM Films, 1990) (videotape).
2. W. Durant. *The Life of Greece* (New York: Simon & Schuster, 1939, 1966), 198.

3. W. Bennis, *On Becoming a Leader* (Reading, Mass.: Addison-Wesley, 1989), 51.

4. Bennis, *On Becoming a Leader*, 40.

5. What we have learned from our studies of primarily business enterprises has also been found to be true in other organizations. For a look at the important role that values, capabilities, and confidence play in military leadership, see E. Jacques and S. D. Clement, *Executive Leadership: A Practical Guide to Managing Complexity* (Arlington, Va.: Cason Hall, 1991), 31.

6. M. Rokeach, *The Nature of Human Values* (New York: Free Press, 1973), 5.

7. Rokeach, *The Nature of Human Values*, 14–15.

8. Extensive descriptions of values clarification exercises are contained in S. B. Simon, *Values Clarification: A Handbook of Practical Strategies for Teachers and Students* (New York: Hart, 1972); M. Smith, *A Practical Guide to Values Clarification* (San Diego, Calif.: University Associates, 1977). For a contemporary treatment of this issue in education, see T. Lickona, *Educating for Character: How Our Schools Can Teach Respect and Responsibility* (New York: Bantam Books, 1991).

9. We were first introduced to a version of this exercise by Professor Charles O'Reilly of the Haas School of Business, University of California, Berkeley.

10. S. Steele, *The Content of Our Character: A New Vision of Race in America* (New York: Harper Perennial, 1990).

11. W. G. Scott and D. K. Hart, *Organizational Values in America* (New Brunswick, N.J.: Transaction, 1990), 190–191.

12. J. M. Burns, *Leadership* (New York: HarperCollins, 1978), 36.

13. For a discussion of this issue, also see B. Z. Posner, J. M. Kouzes, and W. H. Schmidt, "Shared Values Make a Difference," *Human Resource Management 24* (3) (1985): 293–309.

14. A. Colby, L. Kohlberg, E. Speicher-Dubin, and M. Lieberman, "Secondary School Moral Discussion Pro-

grams Led by Social Studies Teachers," *Journal of Moral Education* 6 (2) (1989): 90–117. Also see T. Lickona, *Educating for Character: How Our Schools Can Teach Respect and Responsibility* (New York: Bantam Books, 1991), 228–248.

15. B. Z. Posner, "Individual's Moral Judgment and Its Impact on Group Processes," *International Journal of Management* 3 (2) (1986): 5–11.

16. M. Harmin, "Value Clarity, High Morality: Let's Go for Both," *Educational Leadership* (May 1988): 24–30.

17. For a discussion of Pat Carrigan's accomplishments and leadership practices at Lakewood, see J. M. Kouzes and B. Z. Posner, *The Leadership Challenge: How to Get Extraordinary Things Done in Organizations* (San Francisco: Jossey-Bass, 1987). For a discussion of Carrigan's work at the Bay City plant, see V. Polk and J. Rodgers (producers), *The Leadership Alliance* (Schaumburg, Ill.: Video Publishing House, 1988) (videotape).

18. D. H. Maister, "How's Your Asset?" (Boston: Maister Associates, 1991), 1.

19. Maister, "How's Your Asset?", 2.

20. Maister, "How's Your Asset?", 3.

21. Maister, "How's Your Asset?", 3.

22. A. Bandura, "Conclusion: Reflections on Nonability Determinants of Competence," in R. Sternberg and J. Kolligian, Jr. (eds.), *Competence Considered* (New Haven, Conn.: Yale University Press, 1990), 316.

23. Bandura, in Sternberg and Kolligian (eds.), *Competence Considered*, 315.

24. Bandura, in Sternberg and Kolligian (eds.), *Competence Considered*, 323. Also see M. E. Gist and T. R. Mitchell, "Self-Efficacy: A Theoretical Analysis of Its Determinants and Malleability," *Academy of Management Review* 17 (2) (1992): 183–211.

25. Bandura, in Sternberg and Kolligian (eds.), *Competence Considered*, 327–328. Also see R. F. Mager, "No Self-Efficacy, No Performance." *Training* (Apr. 1992): 32–35.

26. For a further discussion of learning to lead, see Kouzes

and Posner, *The Leadership Challenge* (San Francisco: Jossey-Bass, 1987), 282–290.

27. M. Csikszentmihalyi, *Flow: The Psychology of Optimal Experience* (New York: HarperCollins, 1990), 209–213.

28. For another discussion of the makeup of character, see Lickona, *Educating for Character*, 51.

29. J. M. McPherson, *Abraham Lincoln and the Second American Revolution* (New York: Oxford University Press, 1991), 95.

30. T. Branch, *Parting the Waters: America in the King Years, 1954–1963* (New York: Simon & Schuster, 1988).

31. The questions posed are based upon the work of the original developers of the values clarification process, Louis Rath, Merrill Harmin, and Sidney Simon. See L. Rath, M. Harmin, and S. Simon, *Values and Teaching* (Columbus, Ohio: Merrill, 1966), 30. Also see Simon, *Values Clarification*, 1972; Smith, *A Practical Guide to Values Clarification*, 1977.

32. M. De Pree, *Leadership Is an Art* (New York: Doubleday, 1989), 107.

33. "Experiential Learning" (San Diego, Calif.: Pfeiffer, 1990).

34. For an extensive discussion of personal mission, see R. N. Bolles, *The 1991 What Color Is Your Parachute? A Practical Manual for Job-Hunters and Career-Changers* (Berkeley, Calif.: Ten Speed Press, 1991), 389–406. For additional help on personal mission, also see P. Block, *The Empowered Manager: Positive Political Skills at Work* (San Francisco: Jossey-Bass, 1987), 99–129; S. Covey, *The Seven Habits of Highly Successful People: Restoring the Character Ethic* (New York: Simon & Schuster, 1989).

Chapter Four

1. P. Jordan (producer), *The Leadership Challenge* (Carlsbad, Calif.: CRM Films, 1989) (videotape).

2. R. O. Whitney, personal communication, 18 May 1992.

3. For more information, see A. Morrison, *The New Lead-*

ers: Guidelines on Leadership Diversity in America (San Francisco: Jossey-Bass, 1992).

4. J. P. Kotter and J. L. Heskett, *Corporate Culture and Performance* (New York: Free Press, 1992), 143.

5. Learning International, *Profiles in Customer Loyalty: An Industry-by-Industry Examination of Buyer-Seller Relationships* (Stamford, Conn.: 1989).

6. See, for example, W. H. Schmidt and B. Z. Posner, *Managerial Values and Expectations: The Silent Power in Personal and Organizational Life* (New York: American Management Association, 1982); B. Z. Posner, J. M. Kouzes, and W. H. Schmidt, "Shared Values Make a Difference: An Empirical Test of Corporate Culture," *Human Resource Management* 24 (3) (1985): 293–310; B. Z. Posner and W. H. Schmidt, "An Updated Look at the Values and Expectations of Federal Service Executives," *Public Administration Review* (in press); B. Z. Posner and W. H. Schmidt, "Values and the American Manager: An Update Updated," *California Management Review* 34 (3) (1992): 80–94.

7. J. Castro, "The Simple Life," *Time,* 8 Apr. 1991, 58–63.

8. J. A. Lee, "Changes in Managerial Values," *Business Horizons* (July–Aug. 1988): 29–37.

9. When the values of the sons and daughters of the stereotypical "organization man" profiled in the book by the same name in the mid 1950s were examined, a similar conclusion was reached. See P. Leinberger and B. Tucker, *The New Individualists: The Generation After the Organization Man* (New York: HarperCollins, 1991).

10. B. B. Bunker, "Appreciating Diversity and Modifying Organizational Cultures: Men and Women at Work," in S. Srivastva, D. L. Cooperrider, and Associates (eds.), *Appreciative Management and Leadership: The Power of Positive Thought and Action in Organizations* (San Francisco: Jossey-Bass, 1990), 126–149.

11. R. Fisher and S. Brown, *Getting Together* (Boston: Houghton Mifflin, 1988).

12. M. W. McCall, M. Lomdardo, and A. Morrison, *The*

Lessons of Experience (Lexington, Mass.: Lexington Books, 1988).

13. S. Srivastva and F. J. Barrett, "Foundations for Executive Integrity: Dialogue, Diversity, Development," in S. Srivastva and Associates (eds.), *Executive Integrity: The Search for High Human Values in Organizational Life* (San Francisco: Jossey-Bass, 1988).

14. As quoted in F. Rice, "Champions of Communications," *Fortune*, 3 June 1991, 111.

15. This letter is reprinted as originally written, but the actual company's name has been deleted.

16. A. E. Doody and R. Bingamin, *Reinventing the Wheels* (New York: Ballinger, 1988).

17. R. Whitely, *The Customer-Driven Organization* (Reading, Mass.: Addison-Wesley, 1991).

18. As quoted in J. B. Rosener, "Ways Women Lead," *Harvard Business Review* (Nov.–Dec. 1990): 122.

19. D. Kipnis, *The Powerholders* (Chicago: University of Chicago Press, 1976).

20. D. Jamieson and J. O'Mara, *Managing Workforce 2000: Gaining the Diversity Advantage* (San Francisco: Jossey-Bass, 1991).

21. The Leadership Practices Inventory is available from Pfeiffer & Company, San Diego, Calif.

22. P. F. Drucker, "How to Manage the Boss," *Wall Street Journal*, 1 Aug. 1986, 16.

23. J. A. Sniezek and R. A. Henry, "Accuracy and Confidence in Group Judgment," *Organization Behavior and Human Decision Processes 43* (1989): 1–28; J. A. Sniezek and R. A. Henry, "Revision, Weighting, and Commitment in Consensus Group Judgment," *Organization Behavior and Human Decision Processes 45* (1990): 66–84.

24. B. Z. Posner, "Individual's Moral Judgment and Its Impact on Group Processes," *International Journal of Management 3* (2) (1986): 5–11.

25. W. Bennis, "Leading Followers, Following Leaders," *Executive Excellence* (June 1991), 5–7.

26. See, for example, M. Deutsch, *The Resolution of Con-*

flict (New Haven, Conn.: Yale University Press, 1973);
D. Tjosvold, "Implications of Controversy Research for
Management," *Journal of Management 11* (1985): 21–37;
D. Tjosvold and L. T. McNeely, "Innovation Through
Communication in an Educational Bureaucracy," *Communication Research 15* (1988): 568–581.

27. D. Tjosvold, *Team Organization: An Enduring Competitive Advantage* (New York: Wiley, 1992).

28. Tjosvold, *Team Organization*.

29. A. Bhide and H. H. Stevenson, "Why Be Honest If Honesty Doesn't Pay?" *Harvard Business Review* (Sept.–Oct. 1990): 121–129.

30. Fisher and Brown, *Getting Together*.

31. D. O'Keefe, *Persuasion: Theory and Research* (Newbury Park, Calif.: Sage Publications, 1990).

32. For example, see D. E. Zand, "Trust and Managerial Problem Solving," *Administrative Science Quarterly 17* (2) (1972): 229–239.

33. J. W. Driscoll, "Trust and Participation in Organizational Decision Making as Predictors of Satisfaction," *Academy of Management Journal 21* (1) (1978): 44–56.

34. J. Barefoot, "Suspiciousness, Health, and Mortality: A Follow-Up Study of 500 Older Adults," *Psychosomatic Medicine 49* (Sept.–Oct. 1989): 450–457.

35. D. Armstrong, *Managing by Storying Around* (New York: Doubleday Currency, 1992).

36. Rice, "Champions of Communication."

37. M. A. Allison and E. Allison, *Managing Up, Managing Down* (New York: Simon & Schuster, 1986).

38. J. Sielaff (producer), *The Leadership Edge* (Santa Cruz, Calif.: Lansford Communications, 1989) (videotape).

Chapter Five

1. Adapted from Nguzo Saba Films Teacher's Guide of film "Ujima" (San Francisco: Nguzo Saba Films) as reported in *Friends Can Be Good Medicine* (Sacramento, Calif.: California Department of Mental Health, 1981): 58–59.

2. B. Z. Posner and W. H. Schmidt, "Values Congruence and Differences Between the Interplay of Personal and Organizational Value Systems," *Journal of Business Ethics 12* (1993): 171–177.

3. B. Z. Posner and R. Westwood, "Shared Values: An International Perspective on the Impact of Shared Values," working paper, Santa Clara University, 1993.

4. See, for example, C. Enz and C. R. Schwenk, "Performance and Sharing of Organizational Values," presented at the annual meeting of the Academy of Management, Washington, D.C., 1989; B. Meglino, E. C. Ravlin, and C. L. Adkins, "A Work Values Approach to Corporate Culture: A Field Test of the Value Congruence Process and Its Relationship to Individual Outcomes," *Journal of Applied Psychology 74* (3) (1989): 424–432; C. A. O'Reilly, J. Chatman, and D. Caldwell, "People and Organizational Culture: A Profile Comparison Approach to Assessing Person-Organization Fit," *Academy of Management Journal 34* (3) (1991): 487–516; P. McDonald and J. Gandz, "Getting Value from Shared Values," *Organizational Dynamics* (1992): 64–76: B. Z. Posner, J. M. Kouzes, and W. H. Schmidt, "Shared Values Make a Difference: An Empirical Test of Corporate Culture," *Human Resource Management 24* (3) (1985): 293–310.

5. J. Pfeffer, *Managing with Power: Politics and Influence in Organizations* (Boston: Harvard University Press, 1992).

6. See, for example, J. M. Beyer and T. M. Lodahl, "A Comparative Study of Patterns of Influence in United States and English Universities," *Administrative Science Quarterly 21* (1976): 104–129; J. Pfeffer and W. L. Moore, "Average Tenure of Academic Department Heads: The Effects of Paradigm, Size, and Departmental Demography," *Administrative Science Quarterly 25* (1980): 387–406; J. Pfeffer and W. L. Moore, "Power in University Budgeting: A Replication and Extension," *Administrative Science Quarterly 25* (1980): 637–653; and G. R. Salancik, B. M. Staw, and L. R. Pondy, "Administrative Turnover as a Response to Unmanaged Organizational Interde-

pendence," *Academy of Management Journal* 23 (1980): 422–437.

7. J. Gardner, commencement address, Stanford University, 16 June 1991.

8. A national survey of over 32,000 workers reinforces our findings. See Steelcase, *Office Environment Index: 1989 Summary Report* (Grand Rapids, Mich.: Steelcase, 1989).

9. J. A. Autry, *Love and Profit* (New York: Morrow, 1991), 74.

10. See, for example, F. Richter and D. Tjosvold, "Effects of Student Participation in Classroom Decision Making on Attitudes, Peer Interaction, Motivation, and Learning," *Journal of Applied Psychology* 65 (1981): 74–80; D. Tjosvold, I. R. Andrews, and H. Jones, "Cooperative and Competitive Relationships Between Leaders and Their Subordinates," *Human Relations* 36 (1983): 1,111–1,124; D. Tjosvold, I. R. Andrews, and H. Jones, "Alternative Ways Leaders Can Use Authority," *Canadian Journal of Administrative Sciences* 2 (1985): 307–317; D. Tjosvold, "Power and Social Context in Superior-Subordinate Interaction," *Organizational Behavior and Human Decision Processes* 35 (1985): 281–293; D. Tjosvold, I. R. Andrews, and J. T. Struthers, "Power and Interdependence in Work Groups," *Group & Organization Studies* 16 (3) (1991): 285–299.

11. D. Tjosvold, "Interdependence and Power Between Managers and Employees: A Study of the Leader Relationship," *Journal of Management* 15 (1988): 49–64.

12. A. Kohn, *No Contest: The Case Against Competition* (Boston: Houghton Mifflin, 1986).

13. D. Tjosvold, *The Team Organization* (New York: Wiley, 1991).

14. A. Kohn, *The Brighter Side of Human Nature: Altruism and Empathy in Everyday Life* (New York: Basic Books, 1990).

15. I. Federman, presentation to the Leavey School of Business and Administration. Santa Clara University, 2 Apr. 1991; also reproduced in "Can Turnaround Be This

Easy?" *Journal of Management Inquiry* 1 (1) (1992): 57–60. Subsequent to the story related in the text, Monolithic Memories was merged with Advanced Micro Devices.

16. J. G. Belasco, *Teaching the Elephant to Dance: Empowering Change in Your Organization* (New York: Crown, 1990), 209.

17. S. W. Cook and M. Pelfrey, "Reactions to Being Helped in Cooperating Interracial Groups: A Context Effect," *Journal of Personality and Social Psychology* 49 (5) (1985): 1,231–1,245.

18. R. Levering, presentation to the Bay Area Ethics Consortium, Berkeley, Calif., 30 Jan. 1991.

19. W. Taylor, "The Business of Innovation: An Interview with Paul Cook," *Harvard Business Review* (Mar.–Apr. 1990): 99.

20. C. A. Bartlett and S. Ghoshal, "Matrix Management: Not a Structure, a Frame of Mind," *Harvard Business Review* (July–Aug. 1990): 138–145.

21. W. Ury, *Getting Past No* (New York: Bantam Books, 1991), 29.

22. C. Hampden-Turner, *Charting the Corporate Mind: Graphic Solutions to Business Conflicts* (New York: Free Press, 1990), 7.

23. R. Fisher and S. Brown, *Getting Together: Building a Relationship That Gets to Yes* (Boston: Houghton Mifflin, 1988), 37.

24. A. Colby, L. Kohlberg, E. Speicher-Durbin, and M. Lieberman, "Secondary School Moral Discussion Programs Led by Social Studies Teachers," *Journal of Moral Education* 6 (2) (1989): 90–117.

25. These ideas were suggested by D. Tjosvold, *Team Organization.*

26. F. A. Blanchard, T. Lilly, and L. A. Vaughn, "Reducing the Expression of Racial Prejudice," *Psychological Science* 2 (2) (Mar. 1991): 101–105.

27. Ury, *Getting Past No.*

28. T. J. Peters, "When Values Become Blinders," *San Jose Mercury News*, 12 Oct. 1991, D2.

Chapter Six

1. T. W. Firnstahl, "My Employees Are My Service Guarantee," *Harvard Business Review* (Jul.–Aug. 1989): 28–31, 34.
2. A. Toffler, *Powershift: Knowledge, Wealth, and Violence at the Edge of the 21st Century* (New York: Bantam Books, 1990), 210–211.
3. B. Dumaine, "Who Needs A Boss?", *Fortune*, 7 May 1990, 52–60.
4. J. M. Kouzes and B. Z. Posner, *Team Leadership Practices Inventory* (San Diego: Pfeiffer, 1992).
5. For more information on how leaders liberate the leader within, see J. M. Kouzes and B. Z. Posner, *The Leadership Challenge: How to Get Extraordinary Things Done in Organizations* (San Francisco: Jossey-Bass, 1987).
6. H. S. Astin and C. Leland, *Women of Influence, Women of Vision: A Cross-Generational Study of Leaders and Social Change* (San Francisco: Jossey-Bass, 1991), 120.
7. MICA Executive Survey, "Training Impact on Corporate Competitiveness" (Toronto, Canada: MICA Management Resources, 1991).
8. *America and the New Economy* (Alexandria, Va.: American Society for Training and Development, 1990).
9. O. Port (ed.), "Measuring the Gap Between U.S. and Japanese Auto Makers," *Business Week*, 8 Oct. 1990, 83.
10. B. Geber, "The Resurrection of Ford," *Training* (Apr. 1989): 23–31.
11. J. Stack, *The Great Game of Business* (New York: Doubleday, 1992), 15–16.
12. See, for example, L. A. Schlesinger and J. Zornitsky, "Job Satisfaction, Service Capability, and Customer Satisfaction: An Examination of Their Linkages and Management Implications," *Human Resource Planning* (Spring 1991); L. A. Schlesinger and J. L. Heskett, "Enfranchisement of Service Workers," *California Management Review* (Summer 1991): 83–100.
13. Quoted in T. Peters, "Get Innovative or Get Dead, Part One," *California Management Review* (Fall 1990): 22.

14. J. A. Belasco, "Empowerment as Business Strategy," *Executive Excellence* (June 1991): 15.
15. Belasco, "Empowerment as Business Strategy," 15.
16. J. Sensenbrenner, "Quality Comes to City Hall," *Harvard Business Review* (Mar.–Apr. 1991): 64–75.
17. E. L. Deci, *Intrinsic Motivation* (New York: Plenum Press, 1978).
18. R. E. Wood and A. Bandura, "Impact of Conceptions of Ability on Self-Regulatory Mechanisms and Complex Decision Making," *Journal of Personality and Social Psychology* 56 (1989): 407–415.
19. E. Jacobson, "A Study on New United Motor Manufacturing" (Detroit, Mich.: The General Motors Institute, 1986).
20. A. Bandura and R. E. Wood, "Effect of Perceived Controllability and Performance Standards on Self-Regulation of Complex Decision Making," *Journal of Personality and Social Psychology* 56 (1989): 805–814.
21. J. M. Kouzes and B. Z. Posner, *Readiness Assessment Questionnaire* (Santa Clara, Calif.: Kouzes Posner International, 1992).
22. W. Bennis and B. Nanus, *Leaders: The Strategies for Taking Charge* (New York: HarperCollins, 1985), 203–204.
23. E. J. Langer, *Mindfulness* (Reading, Mass.: Addison-Wesley, 1989); also see "Mindfulness," *American Health* 9 (2) (Mar. 1990): 54–62.
24. E. J. Langer and A. Piper, "The Prevention of Mindlessness," *Journal of Personality and Social Psychology,* 53 (1987): 280–287; also see Langer, *Mindfulness*, 120.
25. I. Nonaka, "The Knowledge-Creating Company," *Harvard Business Review* 69 (6) (Nov.–Dec. 1991): 97.
26. Nonaka, "The Knowledge-Creating Company," 98.
27. J. Hyatt, "Ideas at Work," *Inc.* (May 1991): 59–66.
28. Stack, *The Great Game of Business,* 5.
29. A. Bandura and D. Cervone, "Self-Evaluative and Self-Efficacy Mechanisms Governing the Motivational Effects of Goal Systems," *Journal of Personality and Social Psychology* 45 (1983): 1,017–1,028.

30. Bandura and Cervone, "Self-Evaluative and Self-Efficacy Mechanisms."
31. J. B. Rosener, "Ways Women Lead," *Harvard Business Review* (Nov.–Dec. 1990): 122.
32. Stack, *The Great Game of Business*, 210.
33. B. Dumaine, "Who Needs A Boss?"
34. J. A. Conger, "Leadership: The Art of Empowering Others," *Academy of Management Executive* 3 (1) (1989): 17–24.
35. P. F. Drucker, "The New Productivity Challenge," *Harvard Business Review* 69 (6) (Nov.–Dec. 1991): 69–79.
36. T. A. Stewart, "Brainpower," *Fortune*, 3 June 1991, 50.
37. A. Bandura, *Social Foundations of Thought and Action: A Social-Cognitive View* (Englewood Cliffs, N.J.: Prentice-Hall, 1986).

Chapter Seven

1. R. K. Greenleaf, *Servant Leadership: A Journey into the Nature of Legitimate Power and Greatness* (New York: Paulist Press, 1977), 7.
2. Greenleaf, *Servant Leadership*, 329.
3. J. M. Burns, *Leadership* (New York: HarperCollins, 1978), 20.
4. Greenleaf, *Servant Leadership*, 10.
5. D. A. Garvin, "How the Baldrige Award Really Works," *Harvard Business Review* (Nov.–Dec. 1991): 80–93.
6. W. H. Clover, "Transformational Leaders: Team Performance, Leadership Ratings, and Firsthand Impressions," in K. E. Clark and M. B. Clark (eds.), *Measures of Leadership* (West Orange, N.J.: Leadership Library of America, 1990): 171–184.
7. "Presidential Hot Line," *Inc.* (Feb. 1991): 76.
8. C. K. Goman, *The Loyalty Factor* (New York: MasterMedia, 1991), 41.
9. Garvin, "How the Baldrige Award Really Works."
10. W. Kiechel III, "How to Escape the Echo Chamber," *Fortune*, 18 June 1990, 129–130.

11. Kiechel, "Echo Chamber," 130.
12. J. A. Conger, "Inspiring Others: The Language of Leadership," *Academy of Management Executive 5* (1) (1991): 38.
13. M. M. Osborn and D. Ehninger, "The Metaphor in Public Address," *Speech Monograph 29* (1962): 228.
14. See, for example, E. Borgida and R. E. Nisbett, "The Differential Impact of Abstract vs. Concrete Information on Decisions," *Journal of Applied Technology 7* (3) (1977): 258–271; R. Zemke, "Storytelling: Back to Basics," *Training* (Mar. 1990): 44–50; P. Schwartz, *The Art of the Long View* (New York: Doubleday, 1991); Conger, "Inspiring Others."
15. For example, A. L. Wilkens, "Organizational Stories as Symbols Which Control the Organization," in L. R. Pondy, P. J. Frost, G. Morgan, and T. C. Dandridge (eds.), *Organizational Symbolism* (Greenwich, Conn.: JAI Press, 1983).
16. J. Martin and M. E. Power, "Organizational Stories: More Vivid and Persuasive Than Quantitative Data," in B. M. Staw (ed.), *Psychological Foundations of Organizational Behavior* (Glenview, Ill.: Scott, Foresman, 1982), 161–168.
17. S. Taylor and L. Novelli, Jr., "Some Basic Concepts of Innovation and Story Telling," *Issues & Observation 11* (1) (1991): 6–9.
18. There are many variations of this story. Conger provides a similar example in "Inspiring Others."
19. For an excellent discussion of how leaders reinforce and serve shared values to transmit organizational culture, see E. H. Schein, *Organizational Culture and Leadership* (2nd ed.) (San Francisco: Jossey-Bass, 1992), 228–253.
20. W. H. Peace, "The Hard Work of Being a Soft Manager," *Harvard Business Review* (Nov.–Dec. 1991): 40–47.
21. L. L. Berry and A. Parasuraman, *Marketing Services: Competing Through Quality* (New York: Free Press, 1991), 38.
22. For further discussion of the steps in service recovery, see

C. R. Bell and R. Zemke, *Managing Knock Your Socks Off Service* (New York: AMACOM, 1992), 107–112.

23. Berry and Parasuraman, *Marketing Services*, 41. See pages 39–40 for a discussion of the service reliability-recovery link.

24. D. M. Armstrong, *Managing by Storying Around: A New Method of Leadership* (New York: Doubleday, 1992), 7–9.

25. B. R. Schlenker, *Impression Management* (Pacific Grove, Calif.: Brooks/Cole, 1980).

26. For more information, see K. D. Ryan and D. K. Oestreich, *Driving Fear Out of the Workplace: How to Overcome the Invisible Barriers to Quality, Productivity, and Innovation* (San Francisco: Jossey-Bass, 1991), 35.

Chapter Eight

1. Our research clearly shows that managers who are dynamic and inspiring are significantly more credible than managers who are not. For more information, see the Appendix.

2. F. M. Hudson, *The Adult Years: Mastering the Art of Self-Renewal* (San Francisco: Jossey-Bass, 1991), 1–2.

3. For information on job stress and burnout among American workers, see *Employee Burnout: Causes and Cures — A Research Report, 1992* (Minneapolis, Minn.: Northwestern National Life, 1992), 3–9.

4. S. Walton, with J. Huey, *Sam Walton: Made in America — My Story* (New York: Doubleday, 1992), 30.

5. B. Burlingham, "This Woman Has Changed Business Forever," *Inc.* (June 1990): 34–47.

6. A. Roddick, *Body and Soul: Profits with Principles — The Amazing Success Story of Anita Roddick and the Body Shop* (New York: Crown, 1991), 78.

7. Roddick, *Body and Soul*, 63.

8. Roddick, *Body and Soul*, 225–226.

9. N. Cousins, *Anatomy of an Illness as Perceived by the Patient: Reflections on Healing and Regeneration* (New York: Norton, 1979).

10. N. Cousins, *Head First: The Biology of Hope* (New York: Dutton, 1989), 83.

11. For a more extensive treatment of the attitudes of psychologically hardy individuals, see S. R. Maddi and S. C. Kobasa, *The Hardy Executive: Health Under Stress* (Chicago: Dorsey Professional Books/Dow Jones-Irwin, 1984). For more on the attitudes and practices of resilient people, especially those who overcome abusive childhoods, see S. Wolin and S. Wolin, quoted in "How to Survive (Practically) Anything," *Psychology Today* (Jan.–Feb. 1992); T. Rogers, "Why Some People Transcend Their Traumatic Childhoods," *San Francisco Chronicle*, 2 Jan. 1991, B3; R. B. Flannery, Jr., *Becoming Stress-Resistant Through the SMART Program* (New York: Continuum, 1990).

12. Quoted in D. Goleman, "In New Research, Optimism Emerges as the Key to a Successful Life," *New York Times*, 24 Dec. 1991, B1.

13. P. Koestenbaum, *Leadership: The Inner Side of Greatness* (San Francisco: Jossey-Bass, 1991), 42.

14. Koestenbaum, *Leadership*, 194–195.

15. R. M. Brown, "Rita Mae Brown," in P. L. Berman (ed.), *The Courage of Conviction* (New York: Dodd, Mead, 1985), 23.

16. Brown, "Rita Mae Brown," 23.

17. For a discussion of optimal performance and the issue of balance between challenge and skill, see M. Csikszentmihalyi, *Flow: The Psychology of Optimal Performance* (New York: Free Press, 1990).

18. See Goleman, "In New Research, Optimism Emerges," B1. Also see C. S. Snyder, and others, "The Will and the Ways: Development and Validation of an Individual-Differences Measure of Hope," *Journal of Personality and Social Psychology* 60 (4) (1991): 570–585.

19. See Flannery, *Becoming Stress-Resistant*.

20. See J. M. Kouzes and B. Z. Posner, *The Leadership Challenge: How to Get Extraordinary Things Done in Organizations* (San Francisco: Jossey-Bass, 1987), 79–130.

21. For a discussion of group effectiveness and positive images, see D. L. Cooperrider, "Positive Image, Positive Action: The Affirmative Basis of Organizing," in S. Srivastva, D. L. Cooperrider, and Associates, *Appreciative Management and Leadership: The Power of Positive Thought and Action in Organizations* (San Francisco: Jossey-Bass, 1990), 108, 115. For the original study on group images, see R. Schwartz, "The Internal Dialogue: On the Asymmetry Between Positive and Negative Coping Thoughts," *Cognitive Therapy and Research 10* (1986): 91–125.

22. F. Polak, *The Image of the Future* (New York: Elsevier, 1973), 19. Quoted in Cooperrider, "Positive Image, Positive Action," 111.

23. For studies on the health effects of optimism, see C. Peterson and L. M. Bossio, *Health and Optimism: New Research on the Relationship Between Positive Thinking and Physical Well-Being* (New York: Free Press, 1991). For a detailed discussion of how optimism assessment and training have been used to increase sales performance, see M.E.P. Seligman, *Learned Optimism* (New York: Knopf, 1990).

24. Seligman, *Learned Optimism*, 109.

25. Seligman, *Learned Optimism*, 112.

26. Roddick, *Body and Soul*, 17.

27. P. L. Townsend, "Love and Leadership," *Marine Corps Gazette* (Feb. 1982): 24.

28. J. Autry, *Love and Profit: The Art of Caring Leadership* (New York: Morrow, 1991).

29. R. J. Sternberg and S. Grajek, "The Nature of Love," *Journal of Personality and Social Psychology* 47 (2) (1984): 327.

30. Goleman, "In New Research, Optimism Emerges."

31. See Chapter Five of this book for more on personal support. Also see "Friends Can Be Good Medicine: An Independent Evaluation of the Pilot Project" (Sacramento, Calif.: California Department of Mental Health, 1982).

32. Snyder and others, "The Will and the Ways," 570–585.
33. See T. R. Elliott, T. E. Witty, and S. Herrick, "Negotiating Reality After Physical Loss: Hope, Depression, and Disability," *Journal of Personality and Social Psychology 61* (4) (1991): 608–613. Also see Goleman, "In New Research, Optimism Emerges," B1.
34. Peterson and Bossio, *Health and Optimism*, 30.
35. See J. Talan, "Optimism May Be the Best Medicine," *San Jose Mercury News*, 22 May 1991, 1F, 3F. For research on health and optimism, see Peterson and Bossio, *Health and Optimism*, and Seligman, *Learned Optimism*.
36. Goleman, "In New Research, Optimism Emerges," B6.
37. Goleman, "In New Research, Optimism Emerges," B1.
38. See Seligman, *Learned Optimism*, 93–280.
39. Kouzes and Posner, *The Leadership Challenge*, 100–105, 125–129.
40. See Kouzes and Posner, *The Leadership Challenge*, 217–238. Also see Goleman, "In New Research, Optimism Emerges."
41. Seligman, *Learned Optimism*, 208–209.
42. D. Goleman, "Happy or Sad, a Mood Can Prove Contagious," *New York Times*, 15 Oct. 1991, B5.
43. Seligman, *Learned Optimism*, 211. The ABCDE model is based on the work of pioneering psychologist Albert Ellis. For a complete description of the model, see pages 208–280.

Chapter Nine

1. In 1974, Michael D. Cohen and James G. March coined the phrase "organized anarchy" to describe this type of organization. Recently, a number of new books have appeared whose observations resemble in many ways those of these two scholars. For the original work, see M. D. March and J. G. Cohen, *Leadership and Ambiguity* (New York: McGraw-Hill, 1974), 2–5. For more contemporary discussions of these issues, see T. Peters, *Liberation Management: Necessary Disorganization for the*

Nanosecond Nineties (New York: Knopf, 1992); J. B. Quinn, *Intelligent Enterprise* (New York: Free Press, 1992); W. H. Davidow and M. S. Malone, *The Virtual Corporation* (New York: Harper Business, 1992).

2. For a discussion of the organizational problems caused by high degrees of uncertainty, see J. R. Galbraith, *Organizational Design* (Reading, Mass.: Addison-Wesley, 1977). For a discussion of the psychological issues encountered during uncertainty, see D. Yankelovich, "Managing in an Age of Anxiety," *Industry Week*, 24 Oct. 1977, 52–58.

3. M. J. Adler and W. Gorman (eds.), *The Great Ideas: A Syntopicon of Great Books of the Western World*, vol. 2 (Chicago: Encyclopedia Britannica, 1952), 1,337.

4. W. Bennis, *Why Leaders Can't Lead: The Unconscious Conspiracy Continues* (San Francisco: Jossey-Bass, 1989), xii.

5. V. Polk and J. Rodgers (producers), *The Leadership Alliance* (Schaumburg, Ill.: Video Publishing House, 1988) (videotape).

6. For more information on cognitive complexity, see J. M. Bartunek, J. R. Gordon, and R. P. Weathersby, "Developing 'Complicated' Understanding in Administrators," *Academy of Management Review* 8 (2) (1983): 273–284.

7. K. E. Weick, *The Social Psychology of Organizing* (2nd ed.) (Reading, Mass.: Addison-Wesley, 1979), 261.

8. See. B. Z. Posner, J. M. Kouzes, and W. H. Schmidt, "Shared Values Make a Difference: An Empirical Test of Corporate Culture," *Human Resource Management* 24 (3) (1985): 293–310; also see B. Z. Posner, "Person-Organization Values Congruence: No Support for Individual Differences as a Moderating Influence," *Human Relations* 45 (4) (1992): 351–361.

9. J. P. Kotter and J. L. Heskett, *Corporate Culture and Performance* (New York: Free Press, 1992), 23.

10. Kotter and Heskett, *Corporate Culture and Performance*, 24.

11. See I. L. Janis, *Victims of Groupthink* (Boston: Houghton

Mifflin, 1972). For additional reasons for poor group decisions, also see I. L. Janis, *Crucial Decisions: Leadership in Policymaking and Crisis Management* (New York: Free Press, 1989).

12. Janis, *Crucial Decisions*, 57.

13. J. McKinlay, personal communication, 16 Oct. 1991.

14. G. Leonard, *Mastery: The Keys to Success and Long-Term Fulfillment* (New York: Dutton, 1991), 138.

15. Leonard, *Mastery*, 140.

16. S. Weiss, *Gail Mayville: 1990 Recipient, The Business Enterprise Trust Award* (Stanford, Calif.: Business Enterprise Trust, 1991), 21. For a video on the Mayville case, see David Grubin Productions, *Gail Mayville* (Stanford, Calif.: Business Enterprise Trust).

17. J. P. McKenna, "Bob Galvin Predicts Life After Perfection," *Industry Week*, 21 Jan. 1991, 13.

18. For examples, see J. Diebold, *The Innovators: The Discoveries, Inventions, and Breakthroughs of Our Time* (New York: Dutton, 1990).

19. In her critique of the recovery movement, Wendy Kaminer writes of the connection between freedom and action, saying that totalitarianism "succeeded by organizing masses of disaffected, politically inactive, self-centered people who felt helpless and victimized, believed they didn't matter, and sought 'self-abandonment' in the state." W. Kaminer, *I'm Dysfunctional, You're Dysfunctional: The Recovery Movement and Other Self-Help Fashions* (Reading, Mass.: Addison-Wesley, 1992), 151. In this discussion, Kaminer makes reference to H. Arendt, *The Origins of Totalitarianism* (Orlando, Fla.: Harcourt Brace Jovanovich, 1973), 305–389.

20. D. N. Michael, "Organizational Change: The Wholistic Challenge." Symposium proceedings from "The Possible Society: An Exploration of Practical Policy Alternatives for the Decade Ahead," National Institute of Public Affairs, 26–28 Apr. 1979, 17. This paper was based on an earlier work by the same author, *On Learning to Plan—*

And Planning to Learn (San Francisco: Jossey-Bass, 1973), 18.

21. Michael, "The Possible Society," 18–20, and *On Learning to Plan—And Planning to Learn,* 18.

22. J. W. Gardner, *On Leadership* (New York: Free Press, 1990): 122.

23. Gardner, *On Leadership,* 136.

Appendix

1. J. M. Kouzes and B. Z. Posner, *The Leadership Challenge: How to Get Extraordinary Things Done in Organizations* (San Francisco: Jossey-Bass, 1987).

2. Kouzes and Posner, *The Leadership Challenge,* 27.

3. D. J. O'Keefe, *Persuasion: Theory and Research* (Newbury Park, Calif.: Sage Publications, 1990).

4. R. B. Cialdini, *Influence: How and Why People Agree to Things* (New York: Morrow, 1984).

5. R. M. Kanter, *Men and Women of the Corporation* (New York: Basic Books, 1977).

6. C. A. O'Reilly, "Charisma as Communication: The Impact of Top Management Credibility and Philosophy on Employee Involvement," paper presented to the annual meeting of the Academy of Management, Boston, Aug. 1984.

7. O'Reilly, "Charisma as Communication," 15.

8. The replicated findings are reported in B. Z. Posner and W. H. Schmidt, "The Values of American Managers: An Update Updated," *California Management Review* 34 (3) (1992): 80–94, and B. Z. Posner and W. H. Schmidt, "An Updated Look at the Values and Expectations of Federal Government Executives," *Public Administration Review* (in press). The original studies can be found in W. H. Schmidt and B. Z. Posner, "Values and the American Manager: An Update," *California Management Review* 26 (3) (1984): 202–216, and W. H. Schmidt and B. Z. Posner, "Values and Expectations of Federal Service Executives," *Public Administration Review* 46 (5) (1986): 447–454.

9. O'Keefe, *Persuasion*, 130–132. O'Keefe refers to these three characteristics as trustworthiness, competence, and likability.

10. Throughout our investigations, we typically used the terms *trustworthiness, competence,* and *dynamism* for the characteristics of being honest, competent, and inspiring. We also generally included several synonyms along with these terms. For example, we might use the words *honesty* and *integrity* along with *trustworthiness*; with competence, we might use *capable, effective,* or *productive*; and to dynamism, we might add *inspiring, uplifting,* or *positive* about the future. In this Appendix, we use the terms *honest, competent,* and *inspiring* as in the main text.

ACKNOWLEDGMENTS

We had thought about dedicating this book to Kermit—not the frog, the computer program. *Credibility* was an electronic collaboration. As we wrote the first two drafts, one of us (Barry) was in Australia, while the other (Jim) was at home in California. If not for Kermit, this book might not have made it to the printed page. In some ways, it represents a testimony to the possibilities of future collaborations across continents.

While Barry was "down under," the Graduate School of Management, University of Western Australia, provided the support, encouragement, and resources that made his stay both productive and enjoyable. A special thanks to Myra Cake, Anne Carroll, Brian Carroll, Ray Dallin, Sarah Kidd, André Morkel, Barbara Morkel, Tracey Taylor, and Francesa Webb.

Before *Credibility* became a book, it was a workshop and a video. Janice Van Collie was instrumental in helping us develop an earlier version of the model we present here. Peter

Jordan, president of CRM Films, and video director Steve Katten of the Hathaway Group, guided us through the recordings; they patiently supported our efforts to communicate credibly about credibility. And there are always those who are willing to be first to experiment with new material. That leadership role was enthusiastically assumed by Jerry Hunt of Unisys.

We would also like to thank our collaborators in the research—those who completed our surveys and were gracious in sharing their interview time with us. They are the heart and soul of this book. Their stories and examples bring the numbers and qualities to life. We learned years ago that experience is the best teacher of leadership; these people's histories reinforce this axiom. The names of many of those we interviewed appear in the body of the text. There are others, however, whose stories provide an unseen background; to them we are also grateful.

The most important connection in our electronic network during the early drafts was our partner in leadership research, Debra Scates, director of graduate education and customer service, Leavey School of Business and Administration at Santa Clara University. Debra enabled our incompatible computer files to talk to each other. She turned Mac files into DOS files and vice versa. She also analyzed survey data and enabled us to comprehend what we were finding. Another essential participant in our electronic forum was JoAnn Johnson, whose talents are remarkable. We sent her audiotapes of our interviews, and she returned transcripts to us. Without those precious words, many of which had been barely audible, the stories would have been lost.

All of our colleagues at The Tom Peters Group have been strong supporters throughout. We offer a special thanks to Paul Cohen and Lynne Parode for their editorial contributions and to Natalie Sibert and Barbara Wheeler for their wizardry in desktop publishing.

Our developmental editor, Janet Hunter, used her extraordinary gifts to turn the prose of our second draft into a book. Hers was the task of writing diplomatic memos about how we could improve what we had written and patiently nudging us along to meet deadlines. Often, all we had to say was, "Fix it, Jan," and she would. All this with a newborn son. Fortunately for all, Jan's husband was ever so supportive of our project—and theirs.

Kathy Dalle-Molle checked the facts and secured permissions. She also kept us honest with her expert eye for detail. Sometimes she had to give us the bad news that some of our sources were out of business, could not be found, or had denied us permission. Kathy and Jan are the two who enabled this book to make it to the publisher on time.

Throughout the publishing process, we were warmly supported by our colleagues at Jossey-Bass. We are thankful for their confidence in us and hope that we represent them well. The professionalism of Jossey-Bass associates is unsurpassed. We are especially grateful to our editor, Bill Hicks, who has been a continual source of encouragement and insight. Our sincere thanks also go to Julianne Balmain, Pamela Berkman, Cedric Crocker, Marcella Friel, Michael Martin, Patricia O'Hare, Laura Simonds, and Terri Armstrong Welch.

Writing is at once a very lonely pursuit and a very intimate one. Our families see us at our most frustrated and our most elated. They hear our constant complaining and our nonstop jabbering about this idea and that. They have been ever patient, understanding, and supportive. *Credibility* is really their book, too. Our thanks and our love to Jackie Schmidt-Posner, Amanda Posner, and Donna Kouzes.

J.M.K.
B.Z.P.

THE AUTHORS

JIM KOUZES is chairman emeritus of the Tom Peters Company, a professional services firm that inspires organizations to invent the new world of work using leadership training and consulting solutions. He is also an Executive Fellow at the Center for Innovation and Entrepreneurship at the Leavey School of Business, Santa Clara University. BARRY POSNER is dean of the Leavey School of Business and professor of leadership at Santa Clara University (Silicon Valley, California), where he has received numerous teaching and innovation awards, including his school's and his university's highest faculty awards. Jim and Barry were named by the International Management Council as the 2001 recipients of the prestigious Wilbur M. McFeely Award. This honor puts them in the company of Ken Blanchard, Stephen Covey, Peter Drucker, Edward

Deming, Francis Hesselbein, Lee Iacocca, Rosabeth Moss Kanter, Norman Vincent Peale, and Tom Peters, earlier recipients of the award.

In addition to their award-winning and best-selling book *The Leadership Challenge,* Jim and Barry have coauthored *Encouraging the Heart: A Leader's Guide to Rewarding and Recognizing Others* (1999) and *The Leadership Challenge Planner* (1999). Jim and Barry also developed the highly acclaimed *Leadership Practices Inventory (LPI),* a 360-degree questionnaire assessing leadership behavior; the *LPI* is one of the most widely used leadership assessment instruments in the world. More than 175 doctoral dissertations and academic research projects have been based on the *Five Practices of Exemplary Leadership*® model. CRM Learning has produced a number of leadership and management development videos based on their publications.

Jim and Barry are frequent conference speakers, and each has conducted leadership development programs for scores of organizations, including: Alcoa, Applied Materials, ARCO, AT&T, Australia Post, Bank of America, Bose, Charles Schwab, Cisco Systems, Conference Board of Canada, Consumers Energy, Dell Computer, Deloitte Touche, Egon Zehnder International, Federal Express, Gymboree, Hewlett-Packard, IBM, Johnson & Johnson, Kaiser Foundation Health Plans and Hospitals, Lawrence Livermore National Labs, Levi Strauss & Co., L. L. Bean, 3M, Merck, Mervyn's, Motorola, Network Appliance, Roche Bioscience, Siemens, Sun Microsystems, TRW, Toyota, US Postal Service, United Way, and VISA.

Jim Kouzes is featured as one of the workplace experts in George Dixon's book, *What Works at Work: Lessons from the Masters* (1988), and in *Learning Journeys: Top Management Experts Share Hard-Earned Lessons on Becoming Great*

Mentors and Leaders, edited by Marshall Goldsmith, Beverly Kaye, and Ken Shelton (2000). Not only is he a highly regarded leadership scholar and an experienced executive, he's been cited by the *Wall Street Journal* as one of the twelve most requested non-university executive education providers to U.S. companies. A popular seminar and conference speaker, Jim shares his insights about the leadership practices that contribute to high performance in individuals and organizations, and he leaves his audiences inspired with practical leadership tools and tips that they can apply at work, at home, and in their communities.

Jim directed the Executive Development Center (EDC) at Santa Clara University from 1981 through 1987. Under his leadership the EDC was awarded two gold medals from the Council for the Advancement and Support of Education. He also founded the Joint Center for Human Services Development at San Jose State University, which he managed from 1972 until 1980, and prior to that was on the staff of the University of Texas School of Social Work. His career in training and development began in 1969 when, as part of the Southwest urban team, he conducted seminars for Community Action Agency staff and volunteers in the "war on poverty" effort. Jim received his B.A. degree (1967) with honors from Michigan State University in political science and a certificate (1974) from San Jose State University's School of Business for completion of the internship in organization development.

Jim's interest in leadership began while he was growing up in Washington, D.C. In 1961 he was one of a dozen Eagle Scouts selected to serve in John F. Kennedy's Honor Guard at the presidential inauguration. Inspired by Kennedy, he served as a Peace Corps volunteer from 1967 through 1969. Jim can be reached at 877-866–9691, extension 239, or via e-mail at jim@kouzesposner.com.

Barry Posner, an internationally renowned scholar and educator, is the author or coauthor of more than a hundred research and practitioner-focused articles in such publications as *Academy of Management Journal, Journal of Applied Psychology, Human Relations, Personnel Psychology, IEEE Transaction on Engineering Management, Journal of Business Ethics, California Management Review, Business Horizons,* and *Management Review.* In addition to his books with Jim Kouzes, he has coauthored several books on project management, most recently *Checkered Flag Projects: 10 Rules for Creating and Managing Projects That Win!* Barry is on the editorial review boards for the *Journal of Management Inquiry* and *Journal of Business Ethics.*

Barry received his B.A. degree (1970) with honors from the University of California, Santa Barbara, in political science. He received his M.A. degree (1972) from The Ohio State University in public administration and his Ph.D. degree (1976) from the University of Massachusetts, Amherst, in organizational behavior and administrative theory. He's a highly regarded seminar leader and conference speaker with a warm and engaging style, full of inspiring examples and practical applications. Having consulted with a wide variety of public and private sector organizations around the globe, Barry currently sits on the boards of directors for the American Institute of Architects (AIA) and the San Jose Repertory Theater. He served previously on the boards of Public Allies, Big Brothers/Big Sisters of Santa Clara County, the Center for Excellence in Non-Profits, Sigma Phi Epsilon Fraternity, and several start-up companies. At Santa Clara University he has previously served as associate dean for graduate programs and managing partner for the Executive Development Center.

Barry's interest in leadership began as a student during the turbulent unrest on college campuses in the late 1960s, when he was participating and reflecting on the balance between energetic collective action and chaotic and frustrated anarchy. At one time, he aspired to be a Supreme Court justice, but realizing he would have to study law, he redirected his energies into understanding people, organizational systems, and the liberation of the human spirit. Barry can be reached at 408-554-4523, or via e-mail at bposner@scu.edu.

More information about Jim and Barry, and their work, can be found at their Web site: www.leadershipchallenge.com.

NAME INDEX

SUBJECT INDEX

A

Accessibility, for constituent appreciation, 113
Accountability, and servant leaders, 204–206, 214–215
Action, for hope, 271
Advanced Micro Devices, 30, 303
Agreement, for shared values, 146, 150
Air Force Academy, role modeling at, 190
Ambition, admired less, 19
American Electronics Association, 289
American Enterprise Institute, 42
American Express, 43
American Management Association, 12, 18

American Society for Quality Control, 33, 39, 293–294
Appreciation. *See* Constituent appreciation
Armstrong International, 210
Arrogance, and self-discovery, 261–262
Aspect Telecommunications, 119, 192
AT&T, servant leader at, 191
Attention, for self-confidence, 79–80
Audits: of competence, 83–84; for servant leaders, 215–217
Australia: admired characteristics in, 13; capacity development in, 157; shared values in, 122. *See also* Western Australia
Australia Post, servant leader at, 215

H

Harris Poll, 34–35, 293

Harvard University: and capacity development, 161; and corporate cultures, 90; and optimism, 238; and relationships, 6; and shared values, 139, 142, 264

Harvester Restaurants, and servant leaders, 183–184, 207–209

Hay Group, and listening, 98

Health: and hope, 219–220, 224, 229, 237, 238–240; and trust, 111–112

Herman Miller: and competence audit, 84; and credibility, 22; and servant leader, 196

Heroes, and servant leaders, 211

Hertz Equipment Rental Corporation: and admired characteristics, 17; and self-discovery, 58

Hewlett-Packard: and servant leader, 195; shared values at, 136

Hierarchy, as relationship, 3–5

Hillhaven Corporation, 28

Hitotsubashi University, Institute for Business Research at, 169

Honesty: admired, 14–15, 24, 254; and trust, 108, 109–110

Hong Kong, shared values in, 122

Hope: aspects of sustaining, 218–246; background on, 218–221; demonstrating, 221–229; and dependency, 270–271; discipline of, 55–56, 218–246; love and encouragement for, 233–238; need for, 220–221; and performance, 238–240; and positive images, 219–220, 229–233, 241–242; steps for, 240–246; work balanced with, 227–228

Hudson Institute, 218–219

Humility, for capacity development, 267

I

Images, positive, and hope, 219–220, 229–233, 241–242

Immersion, for self-confidence, 79

Inconsistencies, and servant leaders, 201–203

Independence, for servant leaders, 270

Independent Sector, 273

Innovation, and risk taking, 110–112

Inspiration: admired, 16–17, 18, 21, 255–256; and hope, 231–233

Institute for Policy Studies, 227

Integrity: admired, 12; confidence in, 34

Intensity, and credibility, 49

ITT World Directories, 153

J

Japan: admired characteristics in, 15, 291; capacity development in, 159, 169–170; competition from, 40, 159; cynicism in, 35, 43; scandals in, 37; shared values in, 138

Job enrichment, for capacity development, 180–181

Johnson & Johnson: and listening, 113; and shared values, 126, 144

Jones & Laughlin Steel, 38

K

Kaizen, and learning, 169

Kewdale Structural Engineers (Australia), constituent appreciation at, 102

Korn/Ferry International, 15, 16, 291, 292

L

Language, on relationship, 2–8

Leadership: admired, 12; charac-

Put The Five Practices of Exemplary Leadership®
to Work in Your Organization

The Leadership Practices Inventory (LPI)

Over its nearly 20-year history, the LPI has become the most popular off-the-shelf 360-degree leadership assessment instrument in the world, used by nearly one million leaders worldwide. Repeated analysis of the instrument has proven it to be a reliable and valid measure of a leader's effectiveness. But most important to its creators, the results have also shown that leadership is understandable and learnable.

Leadership Practices Inventory (LPI), Second Edition, Revised

Gives managers and supervisors the skills to master the Five Practices of Exemplary Leadership: Modeling the Way, Inspiring a Shared Vision, Challenging the Process, Enabling Others to Act, and Encouraging the Heart.

LPI ONLINE

LPI Online is a time-saving, interactive tool for administering the *Leadership Practices Inventory (LPI)*.

LPI Online offers simplified, time-saving administration; immediate, streamlined results; and 24/7 web-based access for LPI administrators and participants.

Leadership Practices Inventory-Individual Contributor (LPI-IC), Second Edition, Revised

This instrument is specifically designed for non-management employees, informal leaders, those involved in self-directed teams, project teams, task forces, and cross-functional teams—and helps participants evaluate their own leadership abilities.

WHAT FOLLOWERS EXPECT FROM LEADERS
How to Meet People's Expectations and Build Credibility

Make better use of your commute time. These two one-hour audio cassettes provide concrete examples and specific guidance on how to become a more effective leader.

THE FIVE PRACTICES OF EXEMPLARY LEADERSHIP
When Leaders Are at Their Best

This 16-page article is perfect for leaders with limited time and budget. It provides a concise overview of Kouzes and Posner's model and overall thoughts on leadership.

LEADERSHIP CHALLENGE CARD

This handy pocket-sized card for desks, organizers, and wallets offers quick reference to the model used in *The Leadership Challenge* and the *LPI*.

Plan a Leadership Workshop

The Leadership Challenge® Workshop
This intensive two- or three-day program is based on the best-selling book and designed by its authors.

- Offered by the Tom Peters Company in onsite, public, and custom formats with pre- and post-consulting available for ongoing needs.
- Implemented by some of the world's most recognized companies, including Brooks Brothers, Cisco, Clorox, Rolls-Royce, Seagate Technology, Sun Microsystems, Unilever, and Wells Fargo Bank.

Leadership Is Everyone's Business®

A one-day workshop that develops the leadership practices of individual contributors at all levels of the organization.

To learn more about these learning opportunities, contact the Tom Peters Company in the U.S. and abroad at 888-221-8685, e-mail info@tompeters.com, or visit their website at www.tompeters.com/implementation/solutions/challenge.

Get Connected With the Convenience of Online Learning

Instigo

Working with Instigo, Jim Kouzes produced several highly interactive online seminars. They are now available to you and your organization for your next learning activity.

To learn more, visit www.instigo.com.

Create Excitement With
The Leadership Challenge Video Collection

Video programs offer a compelling format for leadership training in both small groups and large gatherings. These *Leadership Challenge* videos are designed to educate, inspire, and liberate the leader in everyone.

Leadership Challenge: This compelling video shows that leadership is attainable; it is not the private preserve of a few charismatic people but a learnable set of practices.

Leadership in Action: Based on the best-selling book *The Leadership Challenge,* this must-have video describes the five practices common to all successful leaders through a single case study.

Closing the Leadership Gap: This exceptional video reveals how to cultivate and maintain credibility and fill the leadership gap—when leaders say one thing and do another.

Encouraging the Heart: This video illustrates the importance of employee recognition and presents examples of the types of rewards leaders can give to truly motivate top performance.

Credibility: This two-part video series explores the difference between a person in a leadership position, and a person whose direction you are willing to follow.

The Credibility Factor: This program explores the relationship between leaders and their followers, and details the ingredients necessary for quality leadership.

To learn more, visit www.crmlearning.com or call 800-421-0833.